CREATED BY **JOSS WHEDON**

MARIKO **TAMAKI**   NATACHA **BUSTOS**   ELEONORA **BRUNI**

BUFFY THE VAMPIRE SLAYER

Willow

Published by

BOOM!
STUDIOS

Series Designer
Grace Park

Collection Designer
Scott Newman

Logo Designer
Michelle Ankley

Assistant Editor
Gavin Gronenthal

Editor
Jeanine Schaefer

Special Thanks to
Sierra Hahn, **Becca J. Sadowsky**, and **Nicole Spiegel** & **Carol Roeder**.

BOOM! STUDIOS 20th TELEVISION

BUFFY THE VAMPIRE SLAYER: WILLOW, May
2021. Published by BOOM! Studios, a division of Boom
Entertainment, Inc. © 2021 20th Television. Originally
published in single magazine form as BUFFY THE
VAMPIRE SLAYER: WILLOW No. 1-5. © 2020 20th
Television. BOOM! Studios™ and the BOOM! Studios
logo are trademarks of Boom Entertainment, Inc. registered
in various countries and categories. All characters, events,
and institutions depicted herein are fictional. Any similarity
between any of the names, characters, persons, events,
and/or institutions in this publication to actual names,
characters, and persons, whether living or dead, events, and/
or institutions is unintended and purely coincidental. BOOM!
Studios does not read or accept unsolicited submissions of
ideas, stories, or artwork.

BOOM! Studios, 5670 Wilshire Boulevard, Suite 400, Los
Angeles, CA 90036-5679. Printed in China. First Printing.

ISBN: 978-1-68415-688-7,
eISBN: 978-1-64668-232-4

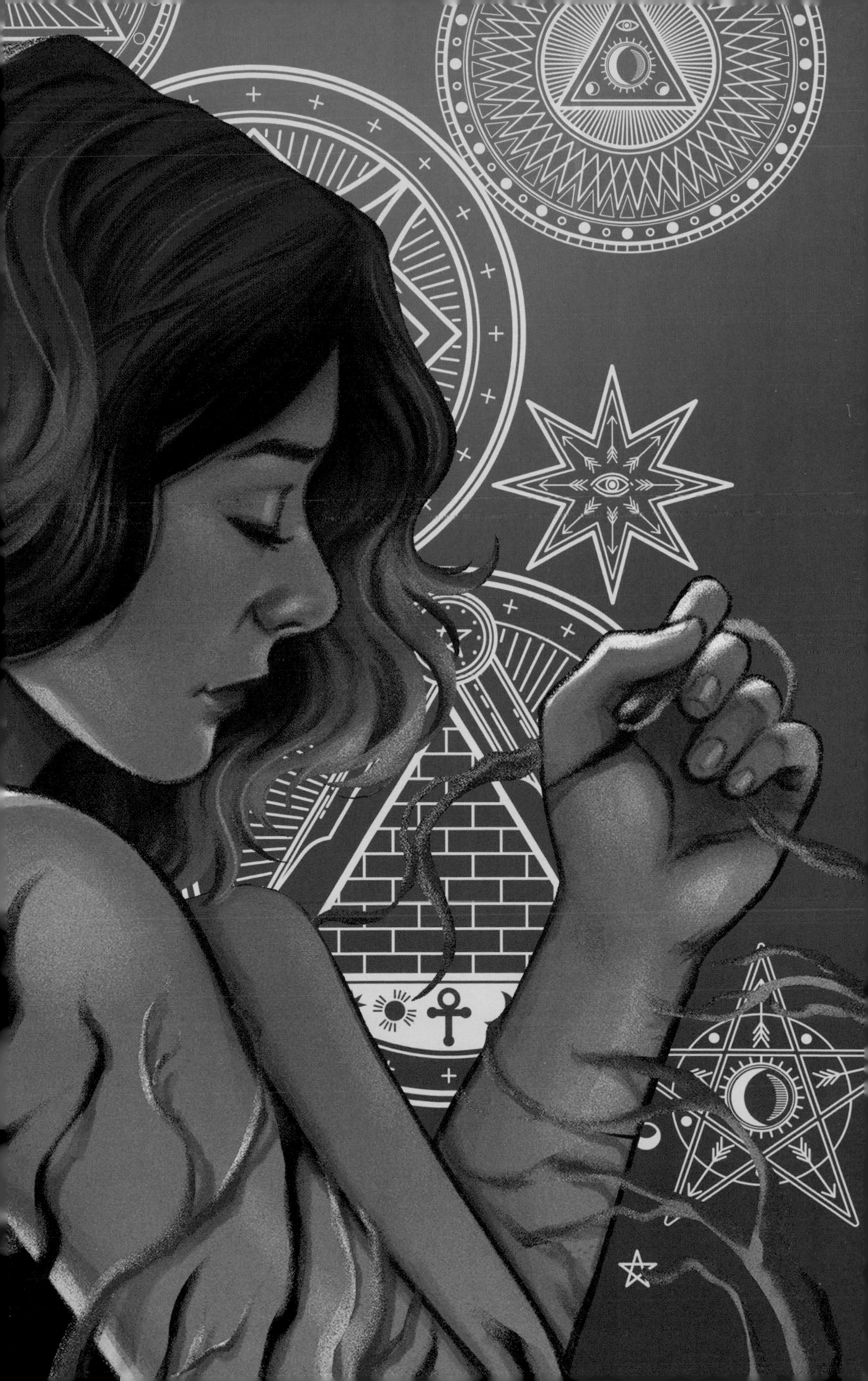

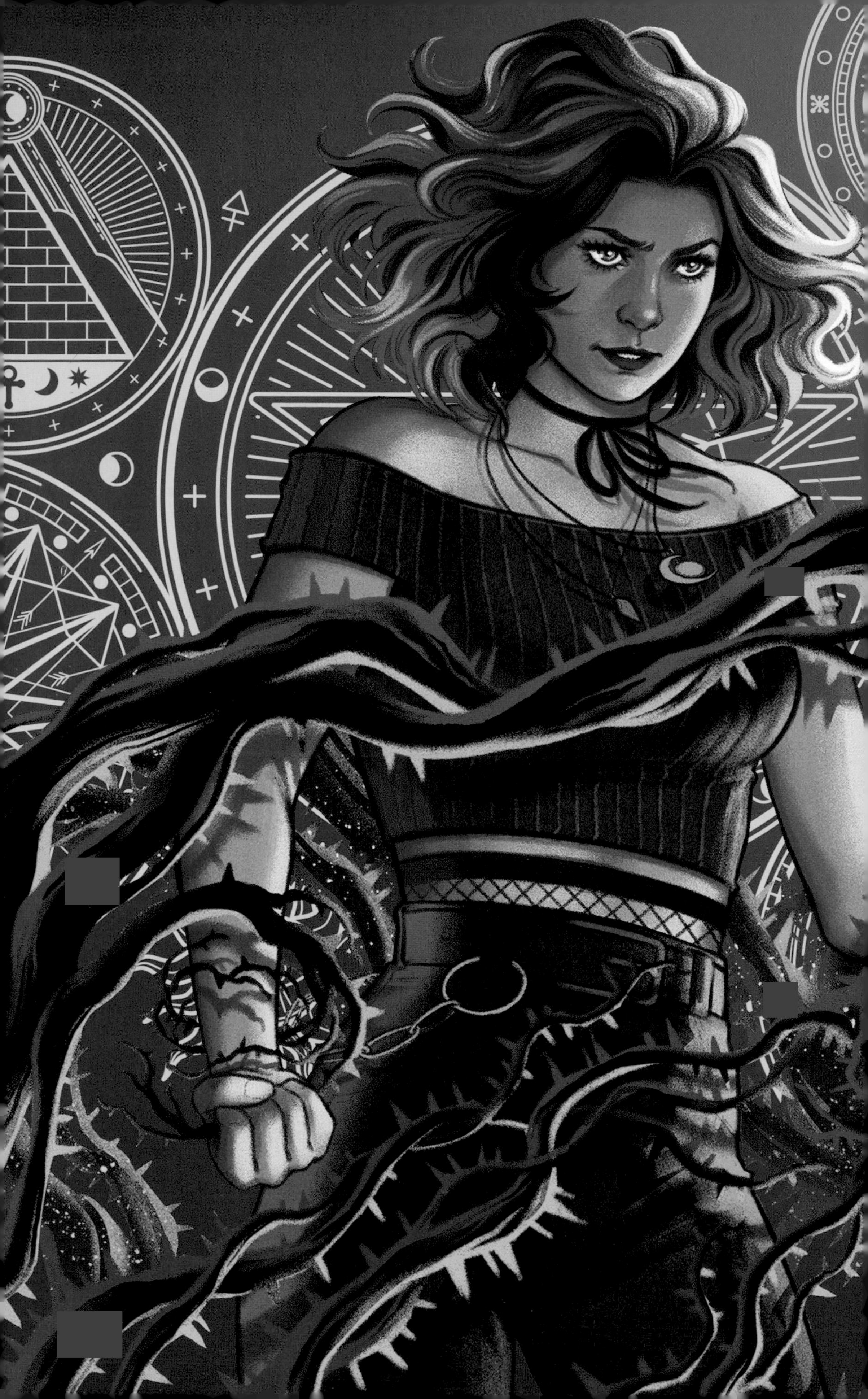

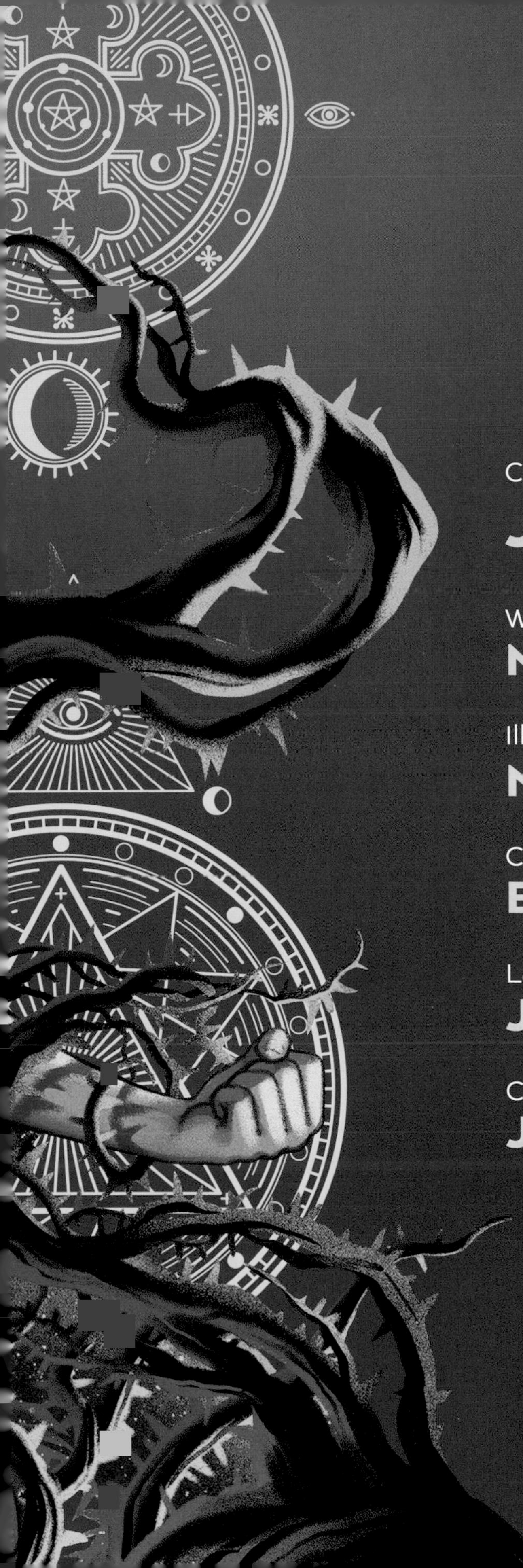

Created by
Joss Whedon

Written by
Mariko Tamaki

Illustrated by
Natacha Bustos

Colored by
Eleonora Bruni

Lettered by
Jodi Wynne

Cover by
Jen Bartel

CHAPTER
ONE

Willow #1 Main Cover by **Jen Bartel**

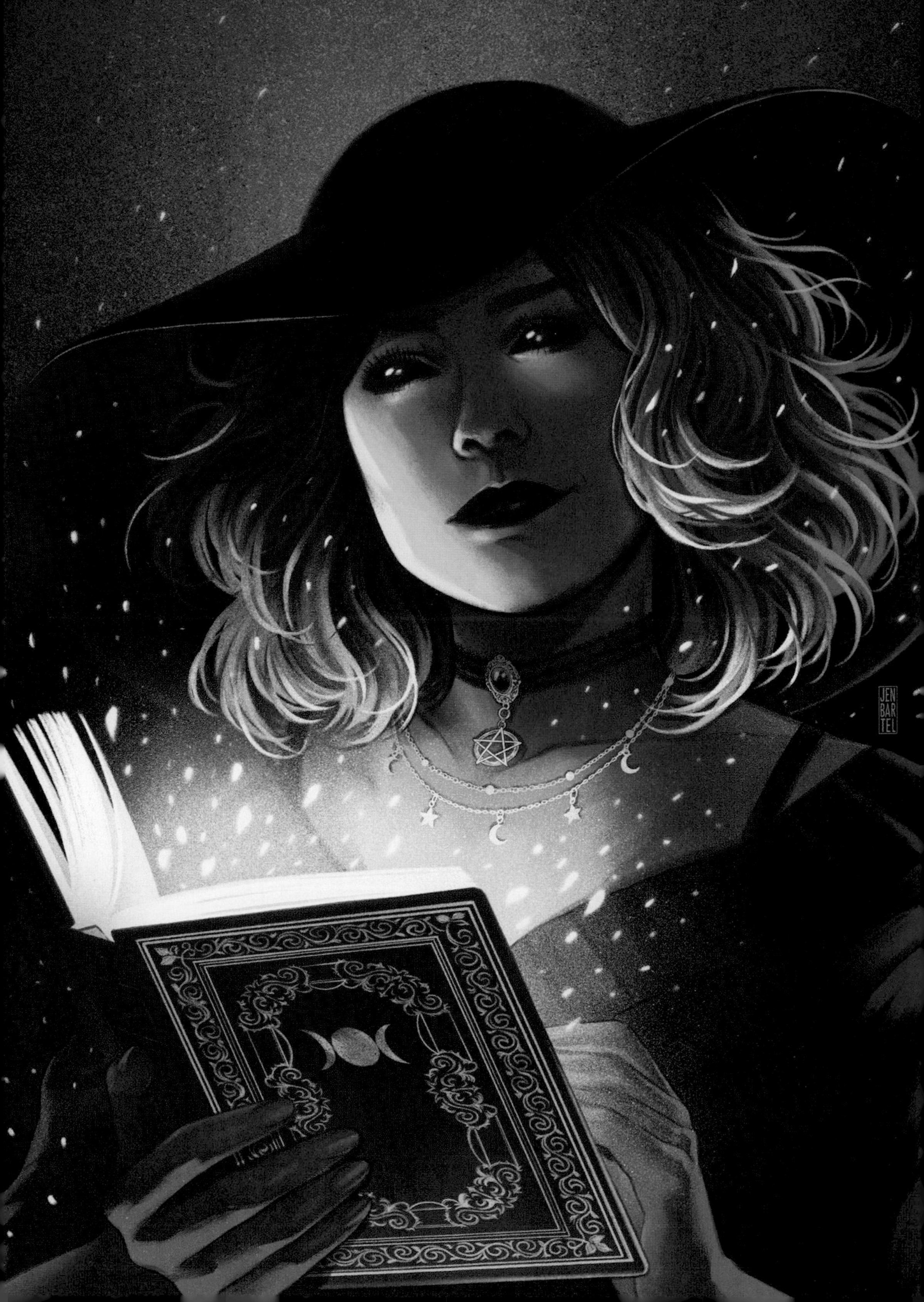
JEN
BAR
TEL

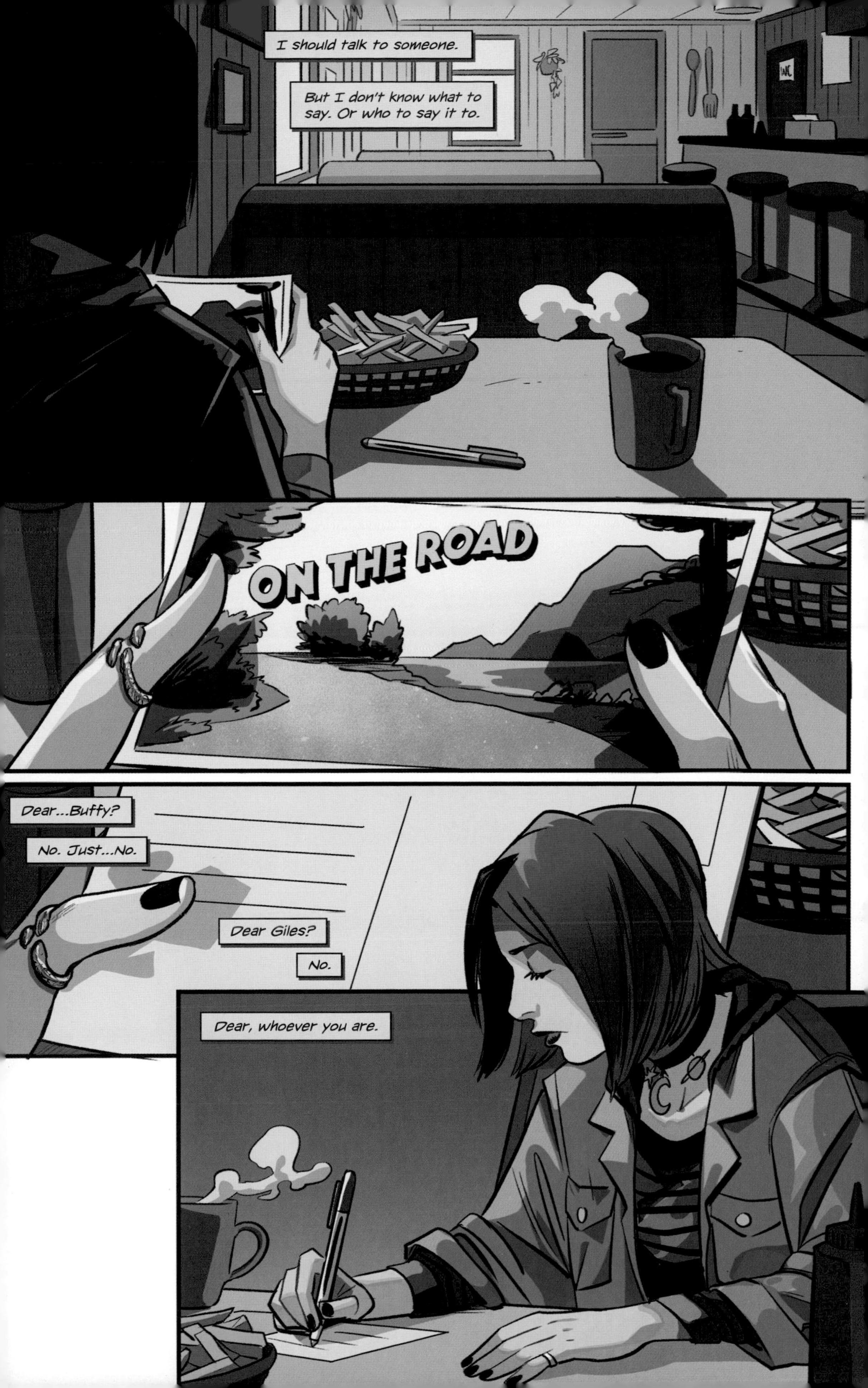

I should talk to someone.
But I don't know what to say. Or who to say it to.
ON THE ROAD
Dear...Buffy?
No. Just...No.
Dear Giles?
No.
Dear, whoever you are.

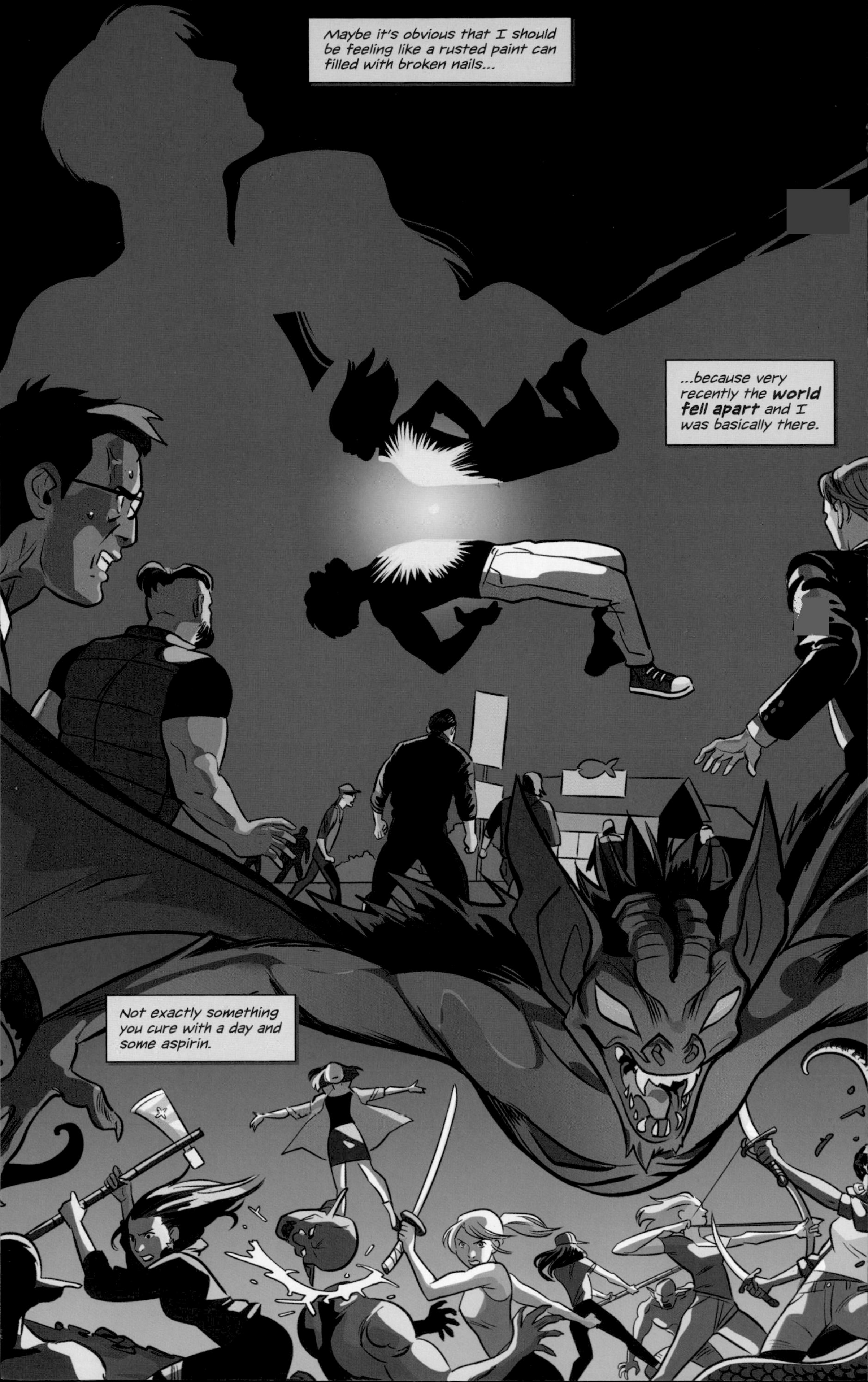
Maybe it's obvious that I should be feeling like a rusted paint can filled with broken nails...
...because very recently the **world fell apart** and I was basically there.
Not exactly something you cure with a day and some aspirin.

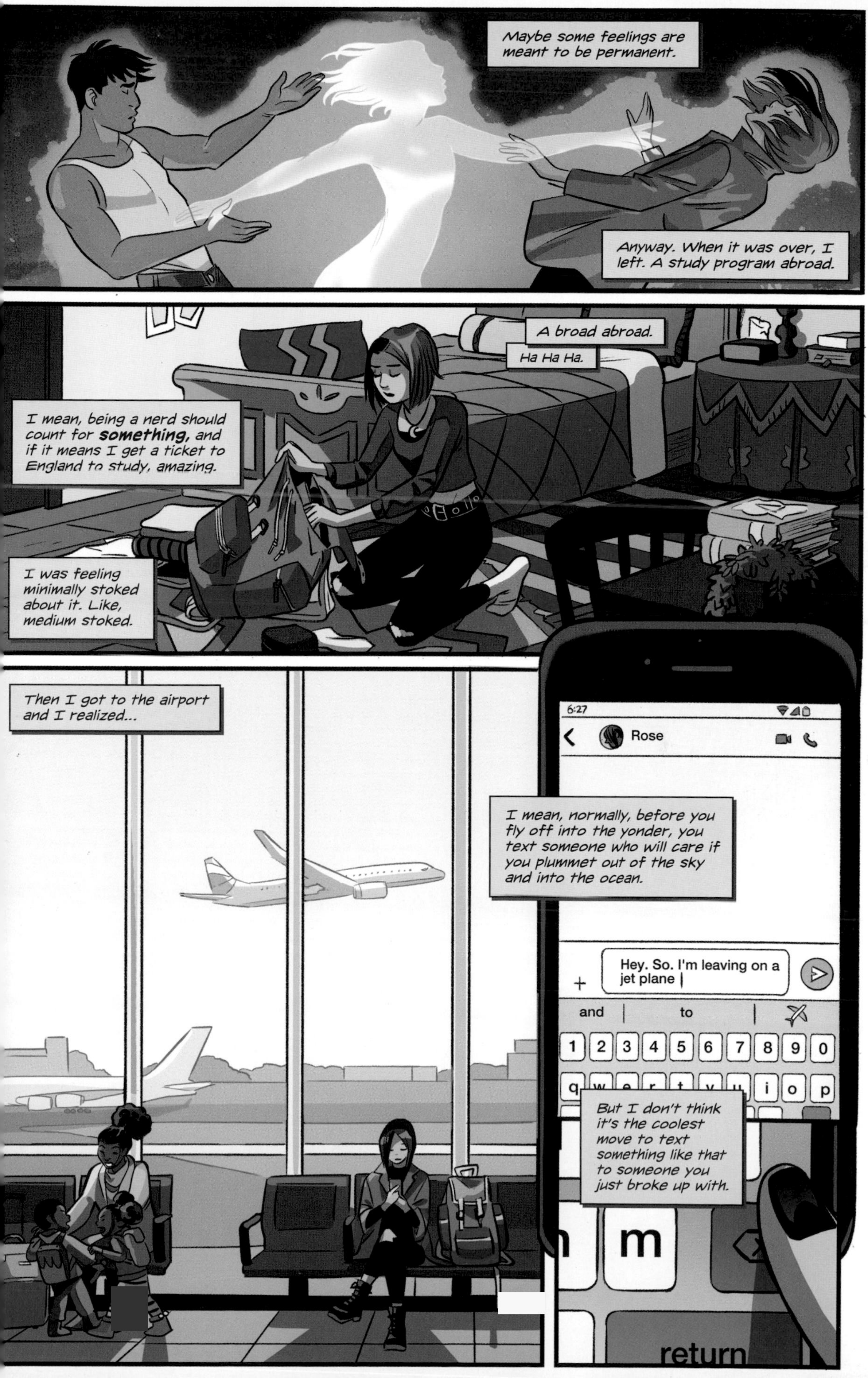
Maybe some feelings are meant to be permanent.
Anyway. When it was over, I left. A study program abroad.
A broad abroad.
Ha Ha Ha.
I mean, being a nerd should count for **something,** and if it means I get a ticket to England to study, amazing.
I was feeling minimally stoked about it. Like, medium stoked.
Then I got to the airport and I realized...
6:27
Rose
I mean, normally, before you fly off into the yonder, you text someone who will care if you plummet out of the sky and into the ocean.
Hey. So. I'm leaving on a jet plane
and
to
But I don't think it's the coolest move to text something like that to someone you just broke up with.
return

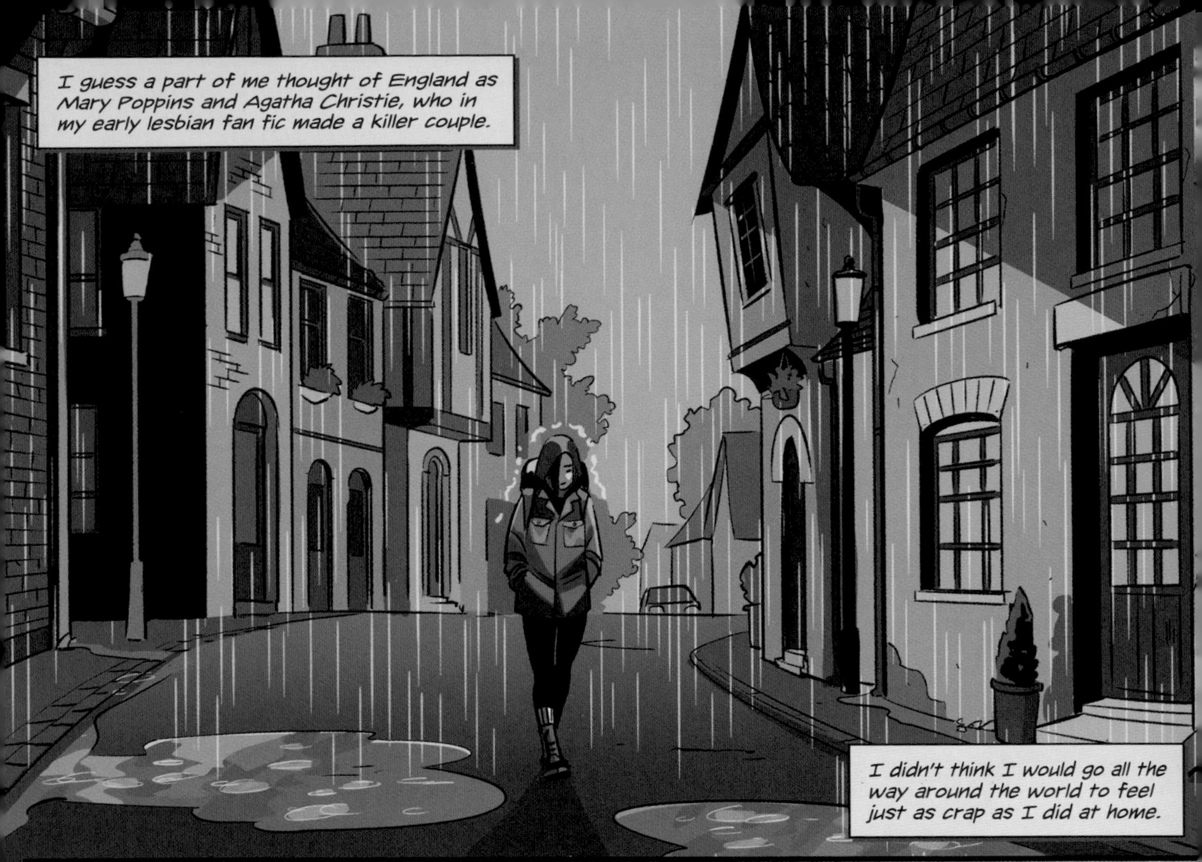
I guess a part of me thought of England as Mary Poppins and Agatha Christie, who in my early lesbian fan fic made a killer couple.
I didn't think I would go all the way around the world to feel just as crap as I did at home.

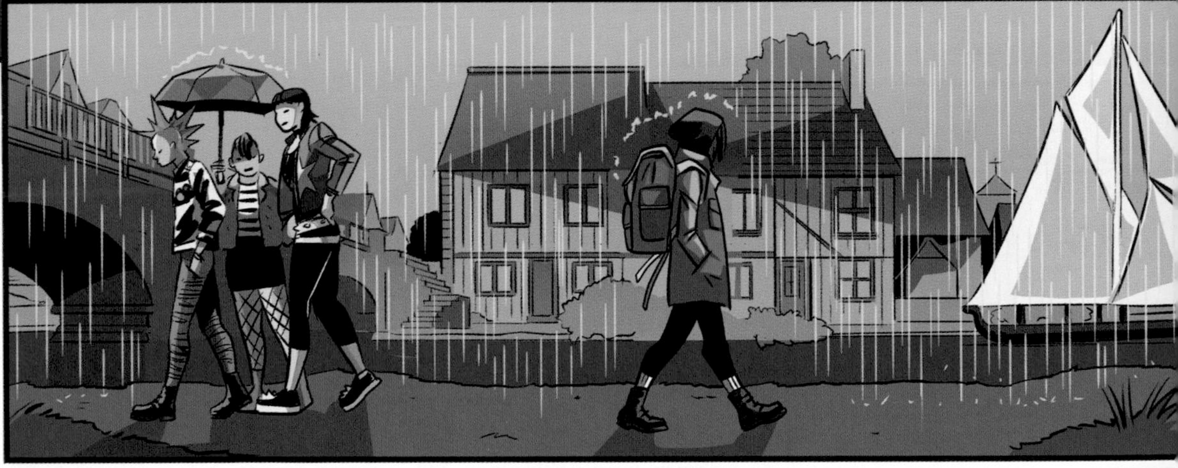

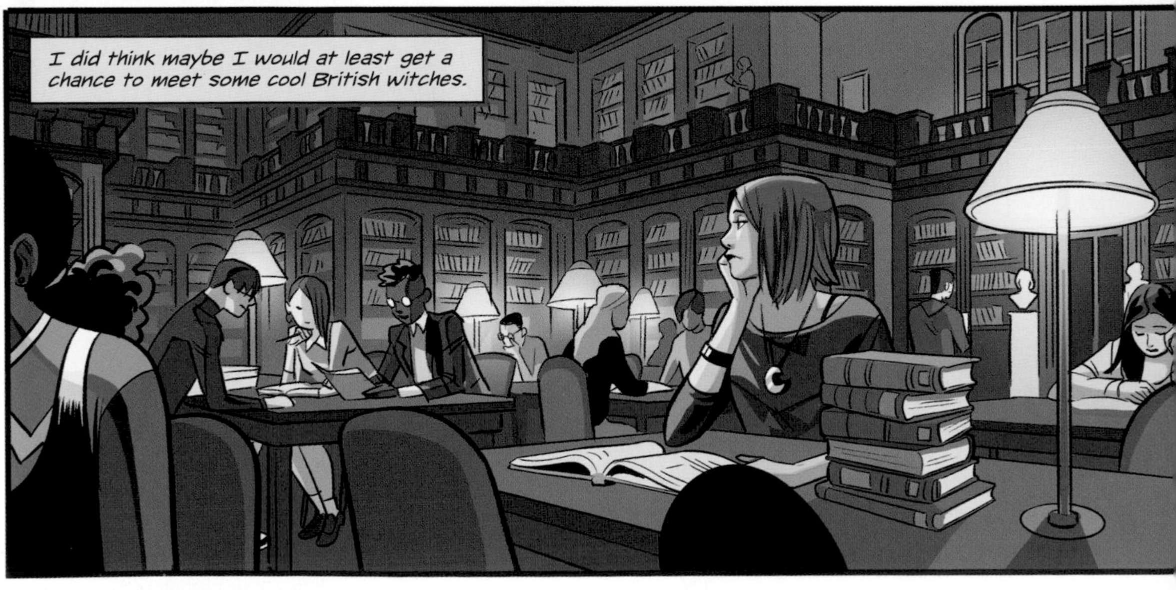
I did think maybe I would at least get a chance to meet some cool British witches.

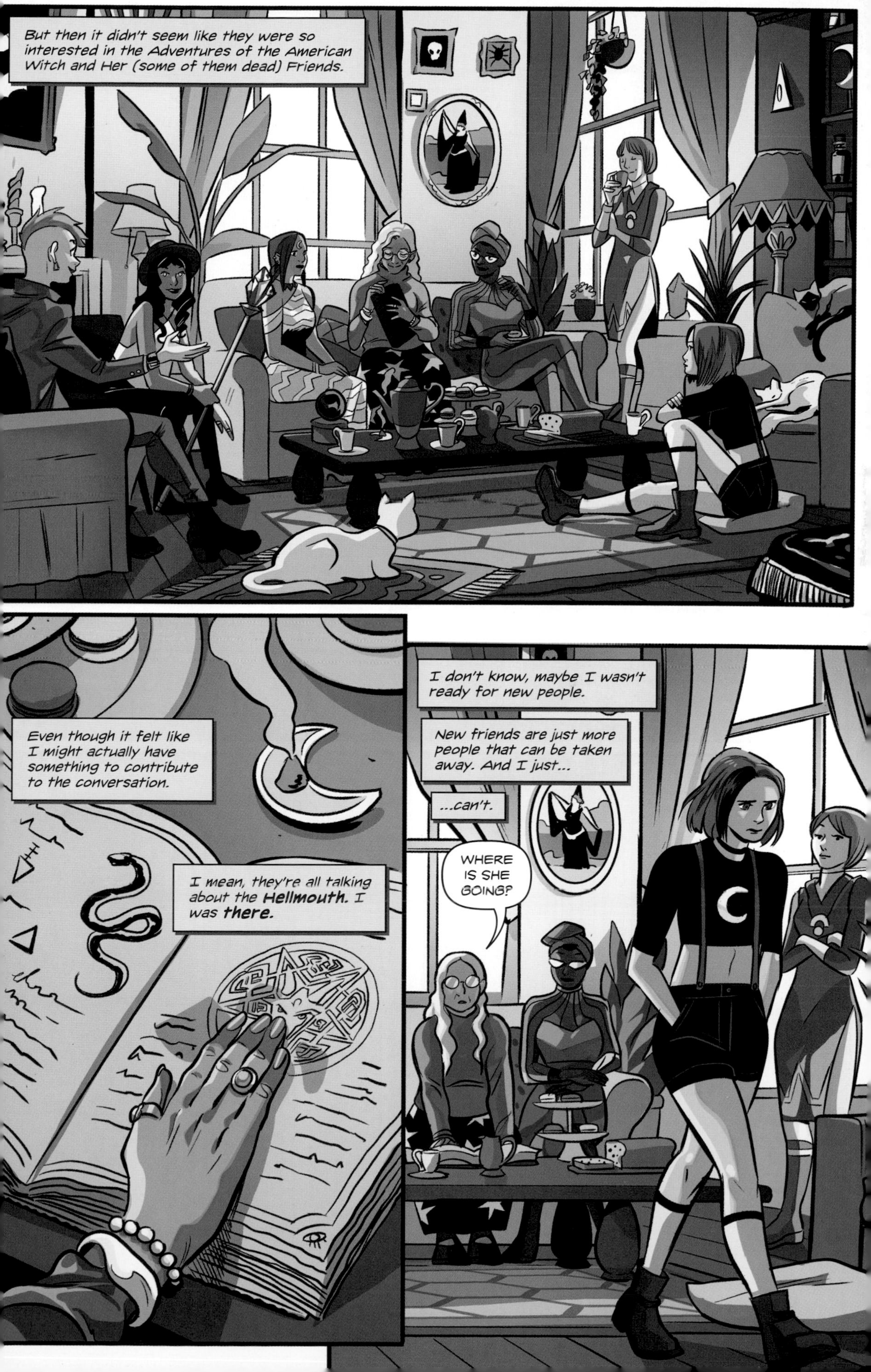
But then it didn't seem like they were so interested in the Adventures of the American Witch and Her (some of them dead) Friends.
Even though it felt like I might actually have something to contribute to the conversation.
I mean, they're all talking about the **Hellmouth.** I was **there.**
I don't know, maybe I wasn't ready for new people.
New friends are just more people that can be taken away. And I just...
...can't.
WHERE IS SHE GOING?

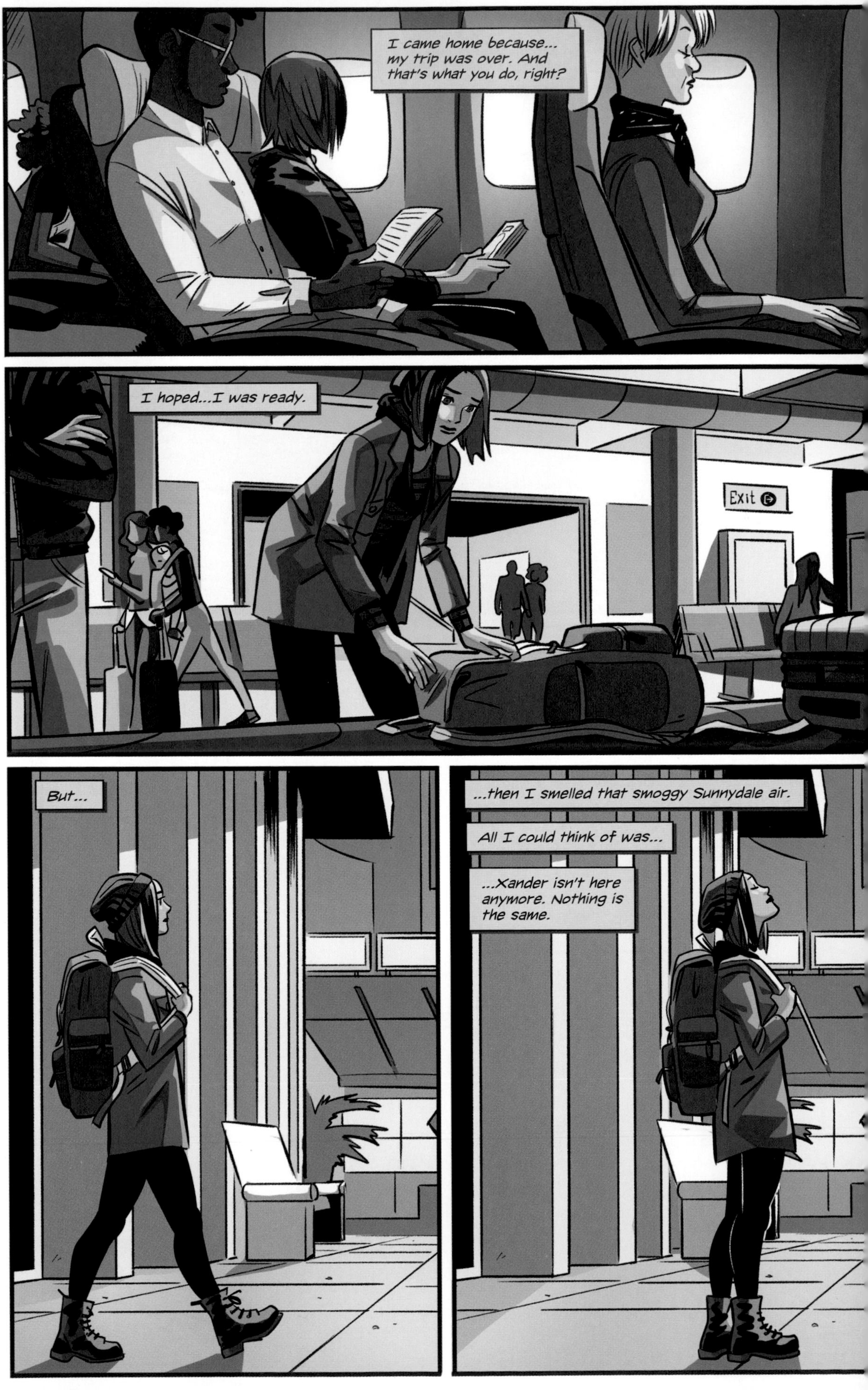
I came home because... my trip was over. And that's what you do, right?
I hoped...I was ready.
Exit
But...
...then I smelled that smoggy Sunnydale air.
All I could think of was...
...Xander isn't here anymore. Nothing is the same.

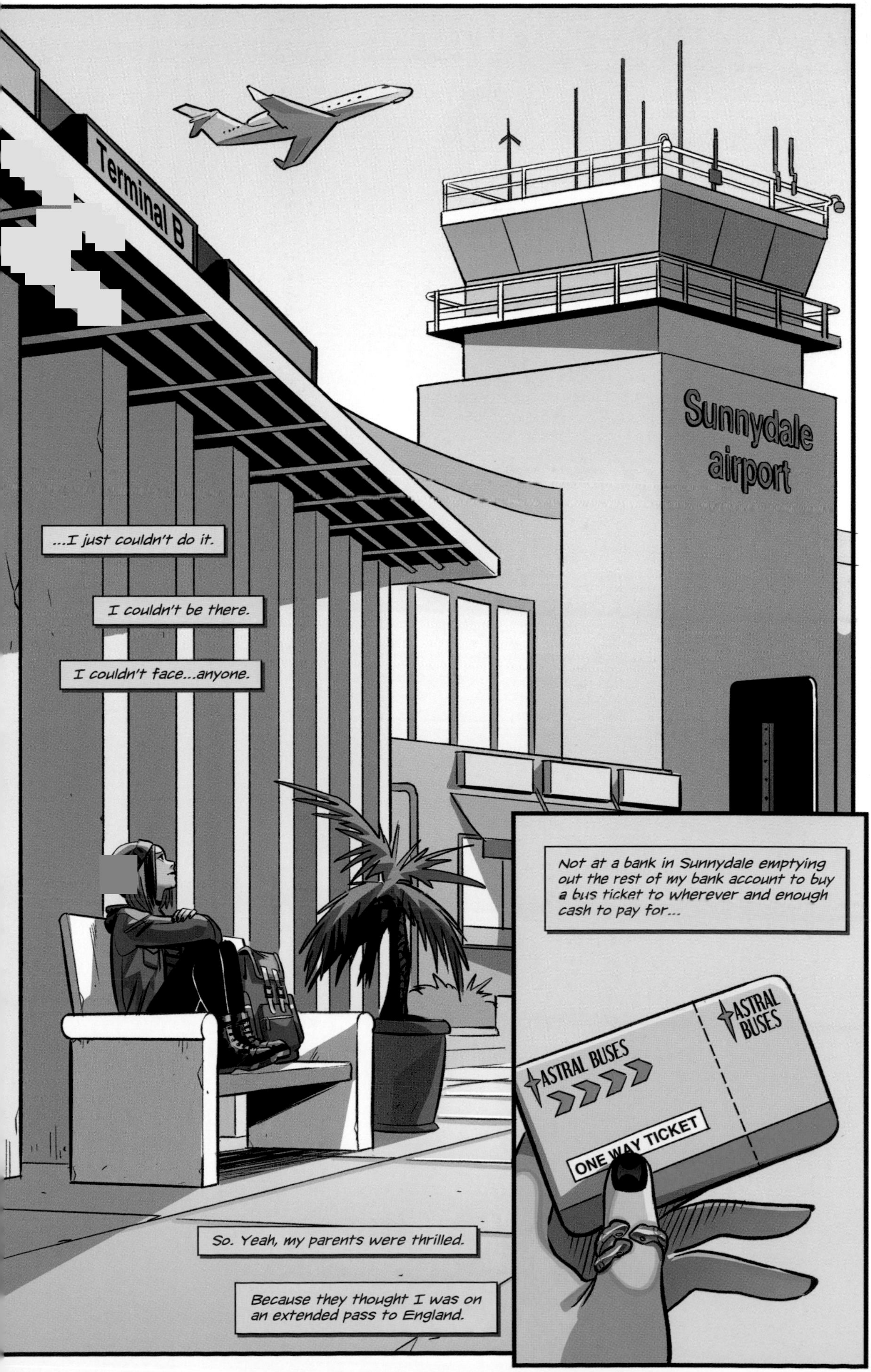
Terminal B
Sunnydale airport
...I just couldn't do it.
I couldn't be there.
I couldn't face...anyone.
So. Yeah, my parents were thrilled.
Because they thought I was on an extended pass to England.
Not at a bank in Sunnydale emptying out the rest of my bank account to buy a bus ticket to wherever and enough cash to pay for...
ASTRAL BUSES
ASTRAL BUSES
ONE WAY TICKET

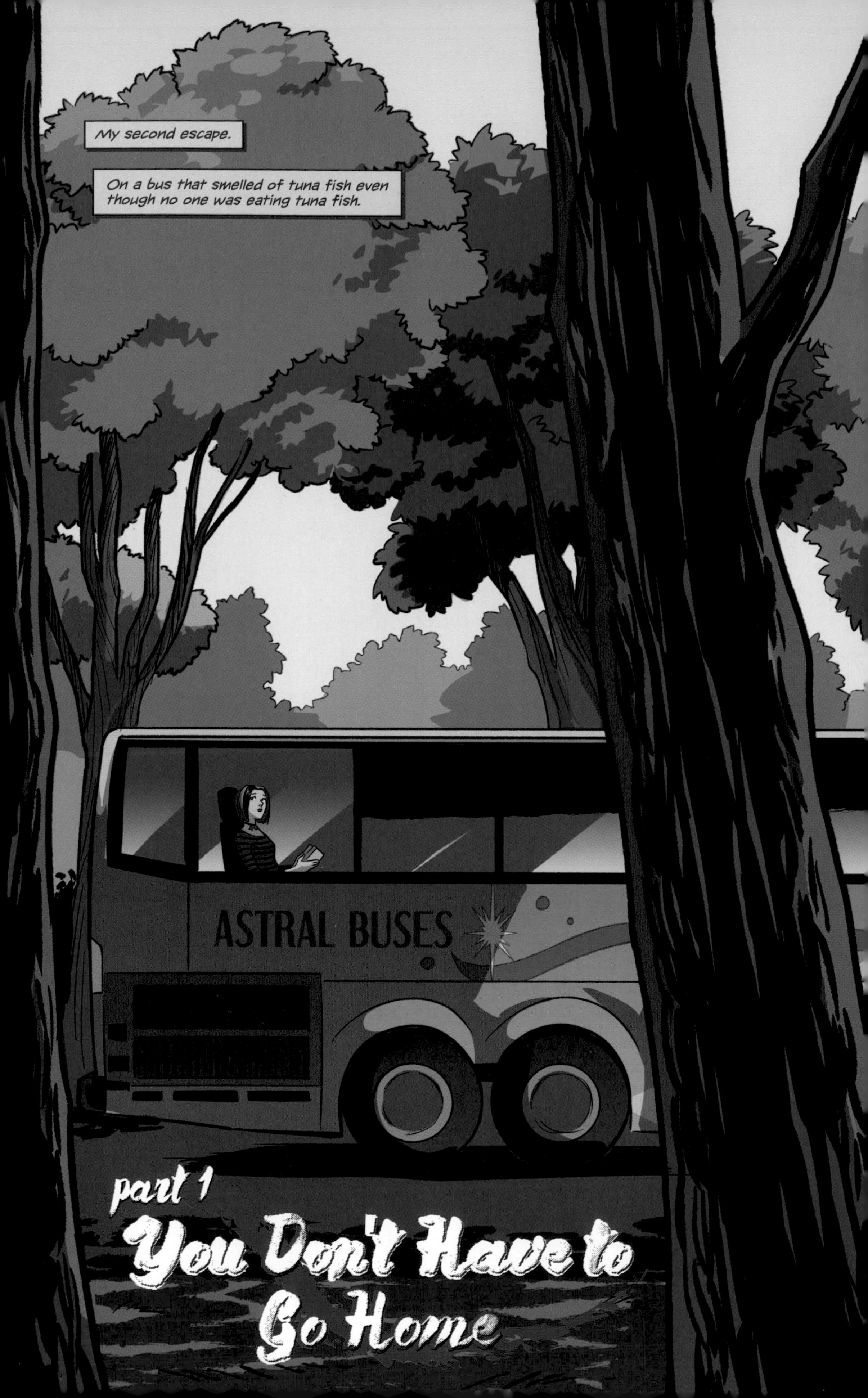
My second escape.
On a bus that smelled of tuna fish even though no one was eating tuna fish.
ASTRAL BUSES
part 1
You Don't Have to Go Home

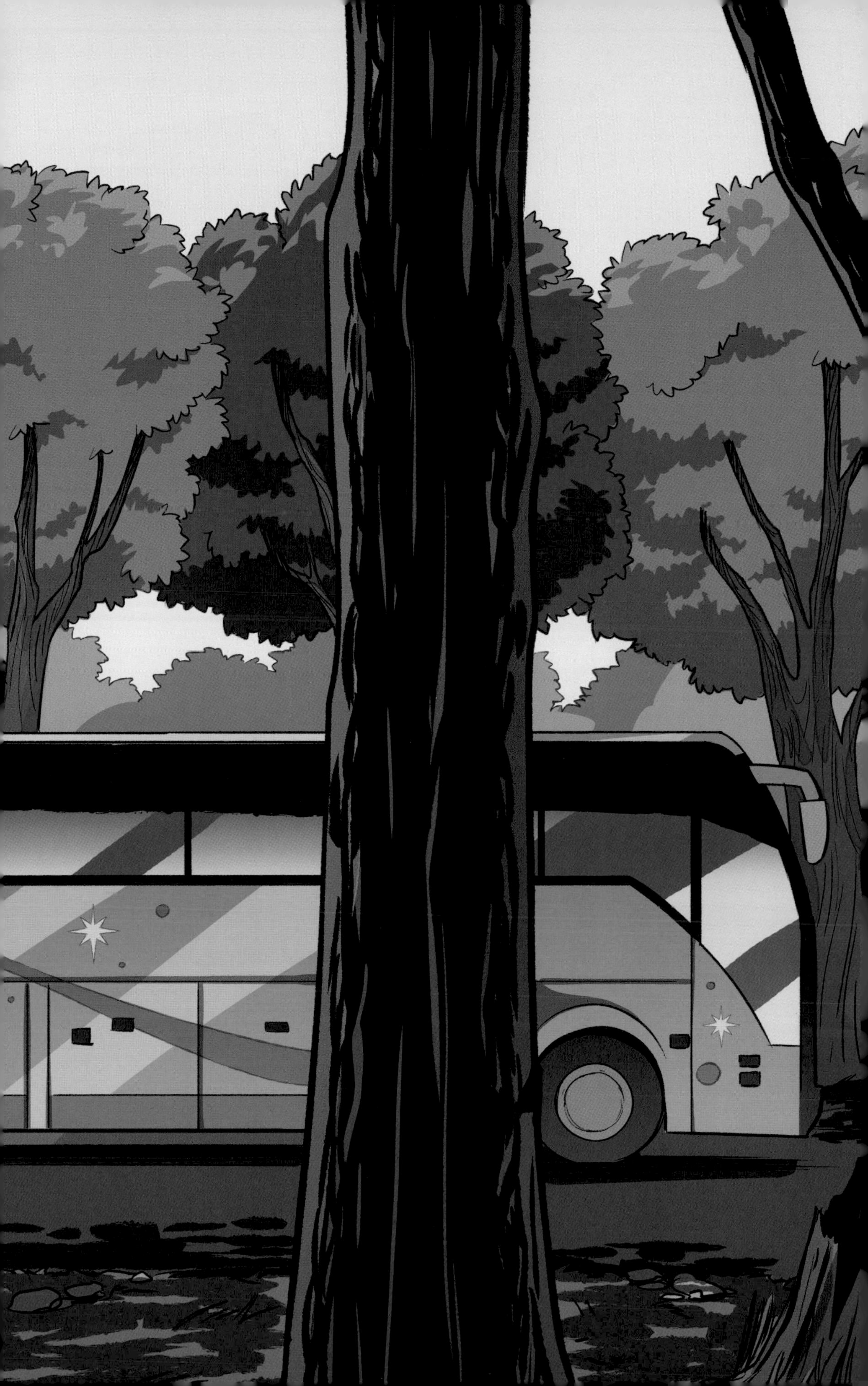

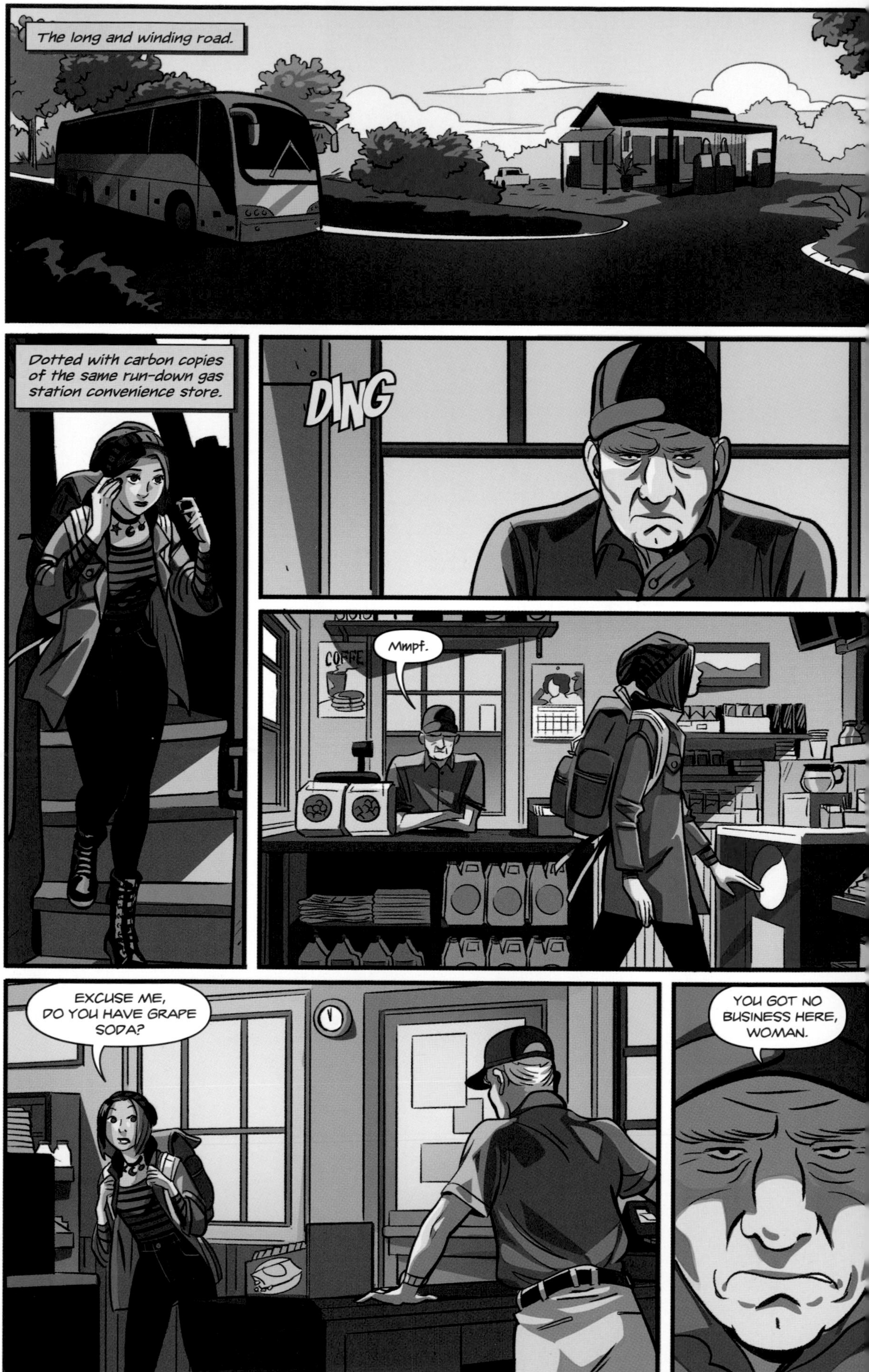
The long and winding road.
Dotted with carbon copies of the same run-down gas station convenience store.
DING
Mmpf.
EXCUSE ME, DO YOU HAVE GRAPE SODA?
YOU GOT NO BUSINESS HERE, WOMAN.

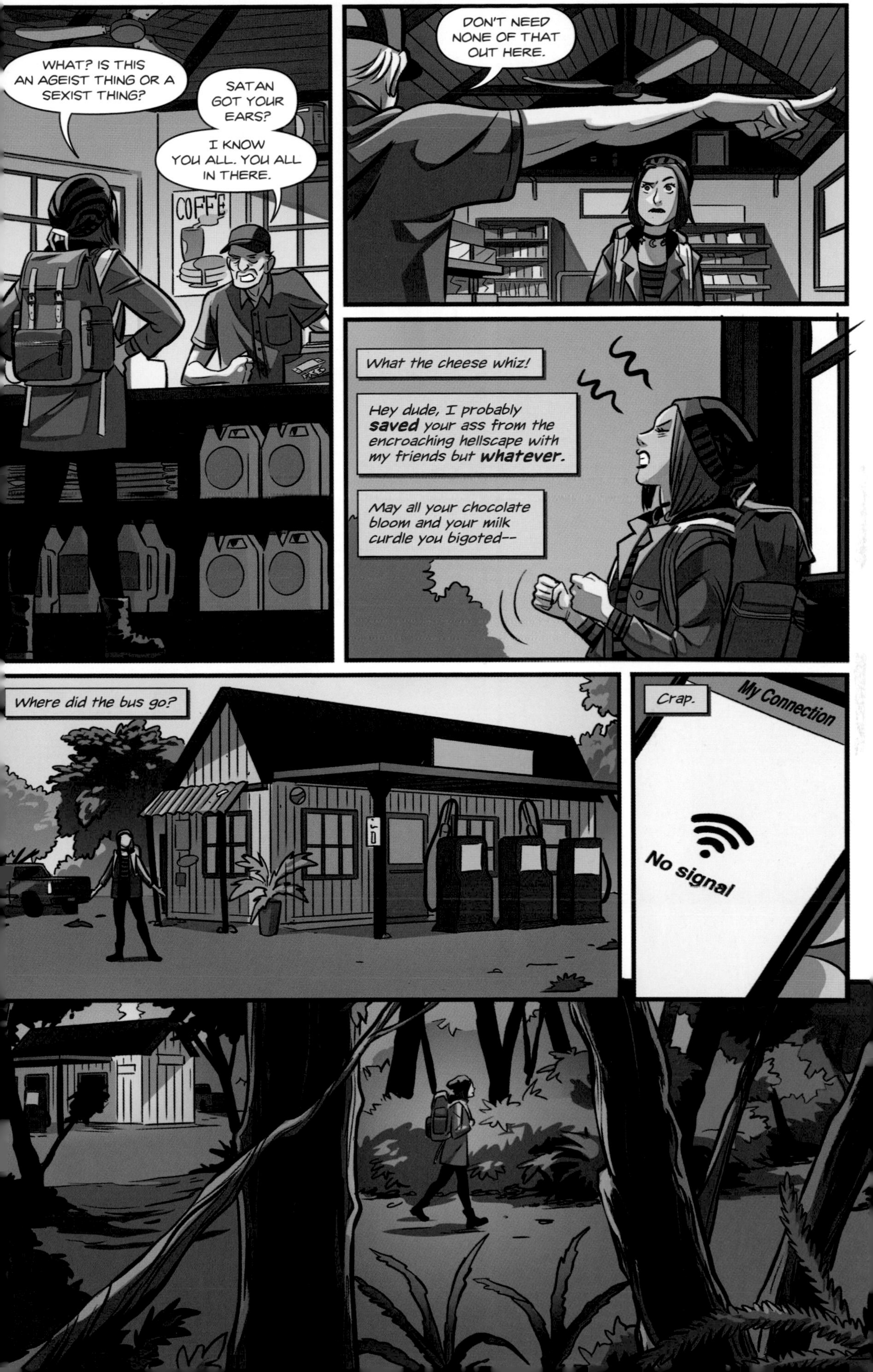
WHAT? IS THIS AN AGEIST THING OR A SEXIST THING?
SATAN GOT YOUR EARS?
I KNOW YOU ALL. YOU ALL IN THERE.
COFFE
DON'T NEED NONE OF THAT OUT HERE.
What the cheese whiz!
Hey dude, I probably saved your ass from the encroaching hellscape with my friends but whatever.
May all your chocolate bloom and your milk curdle you bigoted--
Where did the bus go?
Crap.
My Connection
No signal

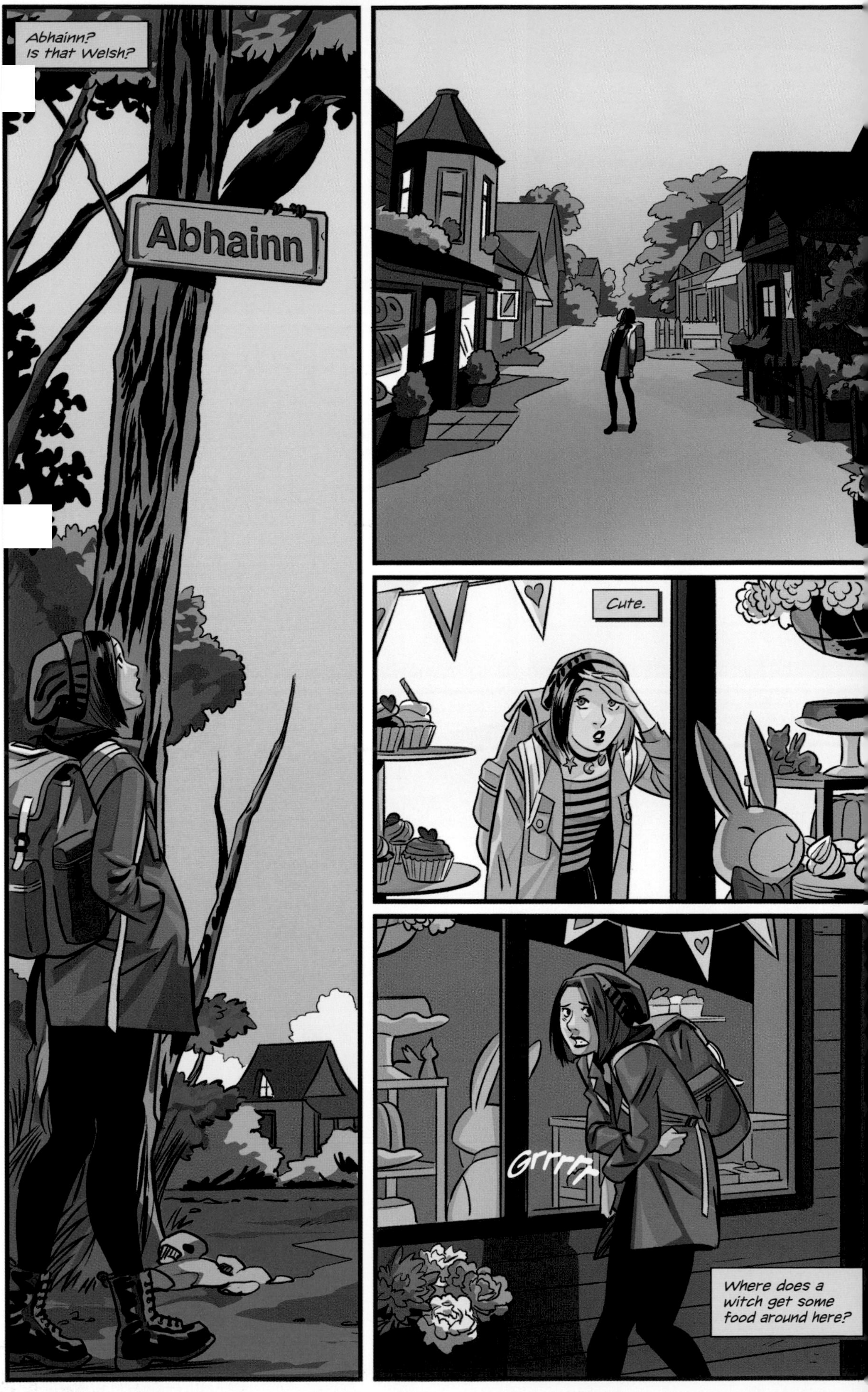
Abhainn?
Is that Welsh?
Abhainn
Cute.
Grrrr
Where does a
witch get some
food around here?

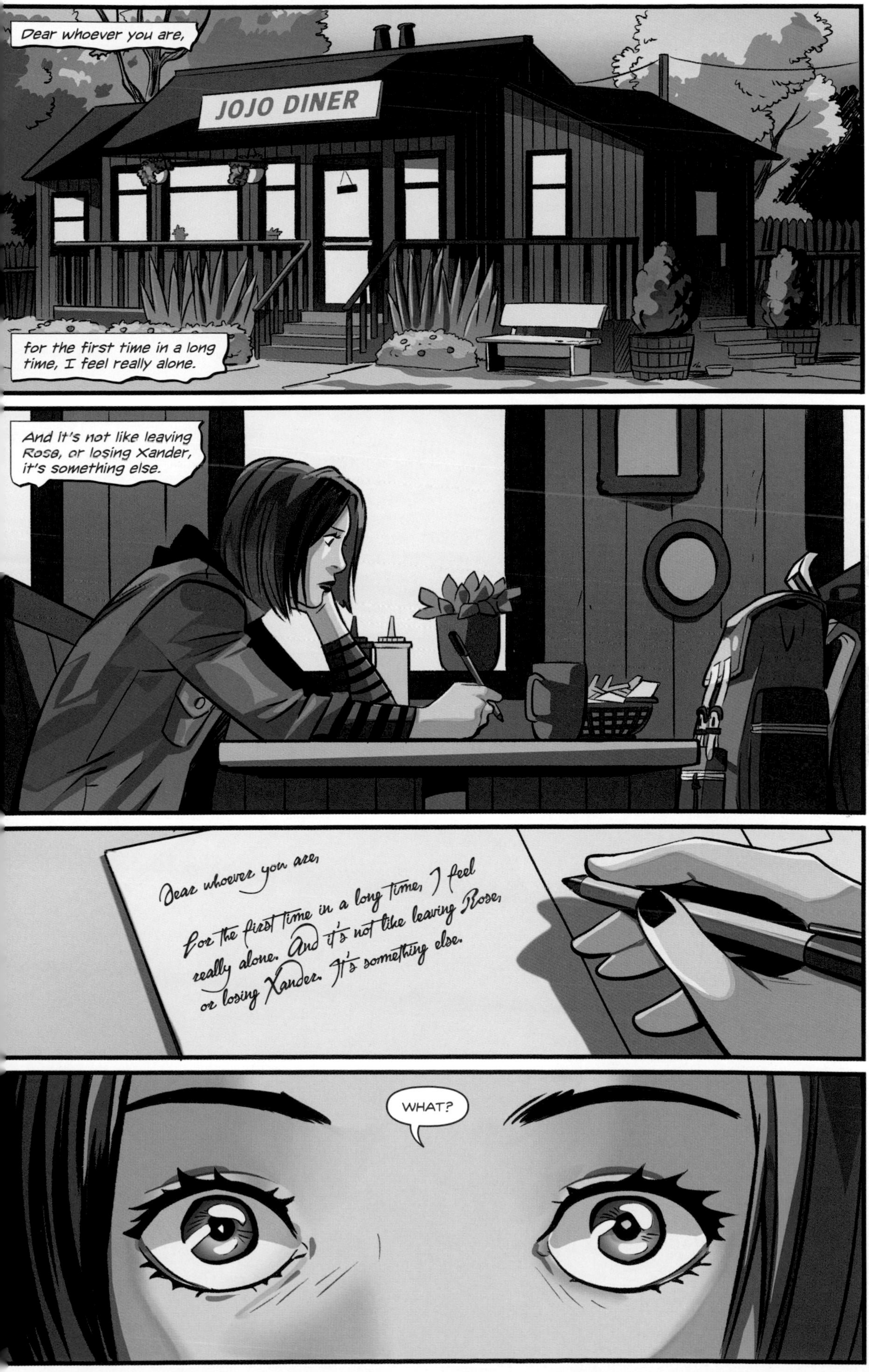
Dear whoever you are,
JOJO DINER
for the first time in a long time, I feel really alone.
And it's not like leaving Rose, or losing Xander, it's something else.
Dear whoever you are,
For the first time in a long time, I feel really alone. And it's not like leaving Rose, or losing Xander. It's something else.
WHAT?

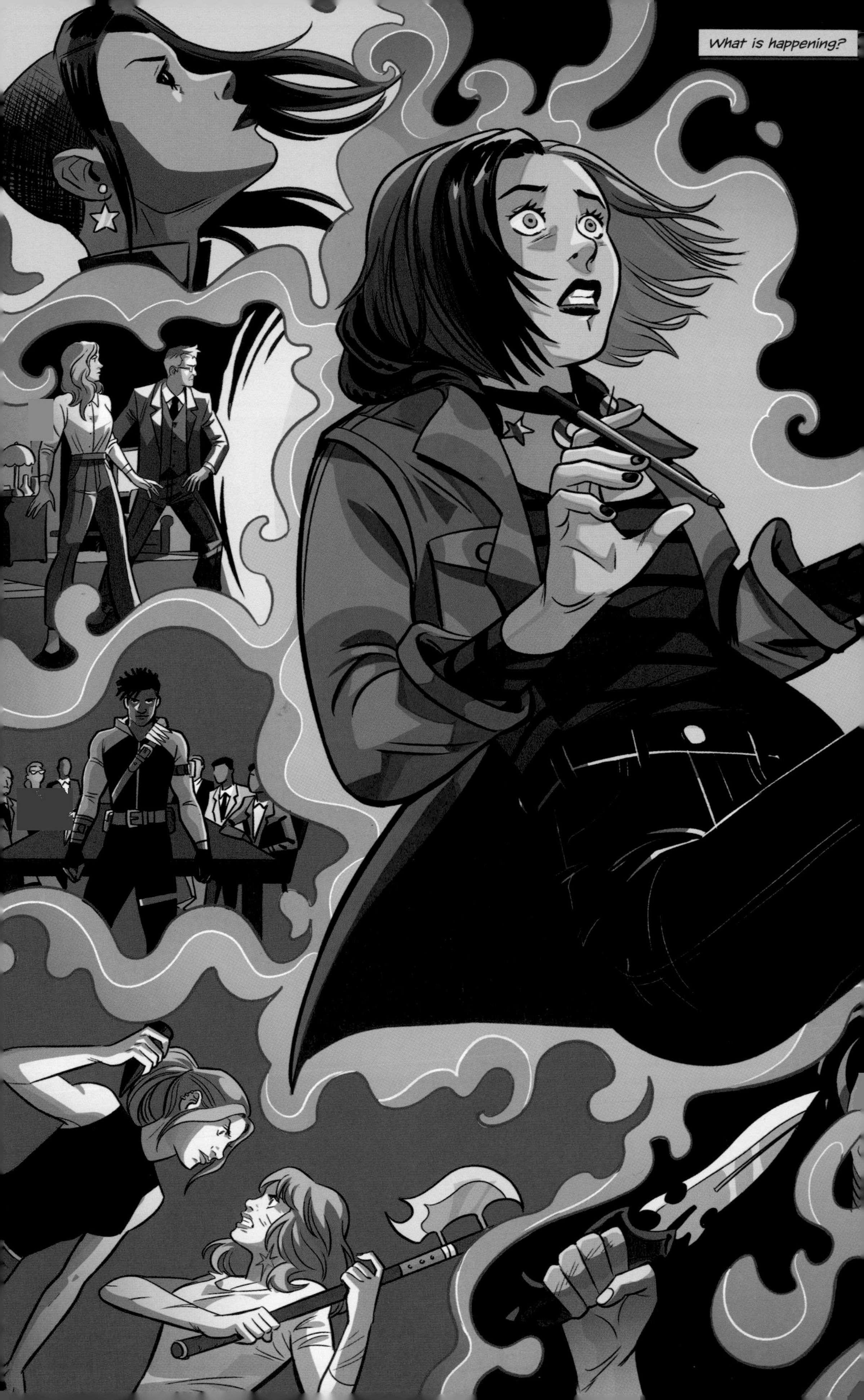
What is happening?

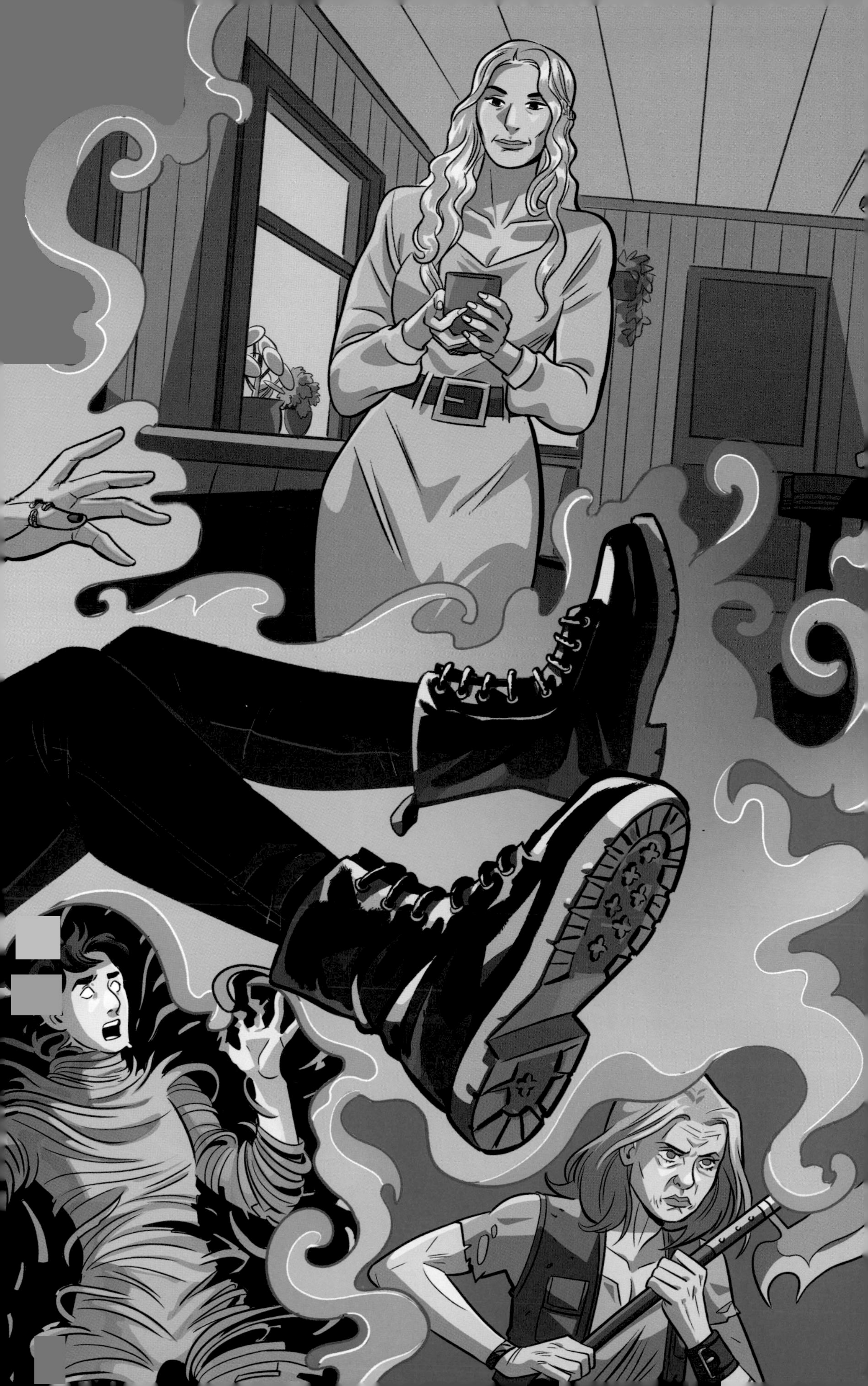

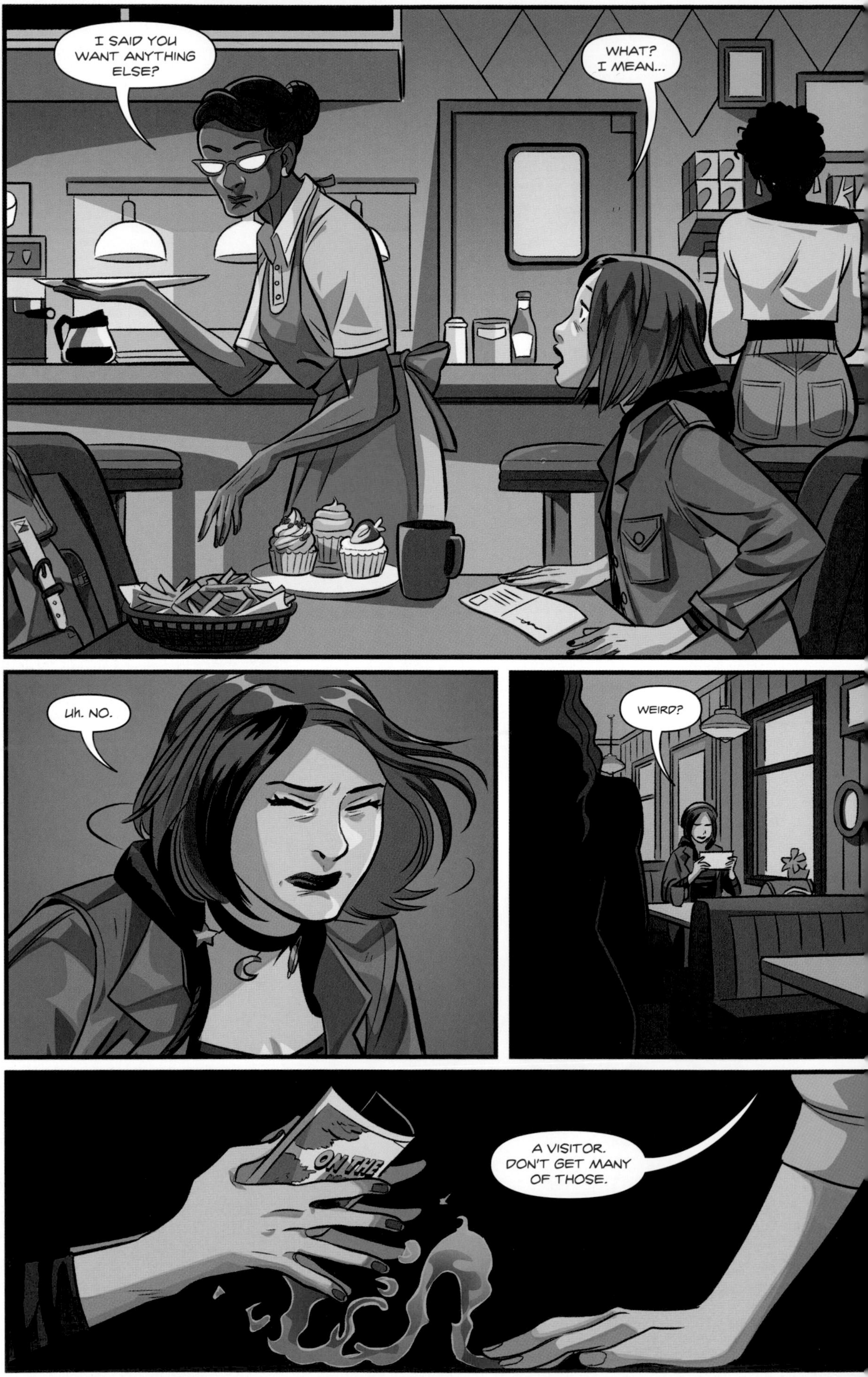
I SAID YOU WANT ANYTHING ELSE?
WHAT? I MEAN...
Uh. NO.
WEIRD?
A VISITOR. DON'T GET MANY OF THOSE.

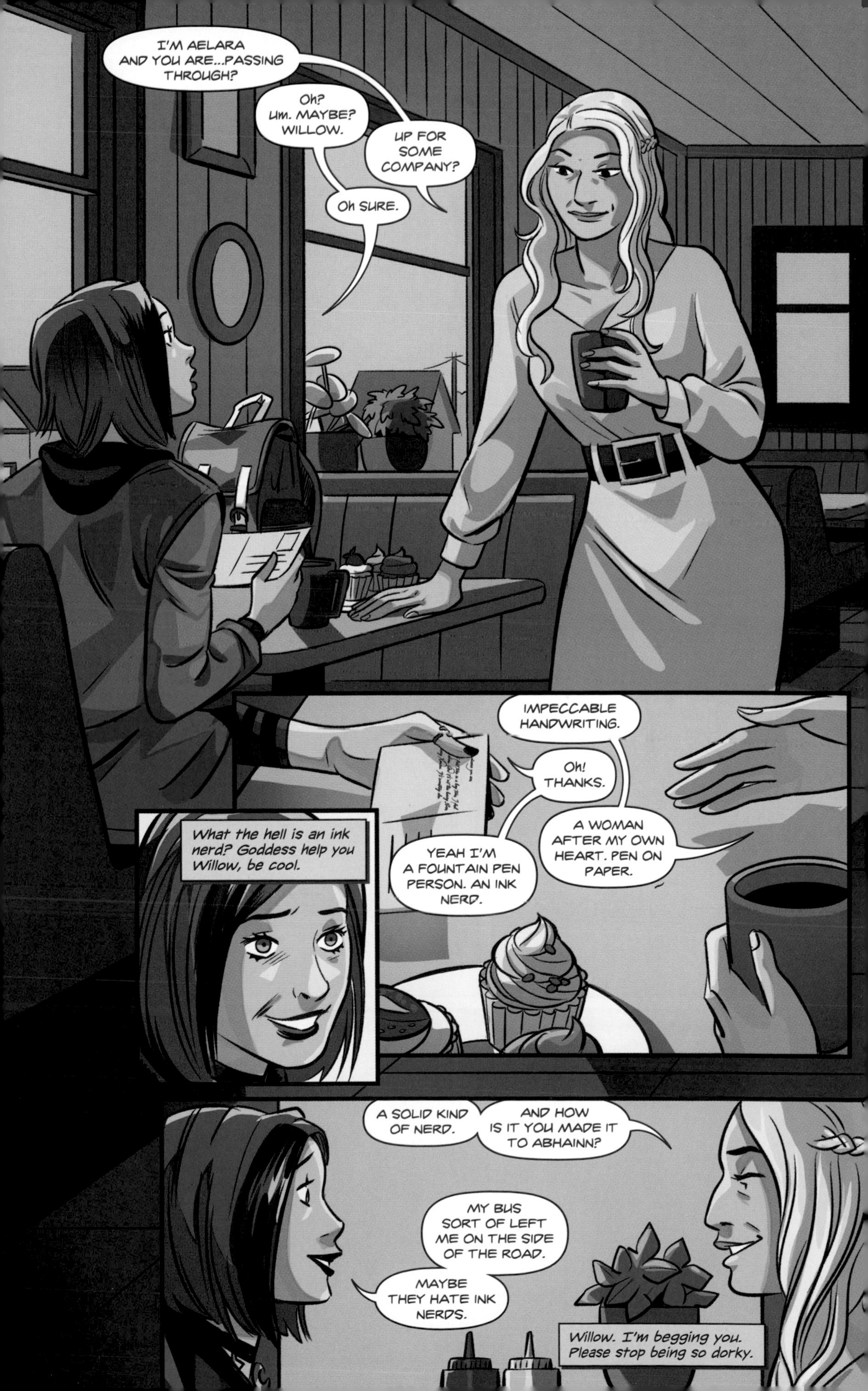
I'M AELARA AND YOU ARE...PASSING THROUGH?
Oh? Um. MAYBE? WILLOW.
UP FOR SOME COMPANY?
Oh SURE.
IMPECCABLE HANDWRITING.
Oh! THANKS.
YEAH I'M A FOUNTAIN PEN PERSON. AN INK NERD.
A WOMAN AFTER MY OWN HEART. PEN ON PAPER.
What the hell is an ink nerd? Goddess help you Willow, be cool.
A SOLID KIND OF NERD.
AND HOW IS IT YOU MADE IT TO ABHAINN?
MY BUS SORT OF LEFT ME ON THE SIDE OF THE ROAD.
MAYBE THEY HATE INK NERDS.
Willow. I'm begging you. Please stop being so dorky.

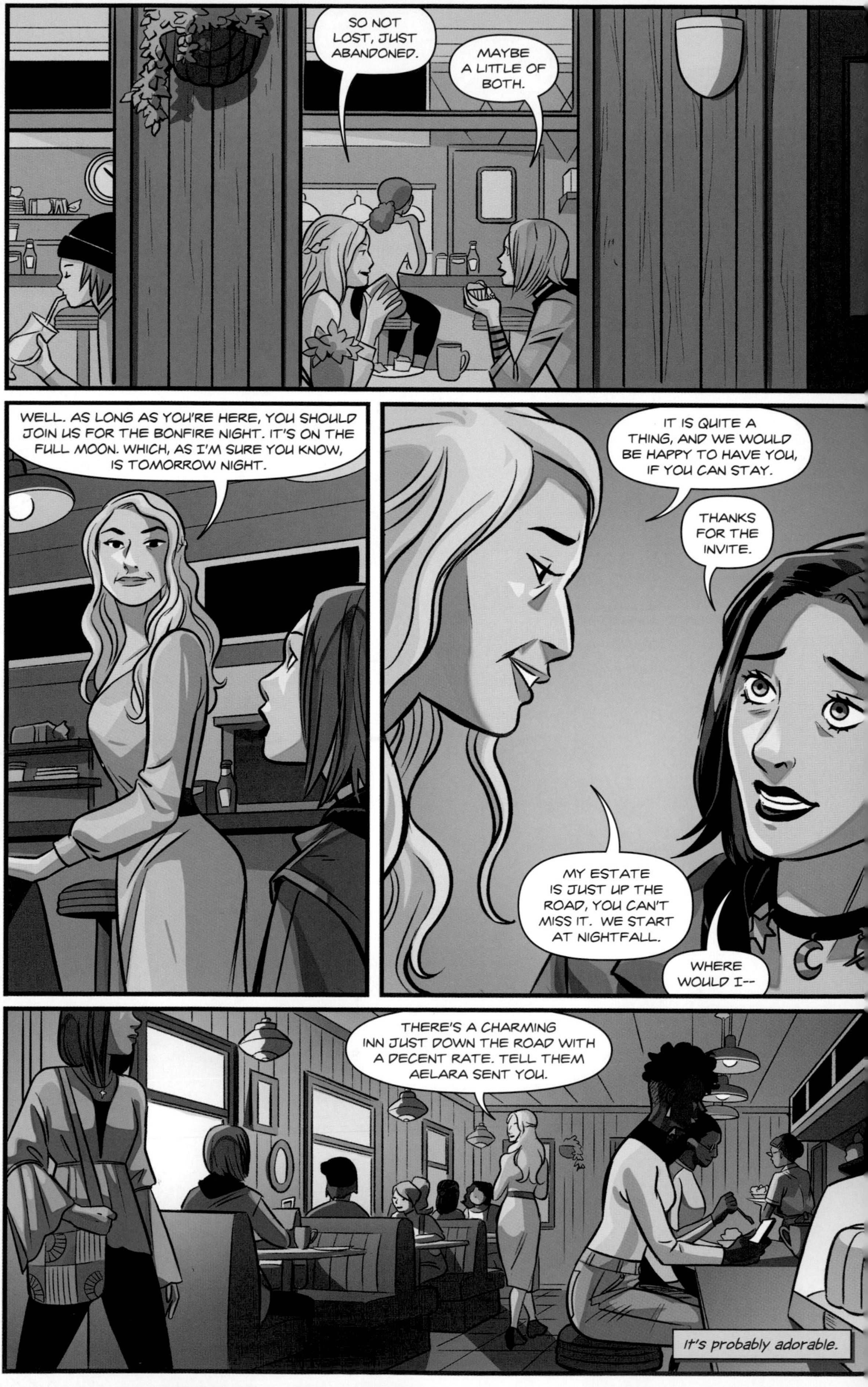
SO NOT LOST, JUST ABANDONED.
MAYBE A LITTLE OF BOTH.
WELL. AS LONG AS YOU'RE HERE, YOU SHOULD JOIN US FOR THE BONFIRE NIGHT. IT'S ON THE FULL MOON. WHICH, AS I'M SURE YOU KNOW, IS TOMORROW NIGHT.
IT IS QUITE A THING, AND WE WOULD BE HAPPY TO HAVE YOU, IF YOU CAN STAY.
THANKS FOR THE INVITE.
MY ESTATE IS JUST UP THE ROAD, YOU CAN'T MISS IT. WE START AT NIGHTFALL.
WHERE WOULD I--
THERE'S A CHARMING INN JUST DOWN THE ROAD WITH A DECENT RATE. TELL THEM AELARA SENT YOU.
It's probably adorable.

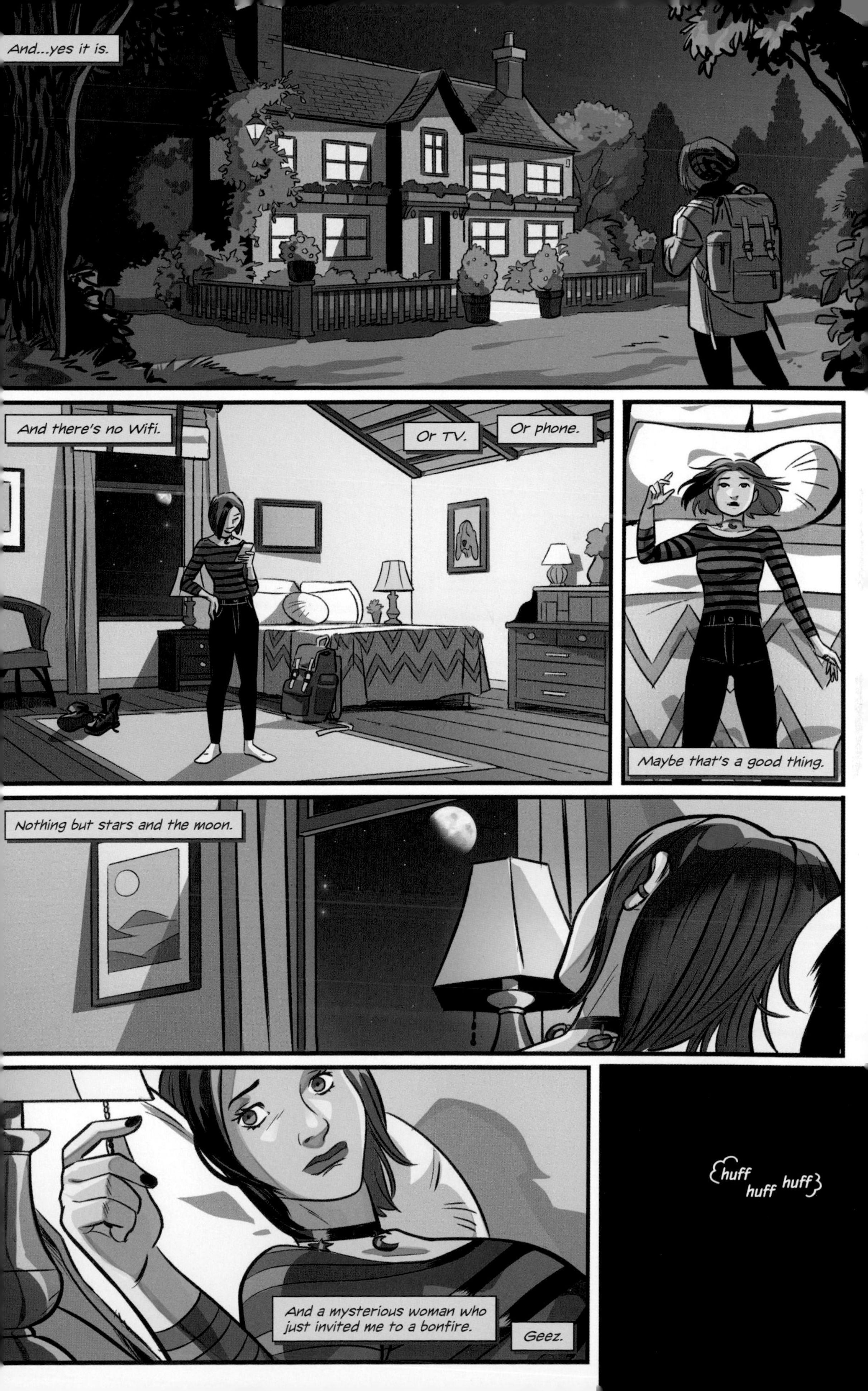
And...yes it is.
And there's no Wifi.
Or TV.
Or phone.
Maybe that's a good thing.
Nothing but stars and the moon.
And a mysterious woman who just invited me to a bonfire.
Geez.
huff huff huff

huff huff huff

CRACK
CRICK

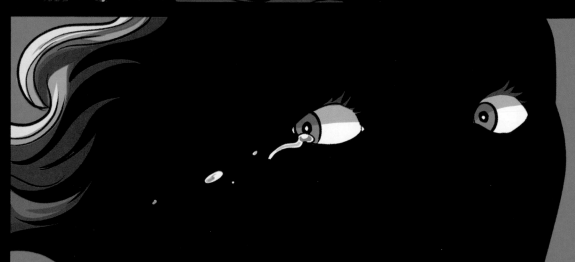

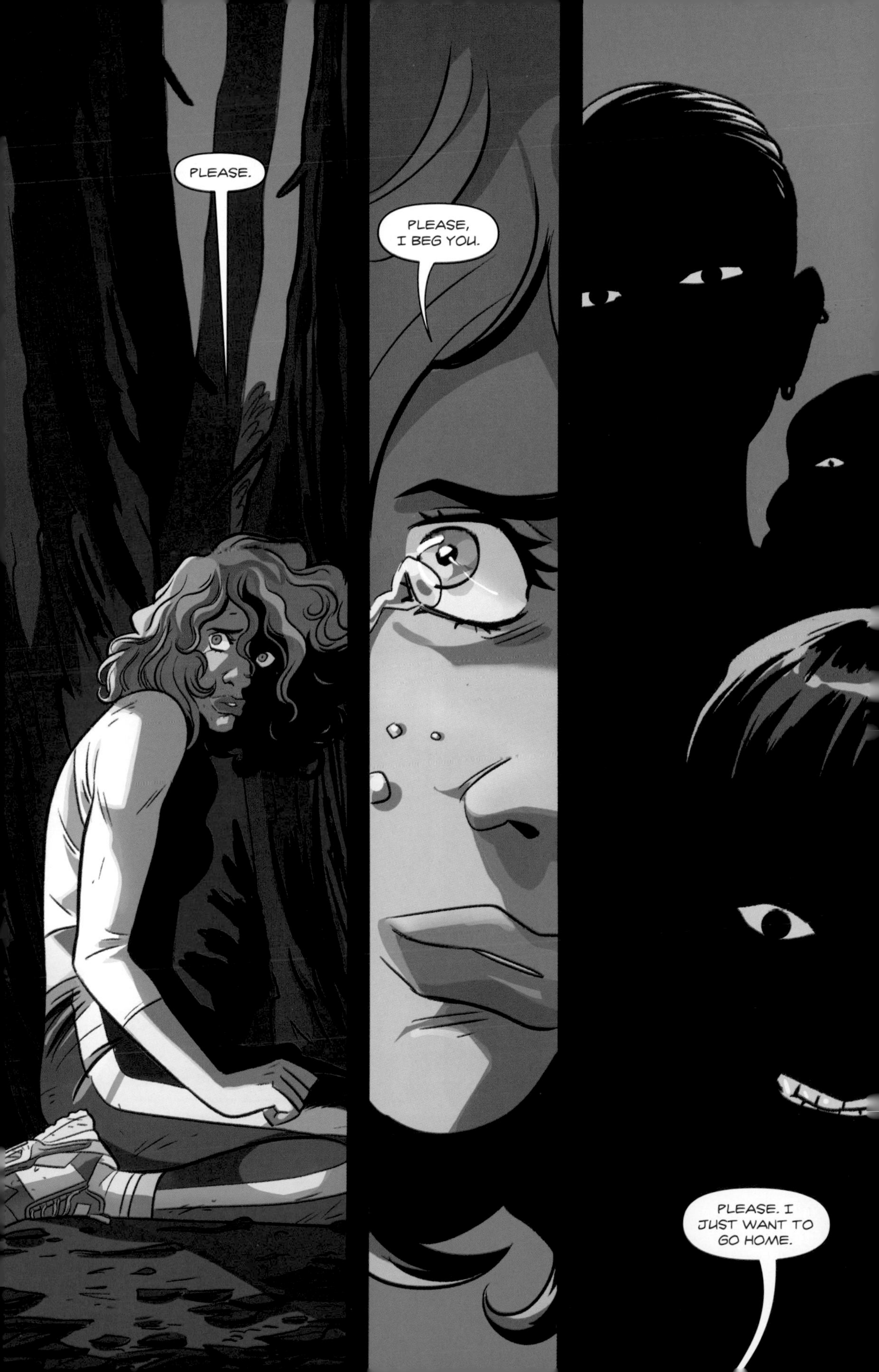
PLEASE.
PLEASE, I BEG YOU.
PLEASE. I JUST WANT TO GO HOME.

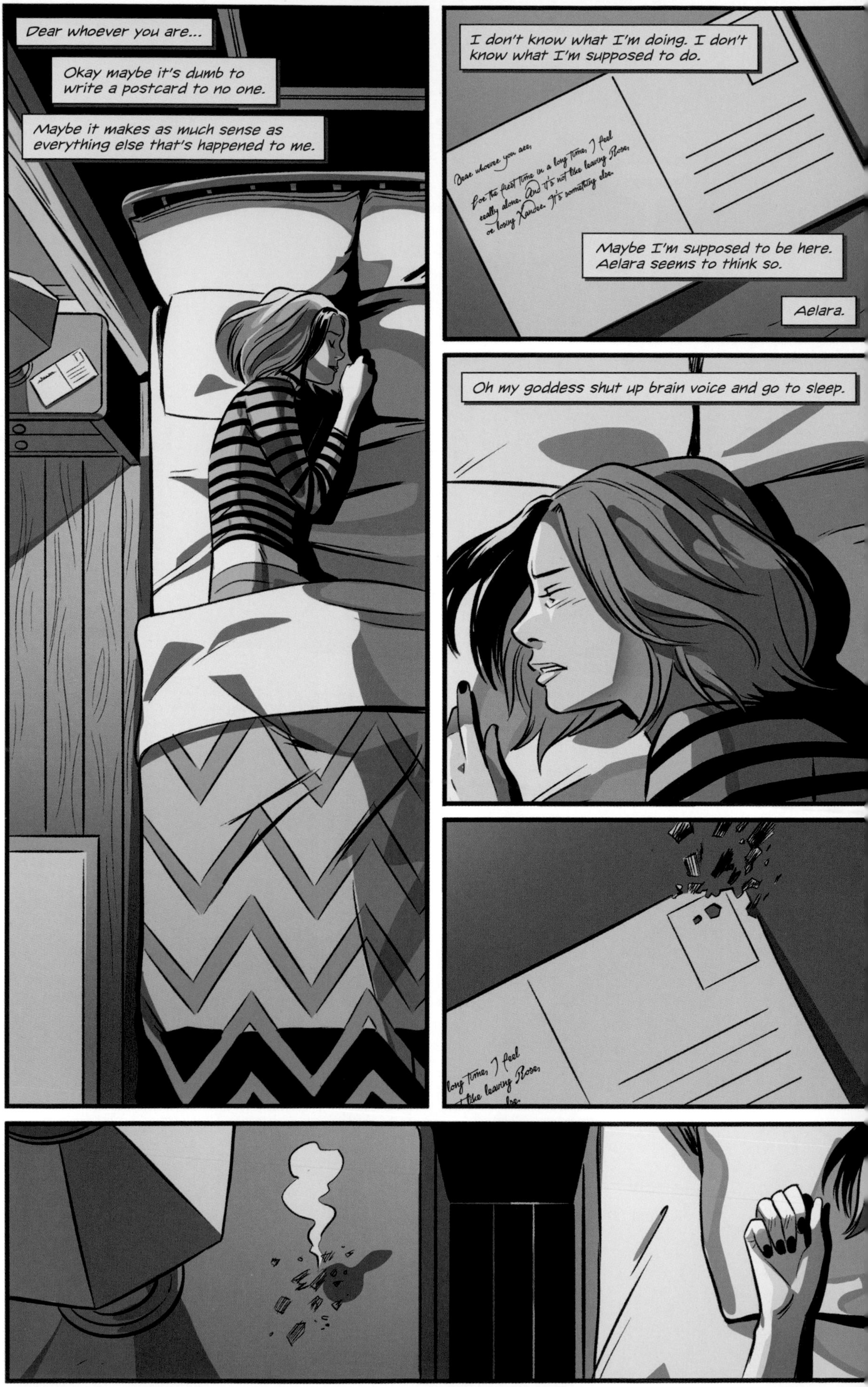
Dear whoever you are...
Okay maybe it's dumb to write a postcard to no one.
Maybe it makes as much sense as everything else that's happened to me.
I don't know what I'm doing. I don't know what I'm supposed to do.
Dear whoever you are,
For the first time in a long time, I feel really alone. And it's not like leaving Rose, or losing Xander. It's something else.
Maybe I'm supposed to be here. Aelara seems to think so.
Aelara.
Oh my goddess shut up brain voice and go to sleep.

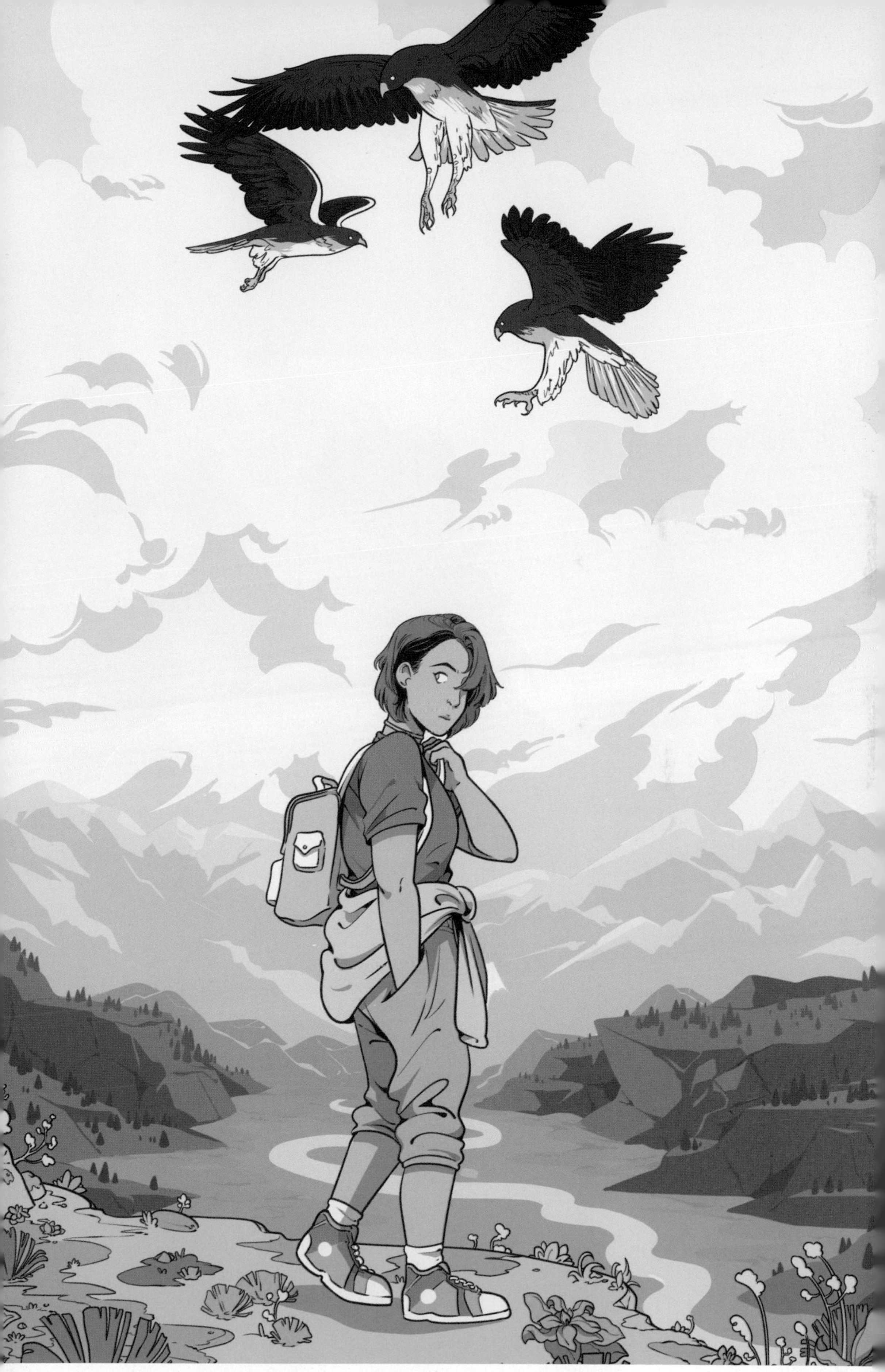

Willow #1 Variant Cover by **Rosemary Valero O'Connell**

CHAPTER
TWO

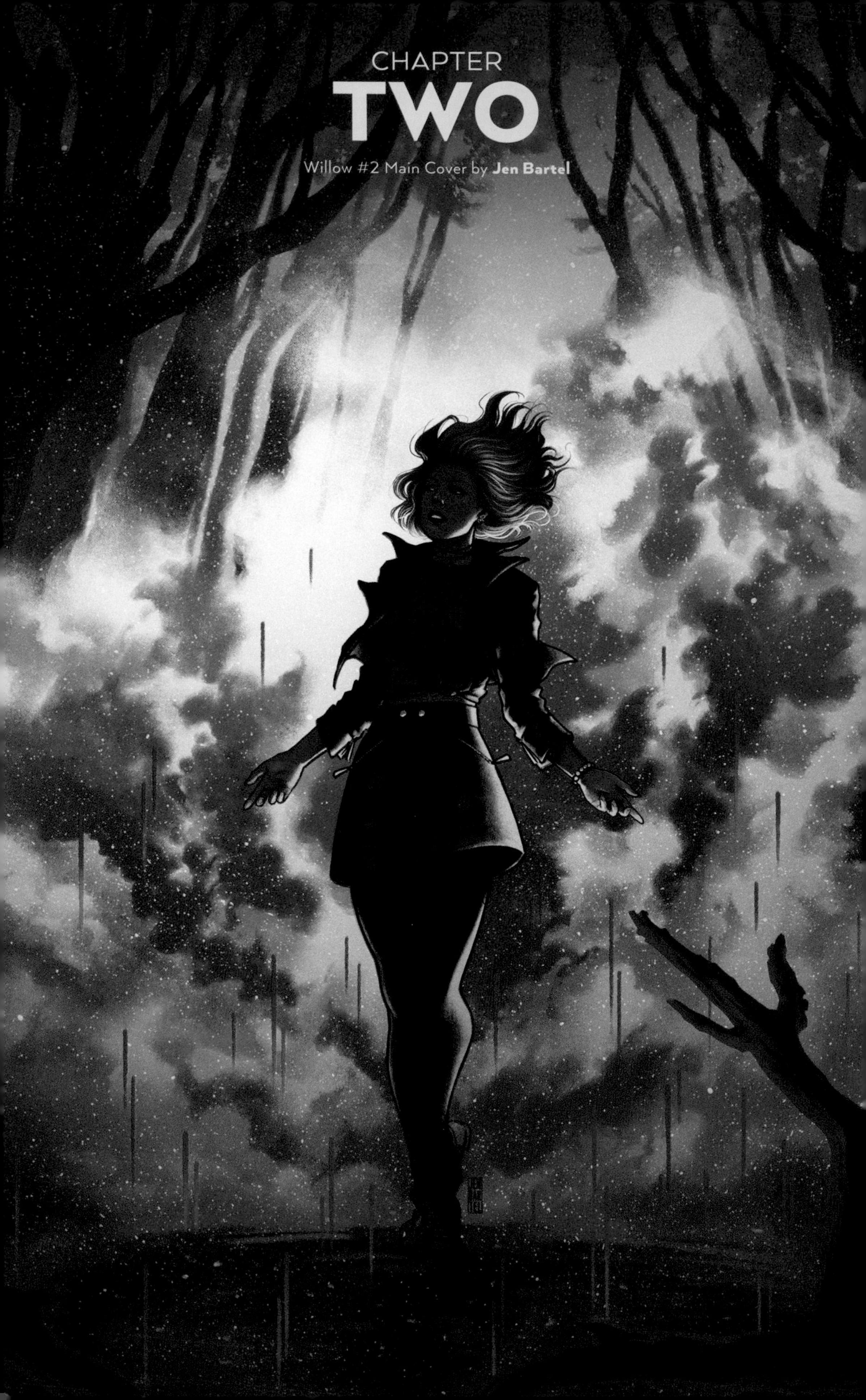

Willow #2 Main Cover by **Jen Bartel**

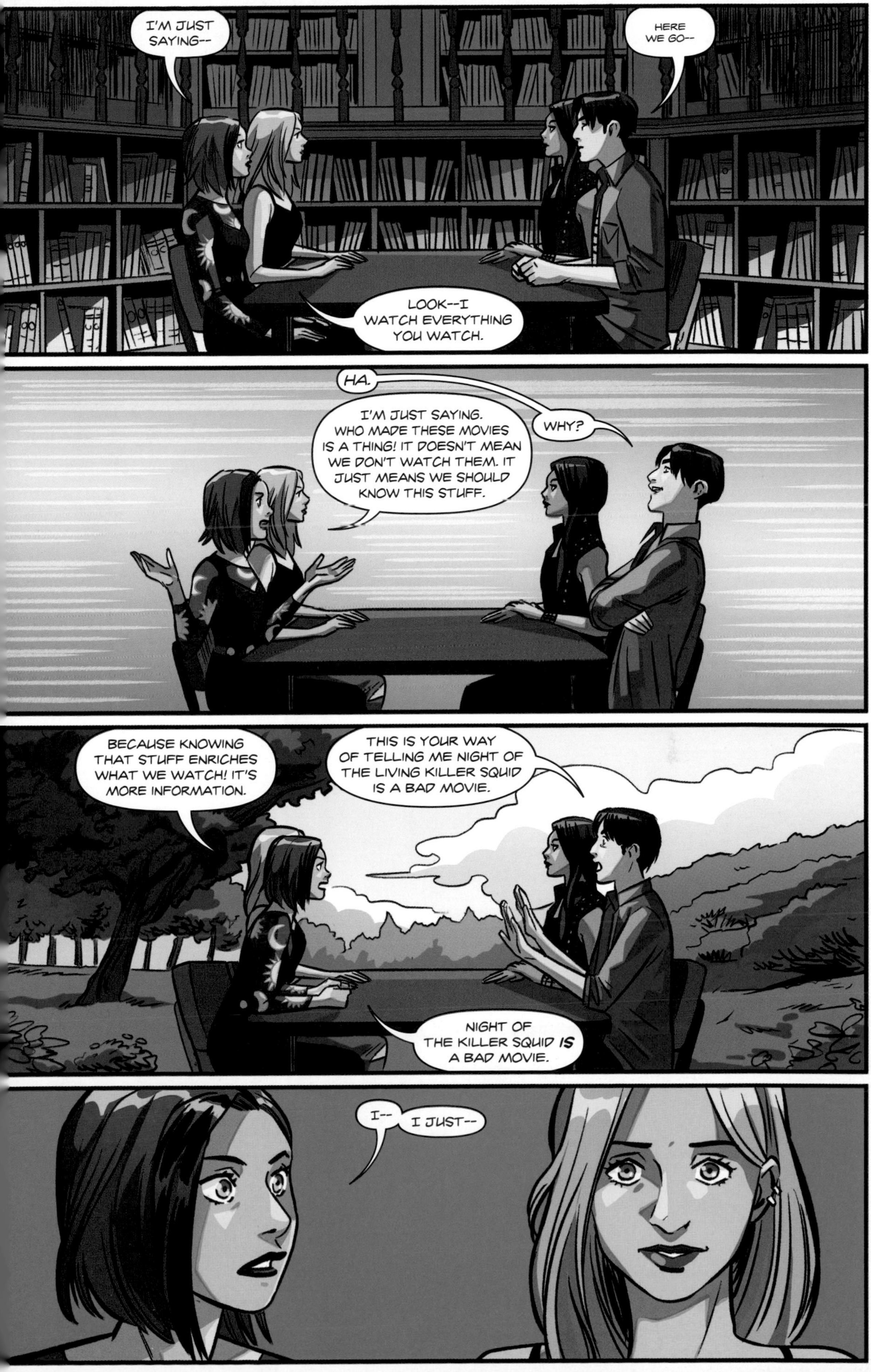
I'M JUST SAYING--
HERE WE GO--
LOOK--I WATCH EVERYTHING YOU WATCH.
HA.
I'M JUST SAYING. WHO MADE THESE MOVIES IS A THING! IT DOESN'T MEAN WE DON'T WATCH THEM. IT JUST MEANS WE SHOULD KNOW THIS STUFF.
WHY?
BECAUSE KNOWING THAT STUFF ENRICHES WHAT WE WATCH! IT'S MORE INFORMATION.
THIS IS YOUR WAY OF TELLING ME NIGHT OF THE LIVING KILLER SQUID IS A BAD MOVIE.
NIGHT OF THE KILLER SQUID *IS* A BAD MOVIE.
I--
I JUST--

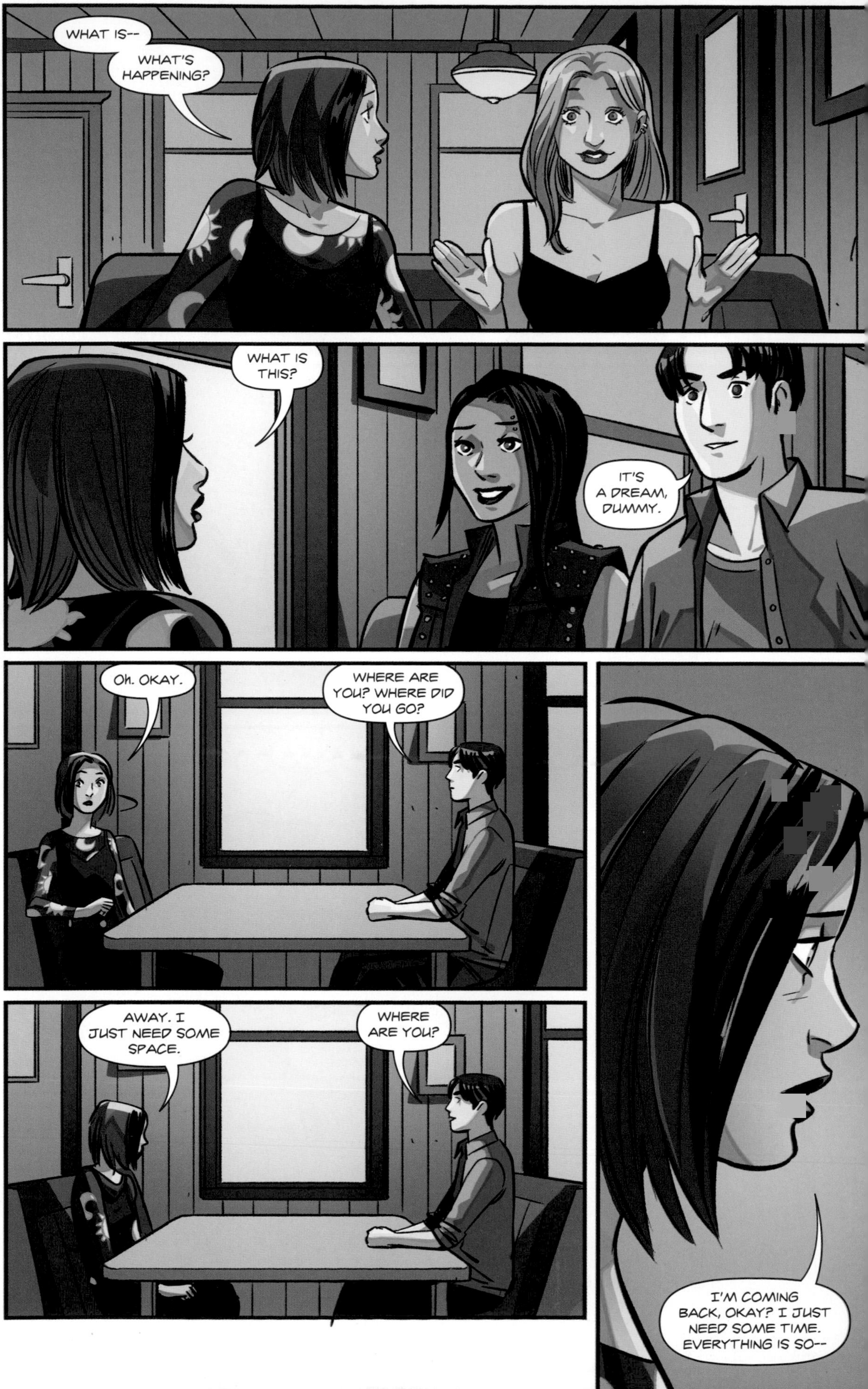
WHAT IS--
WHAT'S HAPPENING?
WHAT IS THIS?
IT'S A DREAM, DUMMY.
Oh. OKAY.
WHERE ARE YOU? WHERE DID YOU GO?
AWAY. I JUST NEED SOME SPACE.
WHERE ARE YOU?
I'M COMING BACK, OKAY? I JUST NEED SOME TIME. EVERYTHING IS SO--

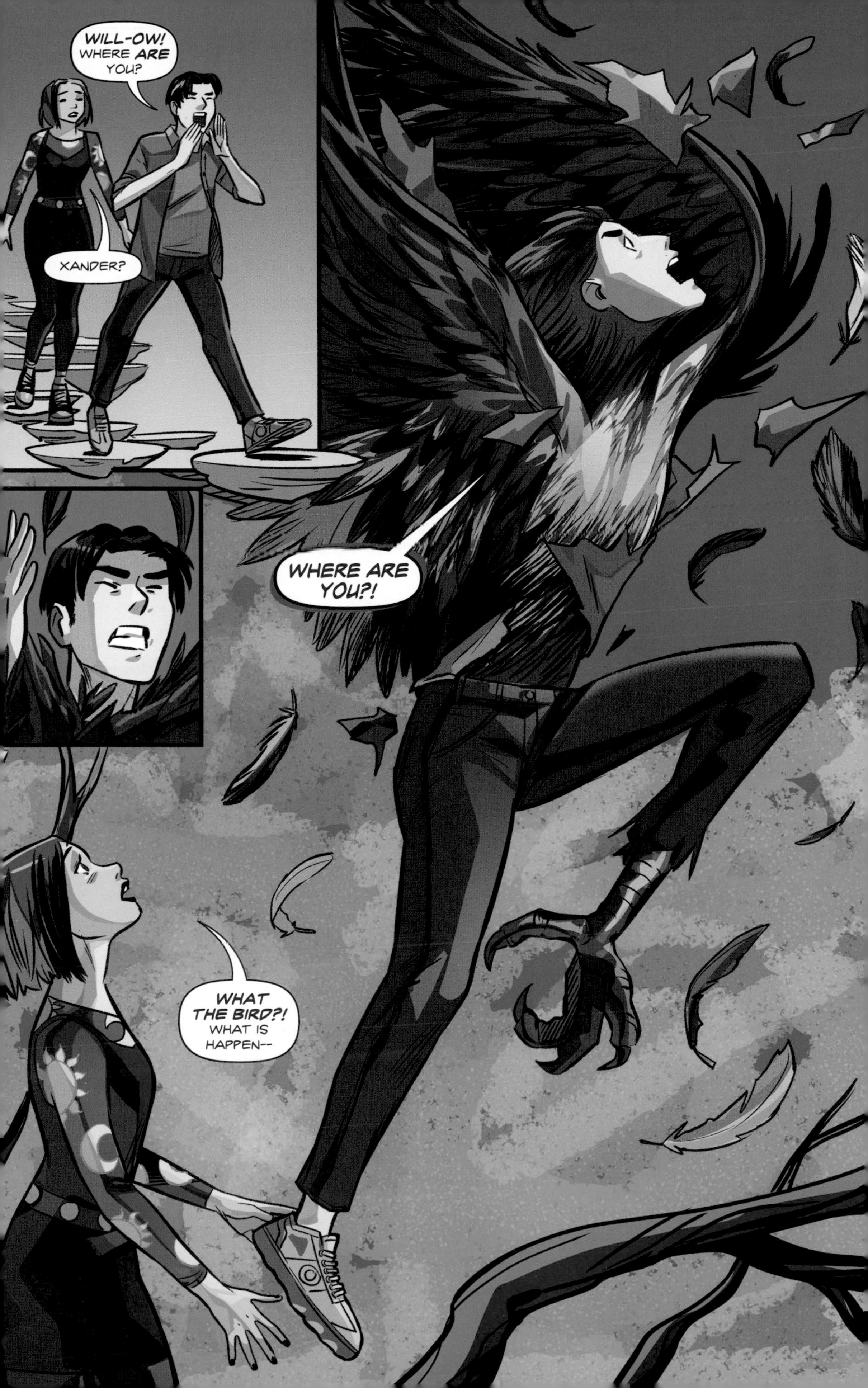
WILL-OW! WHERE ARE YOU?
XANDER?
WHERE ARE YOU?!
WHAT THE BIRD?! WHAT IS HAPPEN--

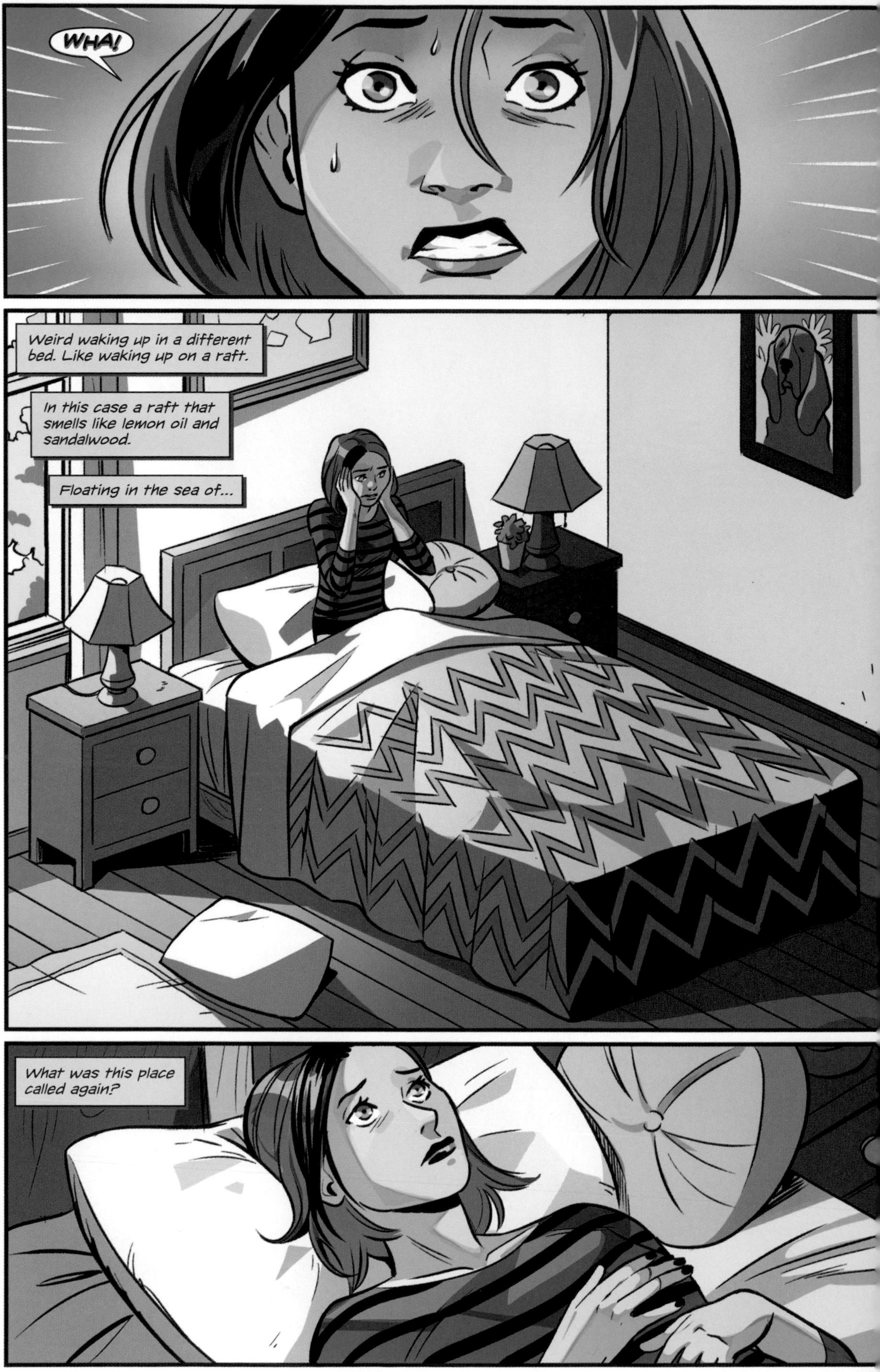
WHA!
Weird waking up in a different bed. Like waking up on a raft.
In this case a raft that smells like lemon oil and sandalwood.
Floating in the sea of...
What was this place called again?

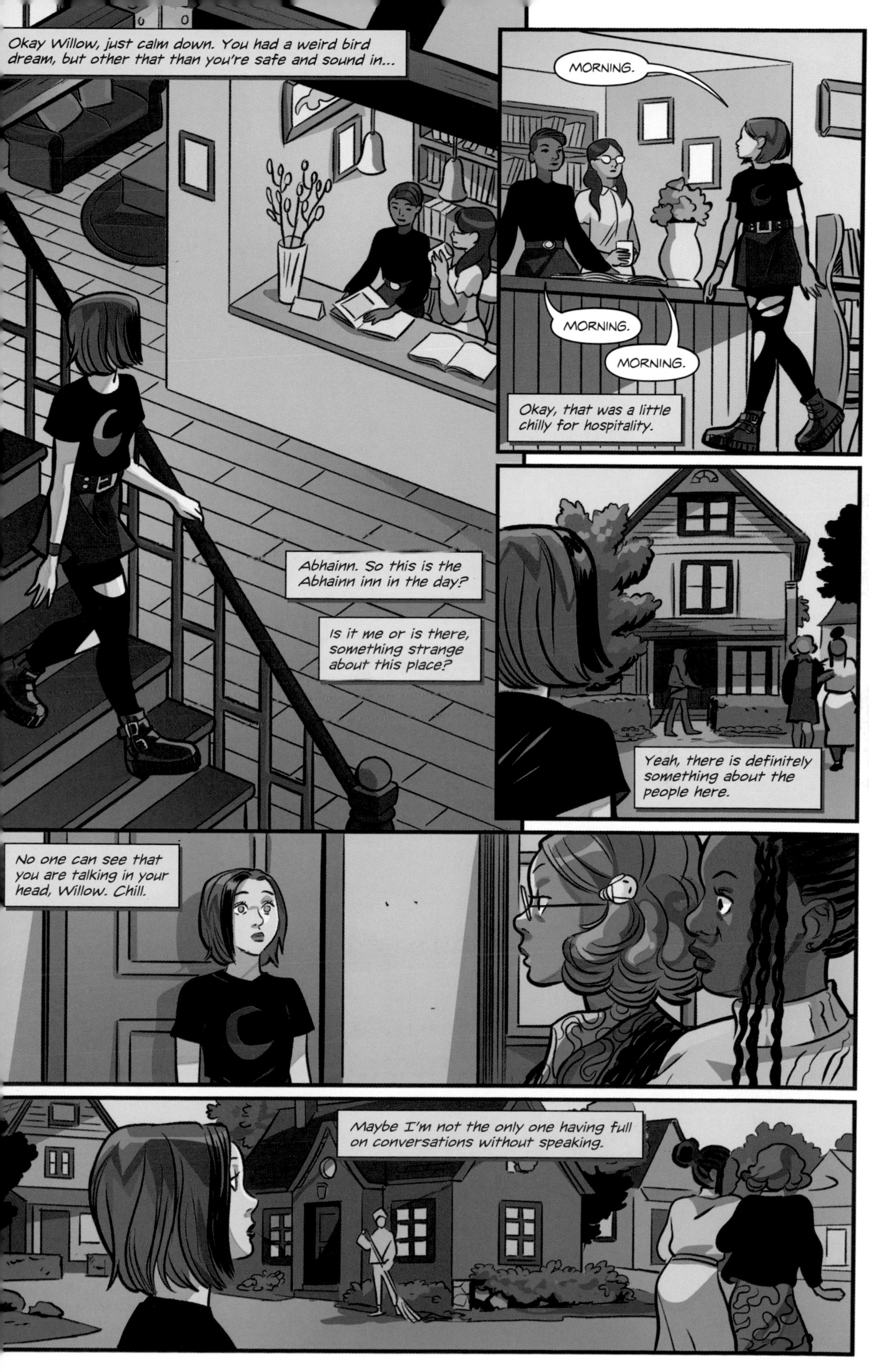
Okay Willow, just calm down. You had a weird bird dream, but other that than you're safe and sound in...
Abhainn. So this is the Abhainn inn in the day?
Is it me or is there, something strange about this place?
MORNING.
MORNING.
MORNING.
Okay, that was a little chilly for hospitality.
Yeah, there is definitely something about the people here.
No one can see that you are talking in your head, Willow. Chill.
Maybe I'm not the only one having full on conversations without speaking.

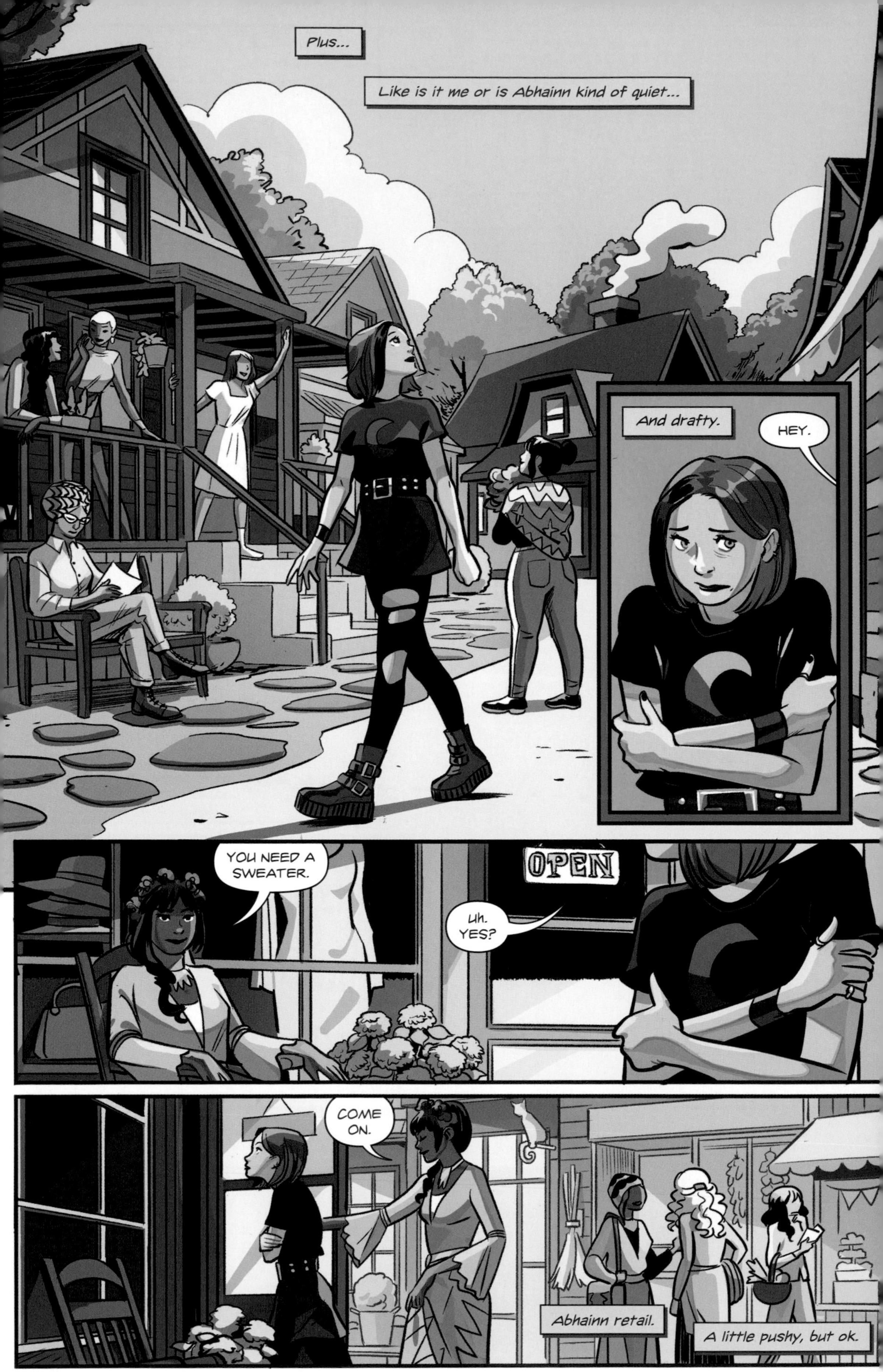
Plus...
Like is it me or is Abhainn kind of quiet...
And drafty.
HEY.
YOU NEED A SWEATER.
OPEN
Uh. YES?
COME ON.
Abhainn retail.
A little pushy, but ok.

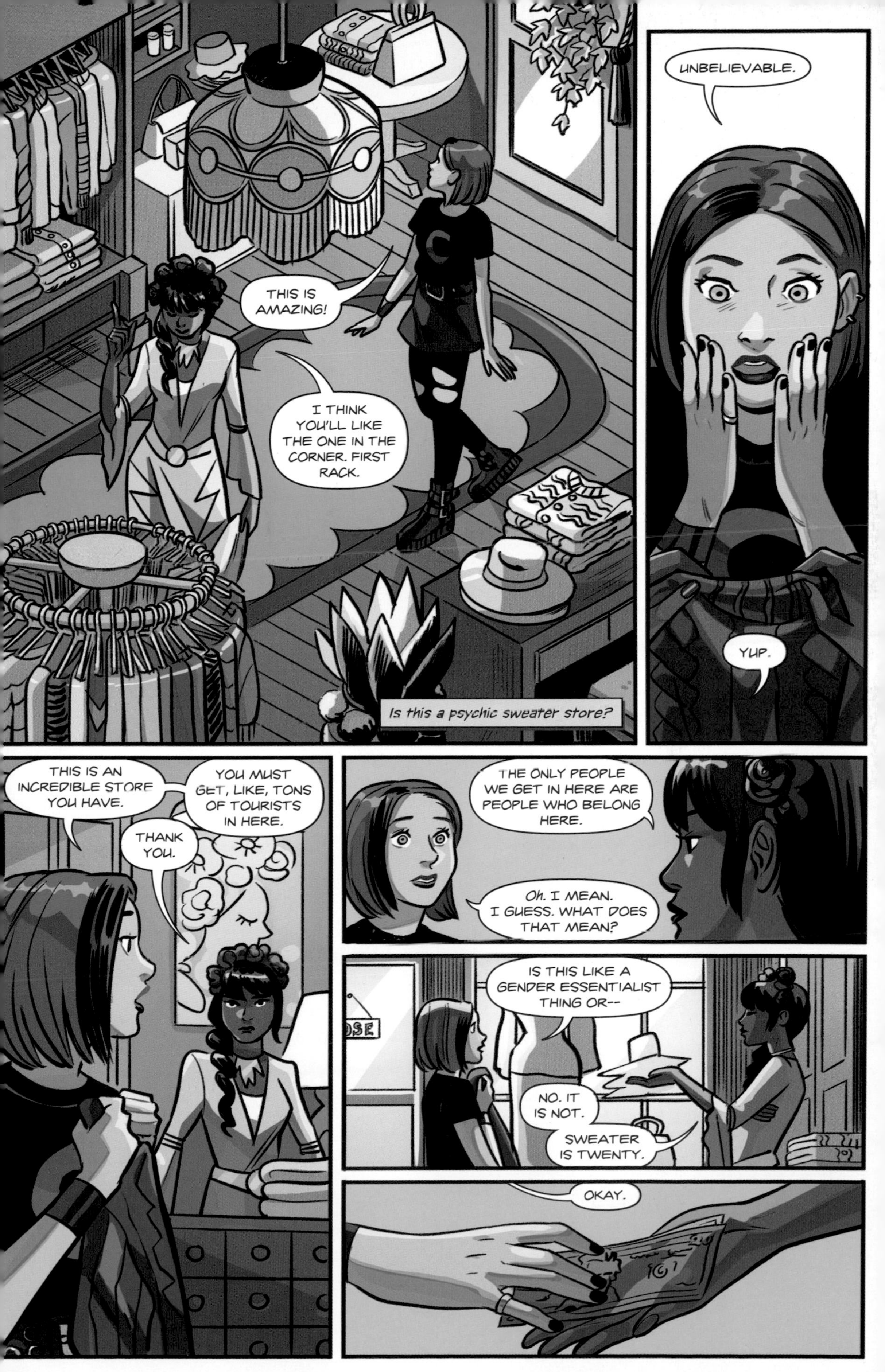
THIS IS AMAZING!
I THINK YOU'LL LIKE THE ONE IN THE CORNER. FIRST RACK.
Is this a psychic sweater store?
UNBELIEVABLE.
YUP.
THIS IS AN INCREDIBLE STORE YOU HAVE.
THANK YOU.
YOU MUST GET, LIKE, TONS OF TOURISTS IN HERE.
THE ONLY PEOPLE WE GET IN HERE ARE PEOPLE WHO BELONG HERE.
Oh. I MEAN. I GUESS. WHAT DOES THAT MEAN?
IS THIS LIKE A GENDER ESSENTIALIST THING OR--
NO. IT IS NOT.
SWEATER IS TWENTY.
OKAY.

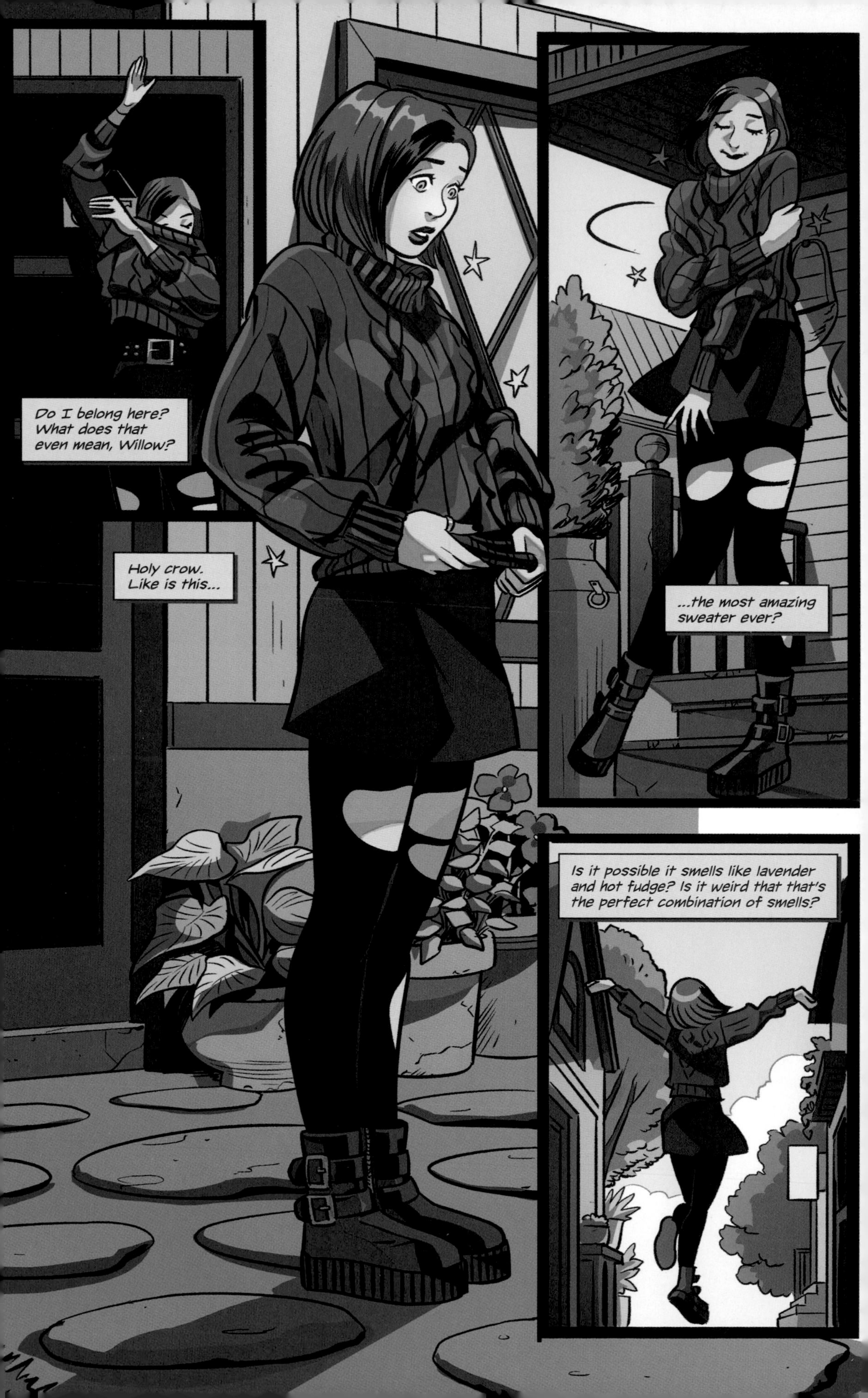
Do I belong here? What does that even mean, Willow?
Holy crow. Like is this...
...the most amazing sweater ever?
Is it possible it smells like lavender and hot fudge? Is it weird that that's the perfect combination of smells?

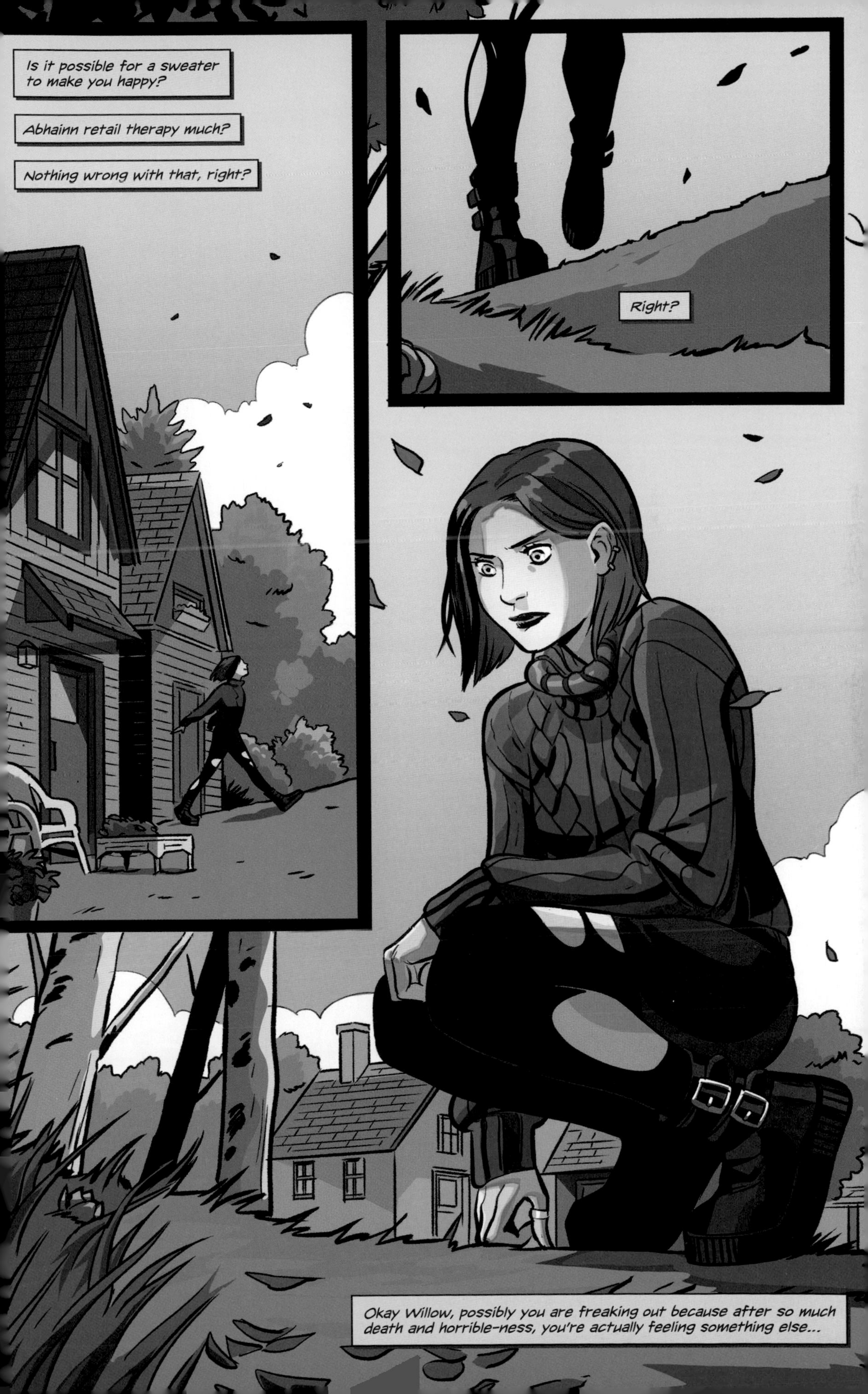
Is it possible for a sweater to make you happy?
Abhainn retail therapy much?
Nothing wrong with that, right?
Right?
Okay Willow, possibly you are freaking out because after so much death and horrible-ness, you're actually feeling something else...

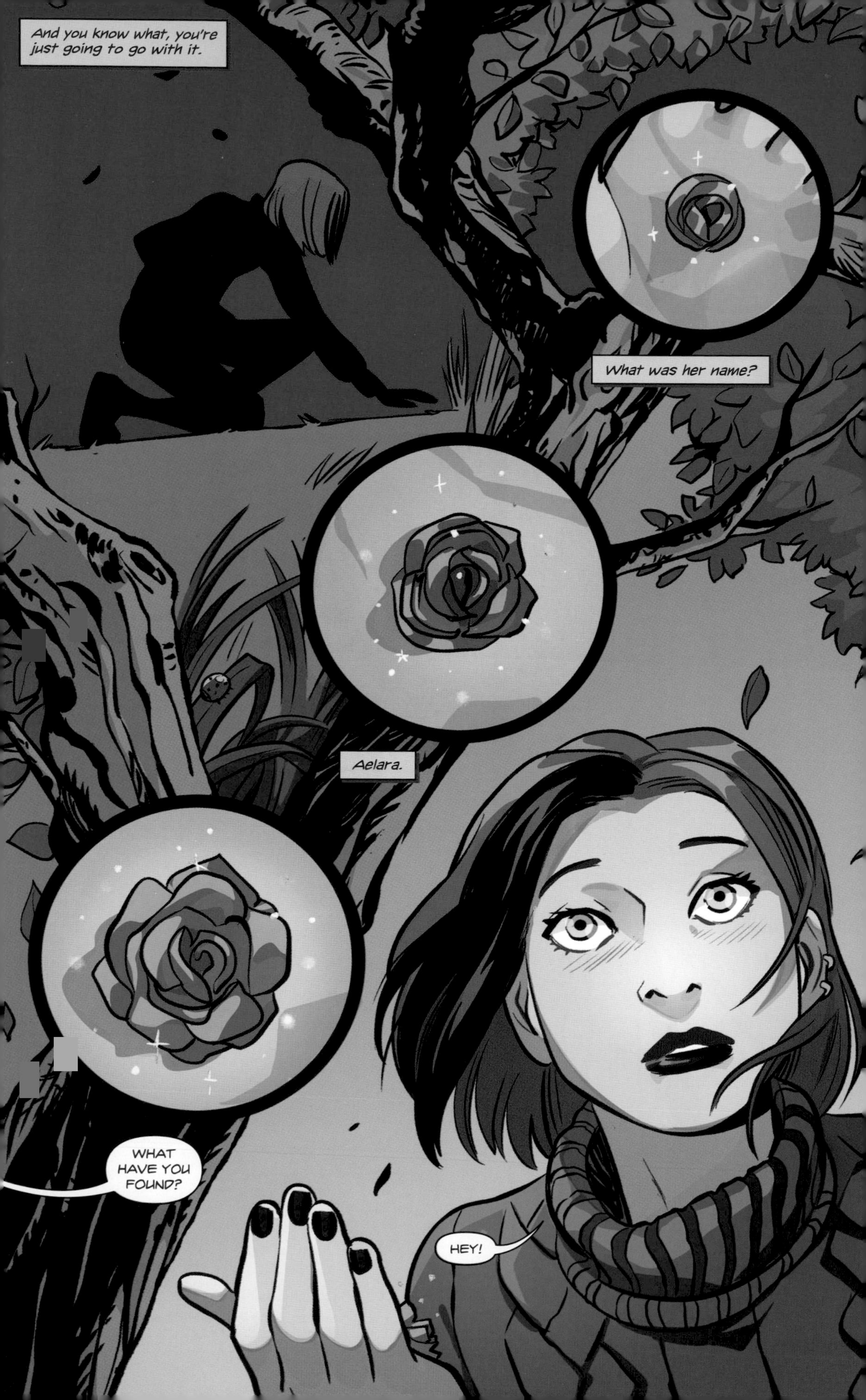
And you know what, you're just going to go with it.
What was her name?
Aelara.
WHAT HAVE YOU FOUND?
HEY!

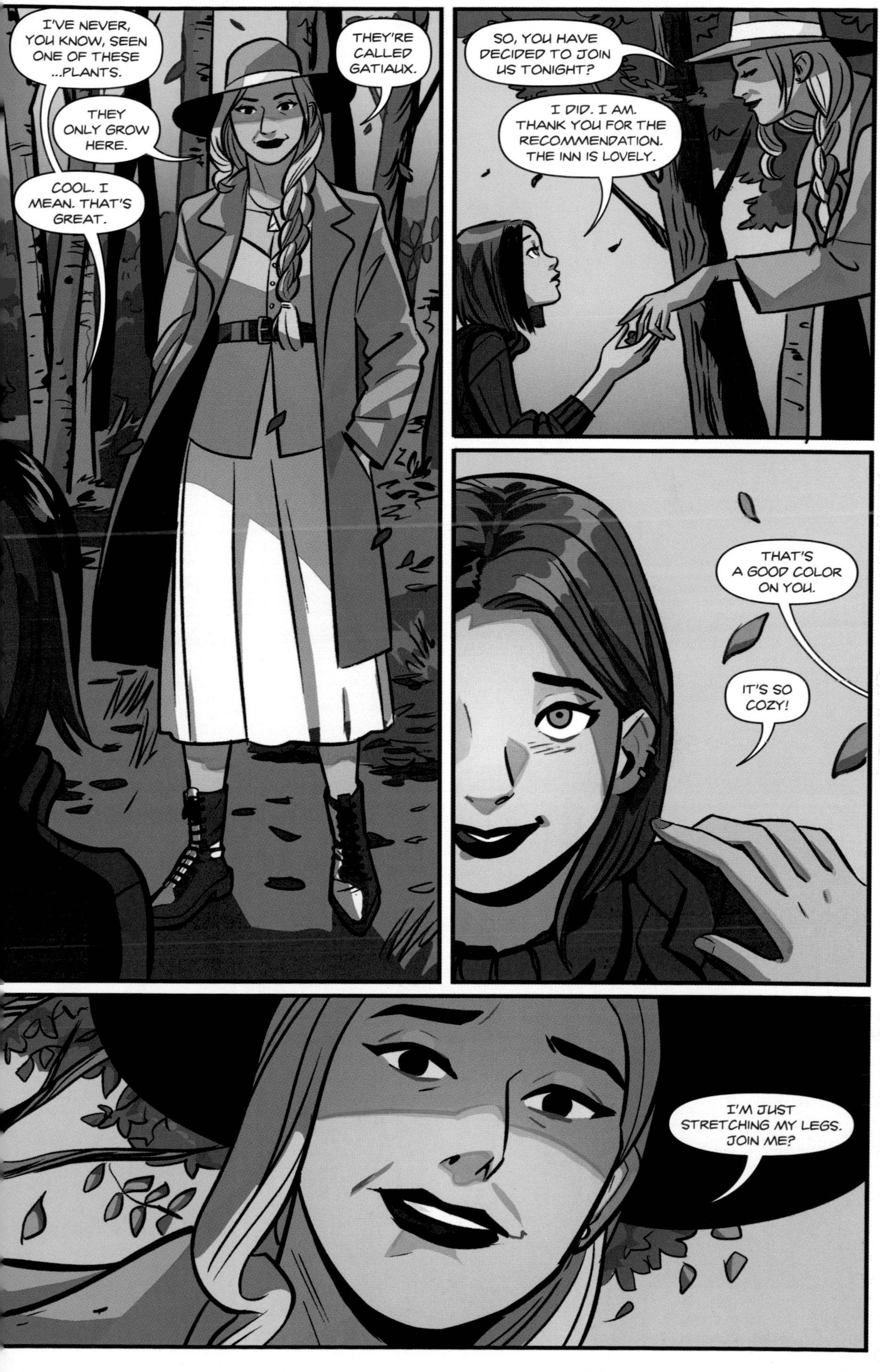
I'VE NEVER, YOU KNOW, SEEN ONE OF THESE ...PLANTS.
THEY'RE CALLED GATIAUX.
THEY ONLY GROW HERE.
COOL. I MEAN. THAT'S GREAT.
SO, YOU HAVE DECIDED TO JOIN US TONIGHT?
I DID. I AM. THANK YOU FOR THE RECOMMENDATION. THE INN IS LOVELY.
THAT'S A GOOD COLOR ON YOU.
IT'S SO COZY!
I'M JUST STRETCHING MY LEGS. JOIN ME?

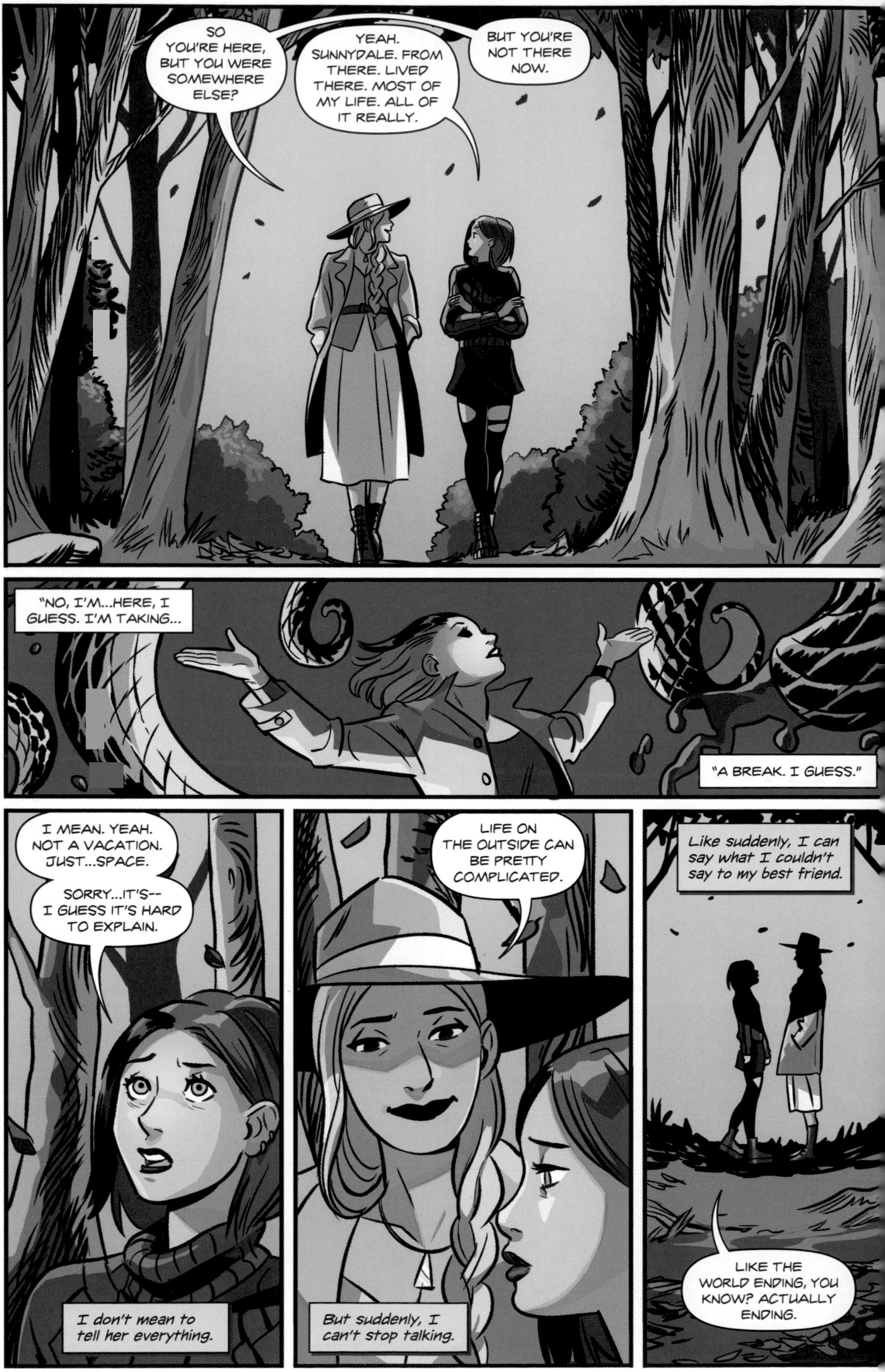
SO YOU'RE HERE, BUT YOU WERE SOMEWHERE ELSE?
YEAH. SUNNYDALE. FROM THERE. LIVED THERE. MOST OF MY LIFE. ALL OF IT REALLY.
BUT YOU'RE NOT THERE NOW.
"NO, I'M...HERE, I GUESS. I'M TAKING...
"A BREAK. I GUESS."
I MEAN. YEAH. NOT A VACATION. JUST...SPACE.
SORRY...IT'S-- I GUESS IT'S HARD TO EXPLAIN.
I don't mean to tell her everything.
LIFE ON THE OUTSIDE CAN BE PRETTY COMPLICATED.
But suddenly, I can't stop talking.
Like suddenly, I can say what I couldn't say to my best friend.
LIKE THE WORLD ENDING, YOU KNOW? ACTUALLY ENDING.

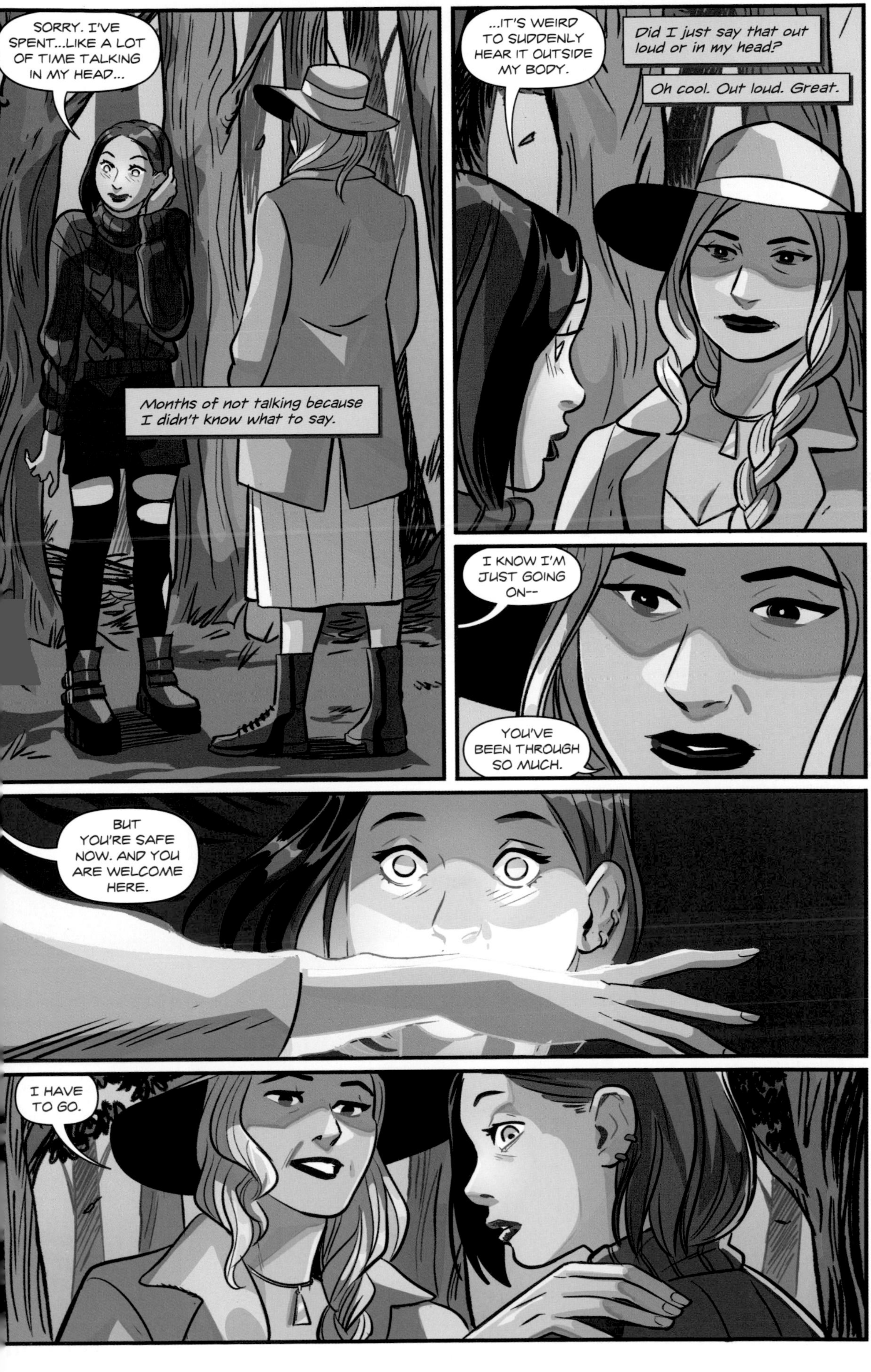
SORRY. I'VE SPENT...LIKE A LOT OF TIME TALKING IN MY HEAD...
Months of not talking because I didn't know what to say.
...IT'S WEIRD TO SUDDENLY HEAR IT OUTSIDE MY BODY.
Did I just say that out loud or in my head?
Oh cool. Out loud. Great.
I KNOW I'M JUST GOING ON--
YOU'VE BEEN THROUGH SO MUCH.
BUT YOU'RE SAFE NOW. AND YOU ARE WELCOME HERE.
I HAVE TO GO.

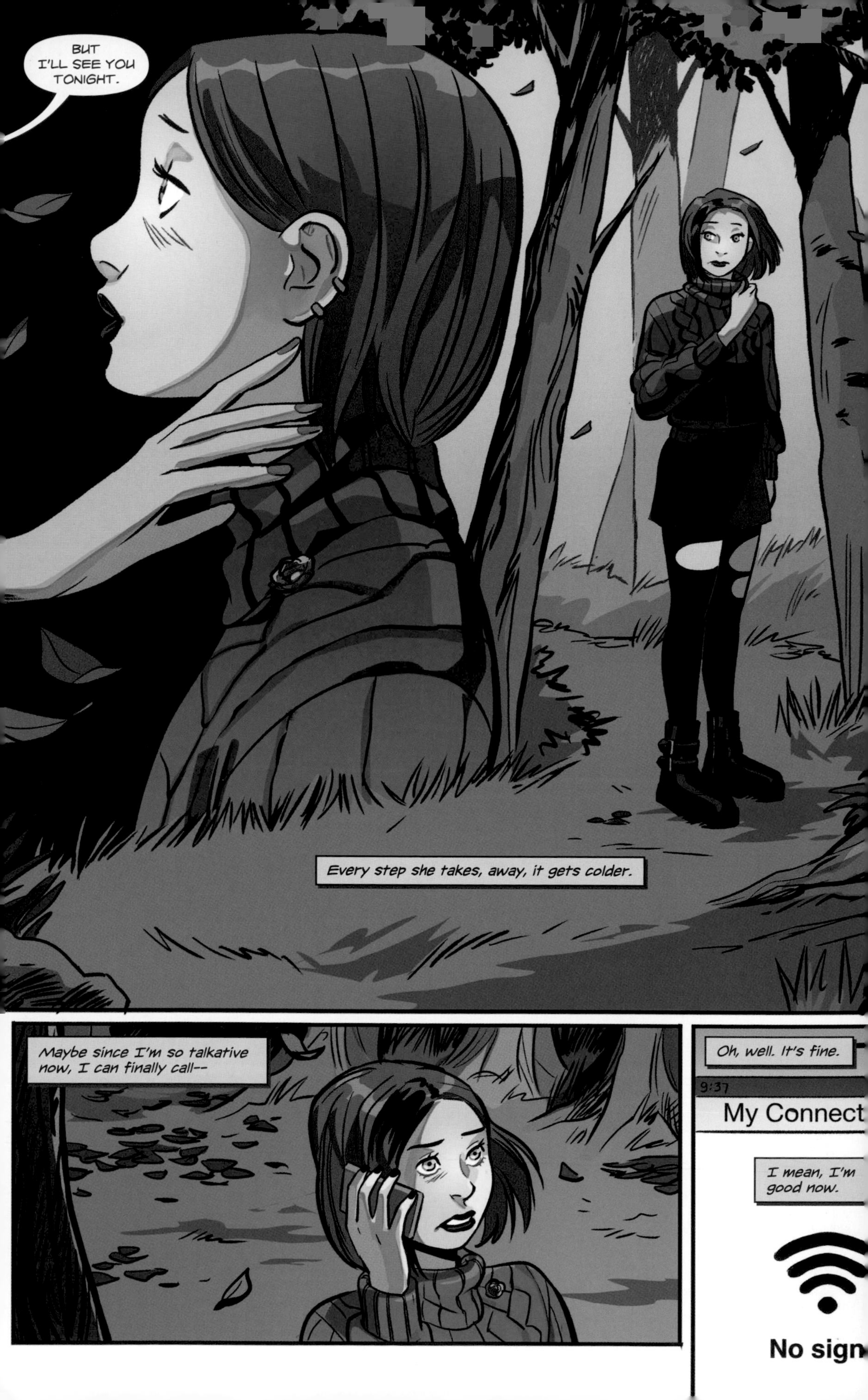
BUT I'LL SEE YOU TONIGHT.
Every step she takes, away, it gets colder.
Maybe since I'm so talkative now, I can finally call--
Oh, well. It's fine.
9:37
My Connect
I mean, I'm good now.
No sign

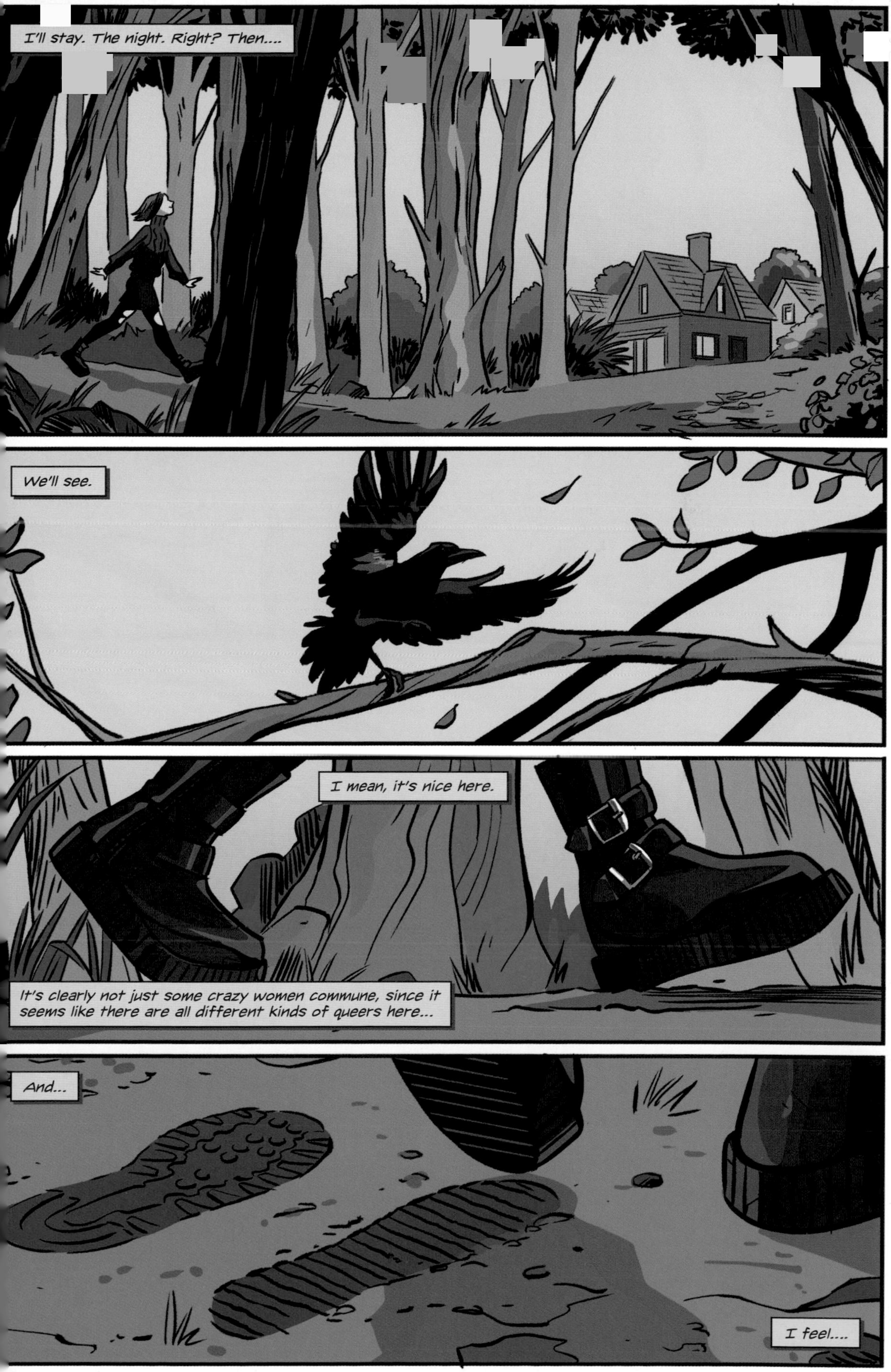
I'll stay. The night. Right? Then....
We'll see.
I mean, it's nice here.
It's clearly not just some crazy women commune, since it seems like there are all different kinds of queers here...
And...
I feel....

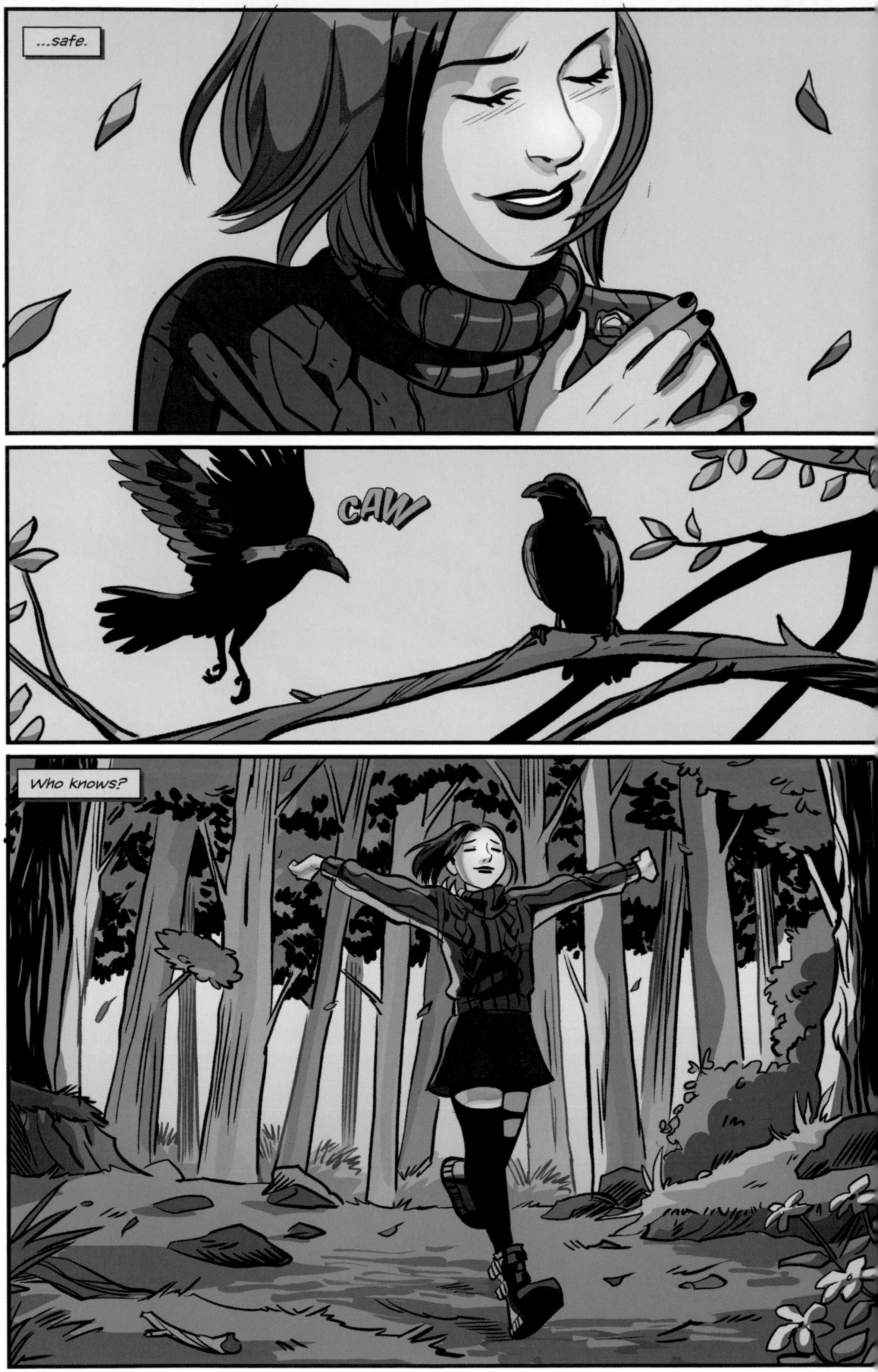
...safe.
CAW
Who knows?

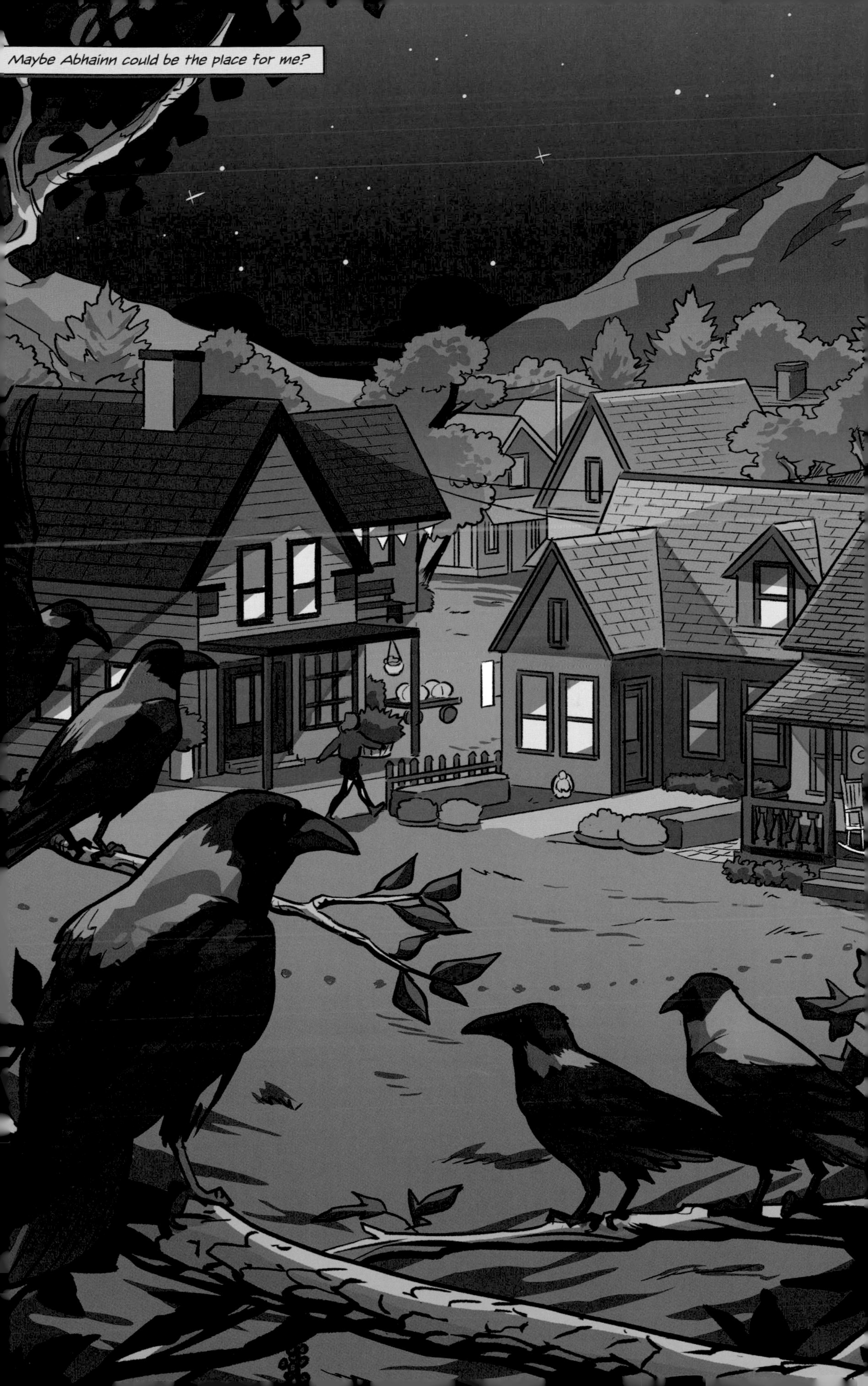
Maybe Abhainn could be the place for me?

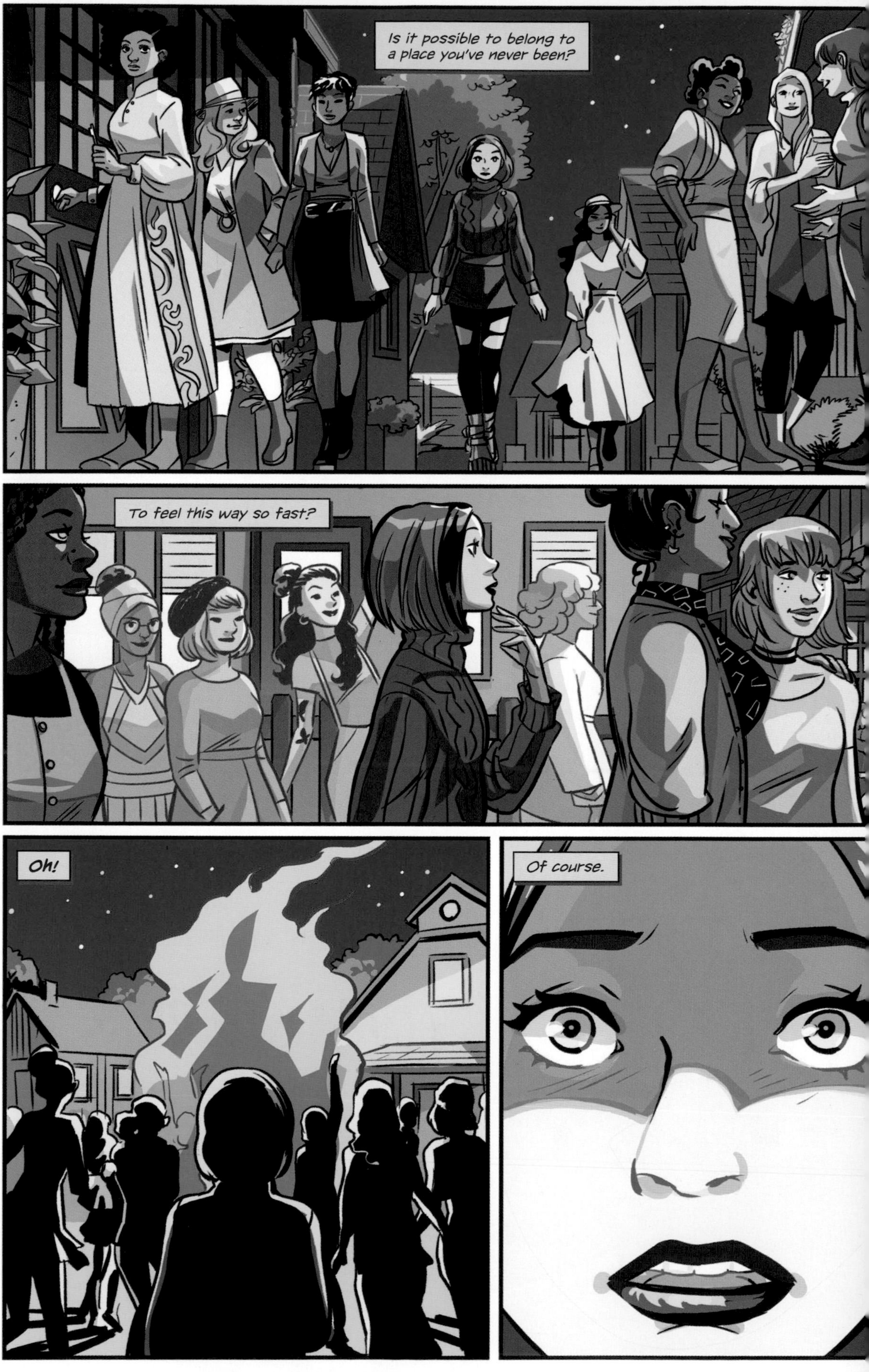
Is it possible to belong to a place you've never been?
To feel this way so fast?
Oh!
Of course.

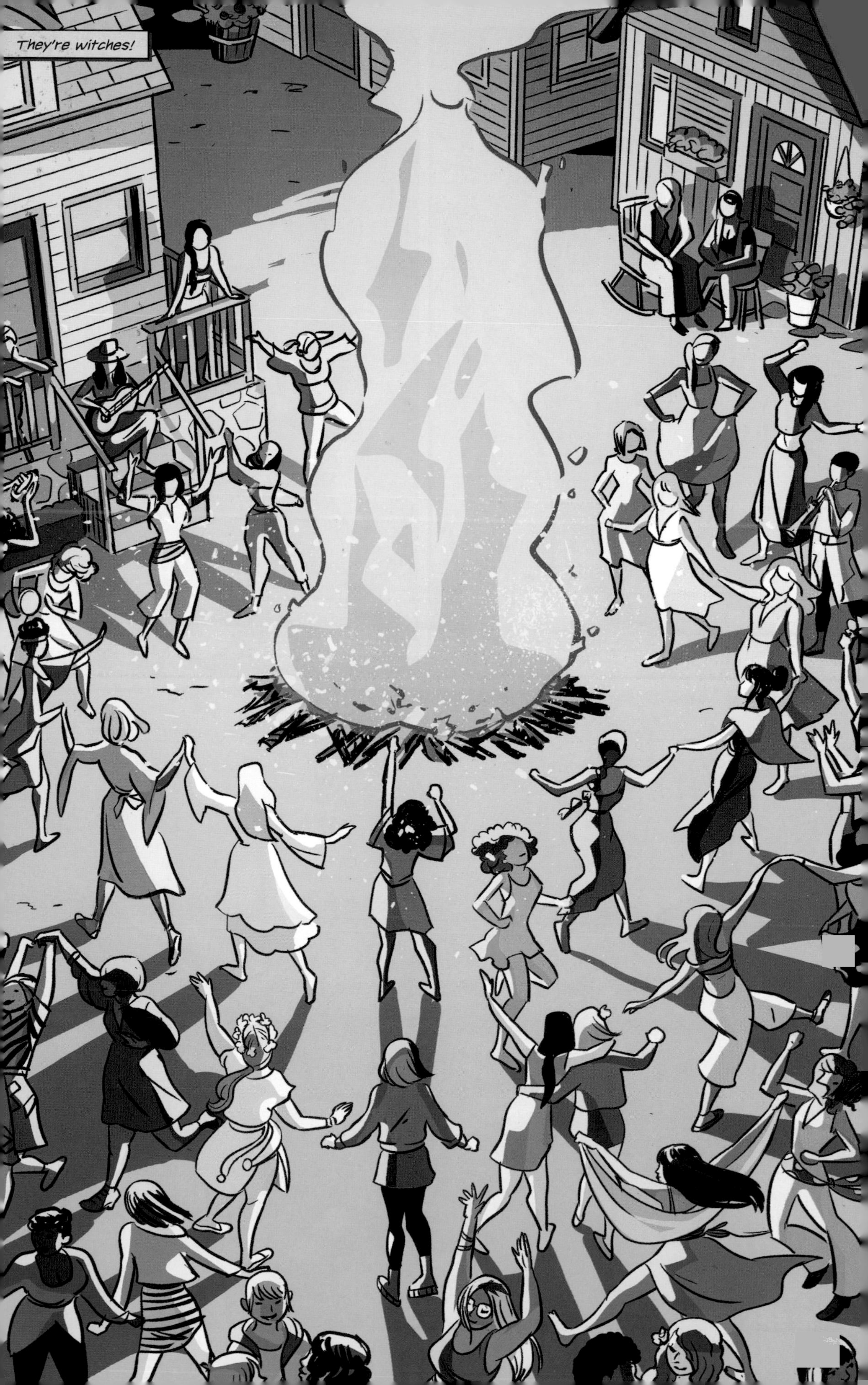
They're witches!

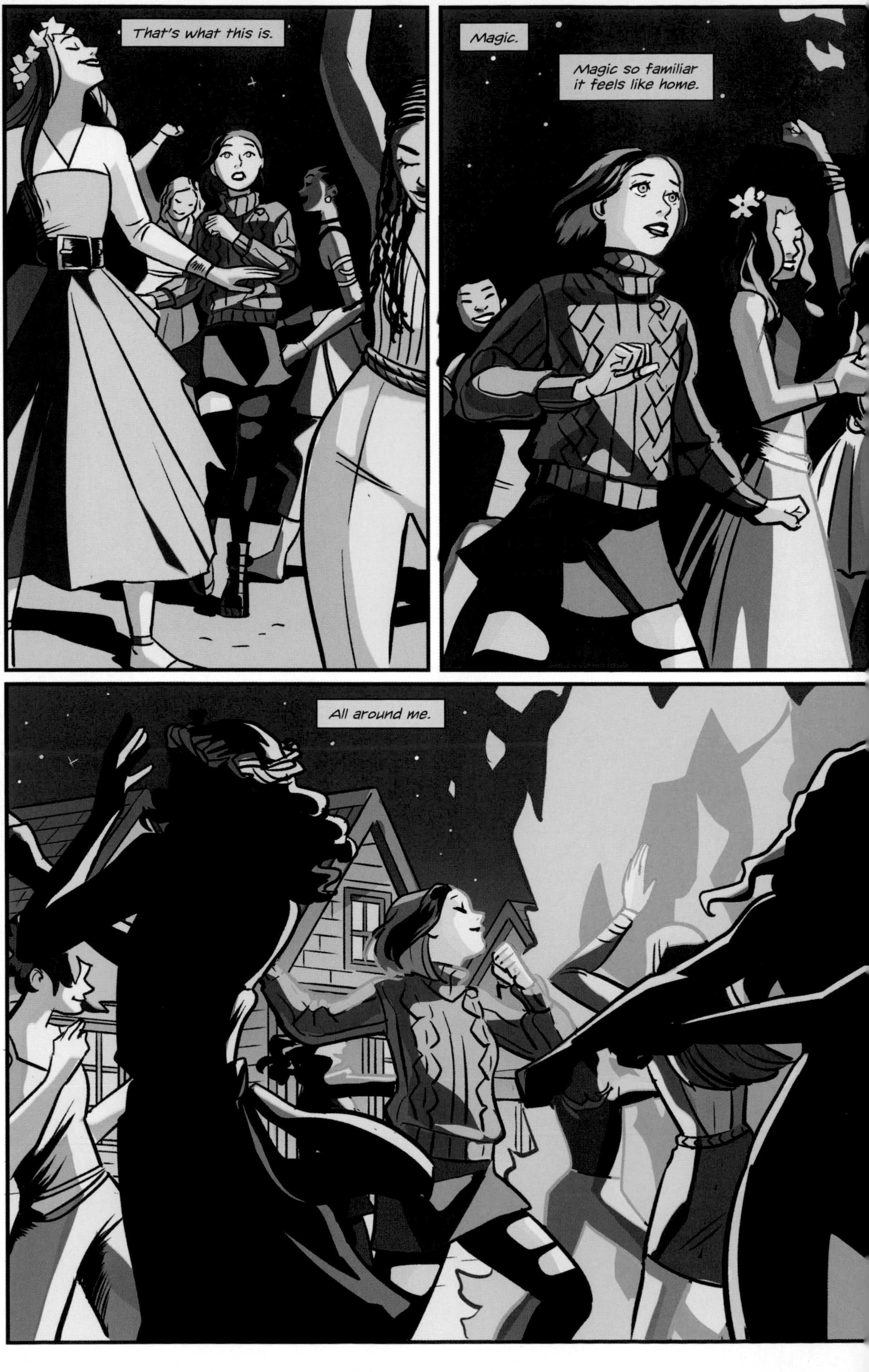
That's what this is.
Magic.
Magic so familiar it feels like home.
All around me.

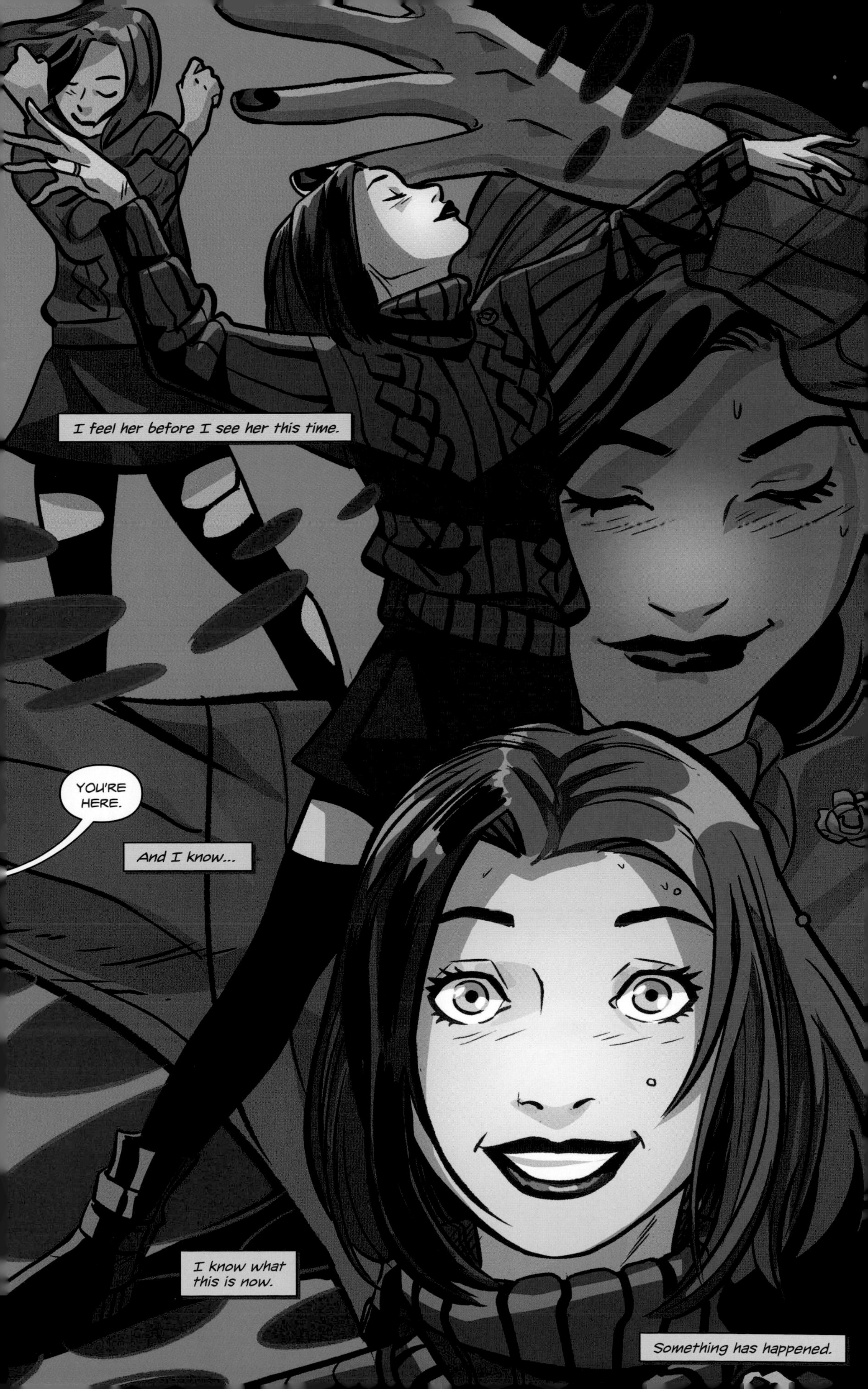
I feel her before I see her this time.
YOU'RE HERE.
And I know...
I know what this is now.
Something has happened.

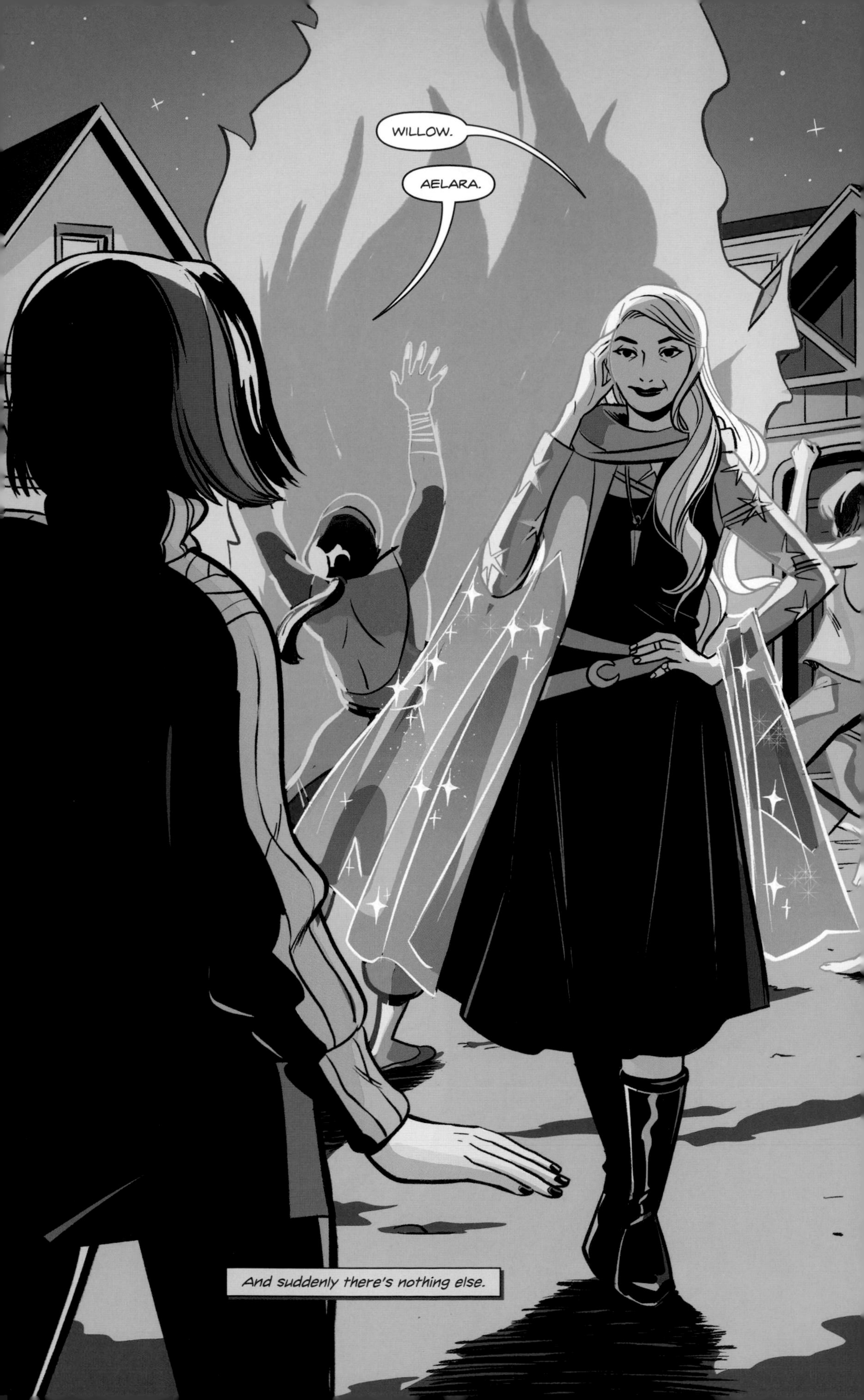
WILLOW.
AELARA.
And suddenly there's nothing else.

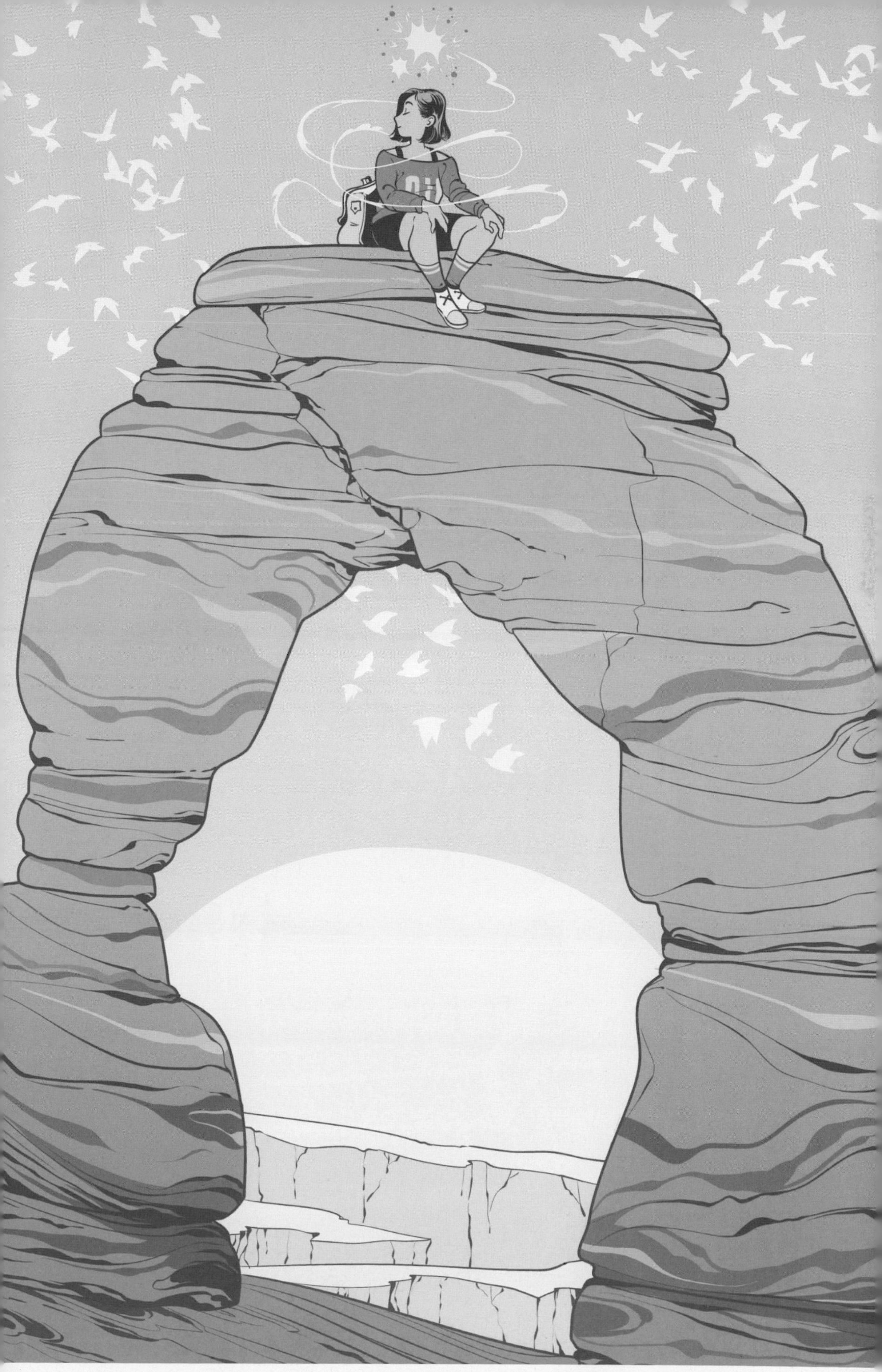

Willow #2 Variant Cover by **Rosemary Valero O'Connell**

CHAPTER THREE

Willow #3 Main Cover by **Jen Bartel**

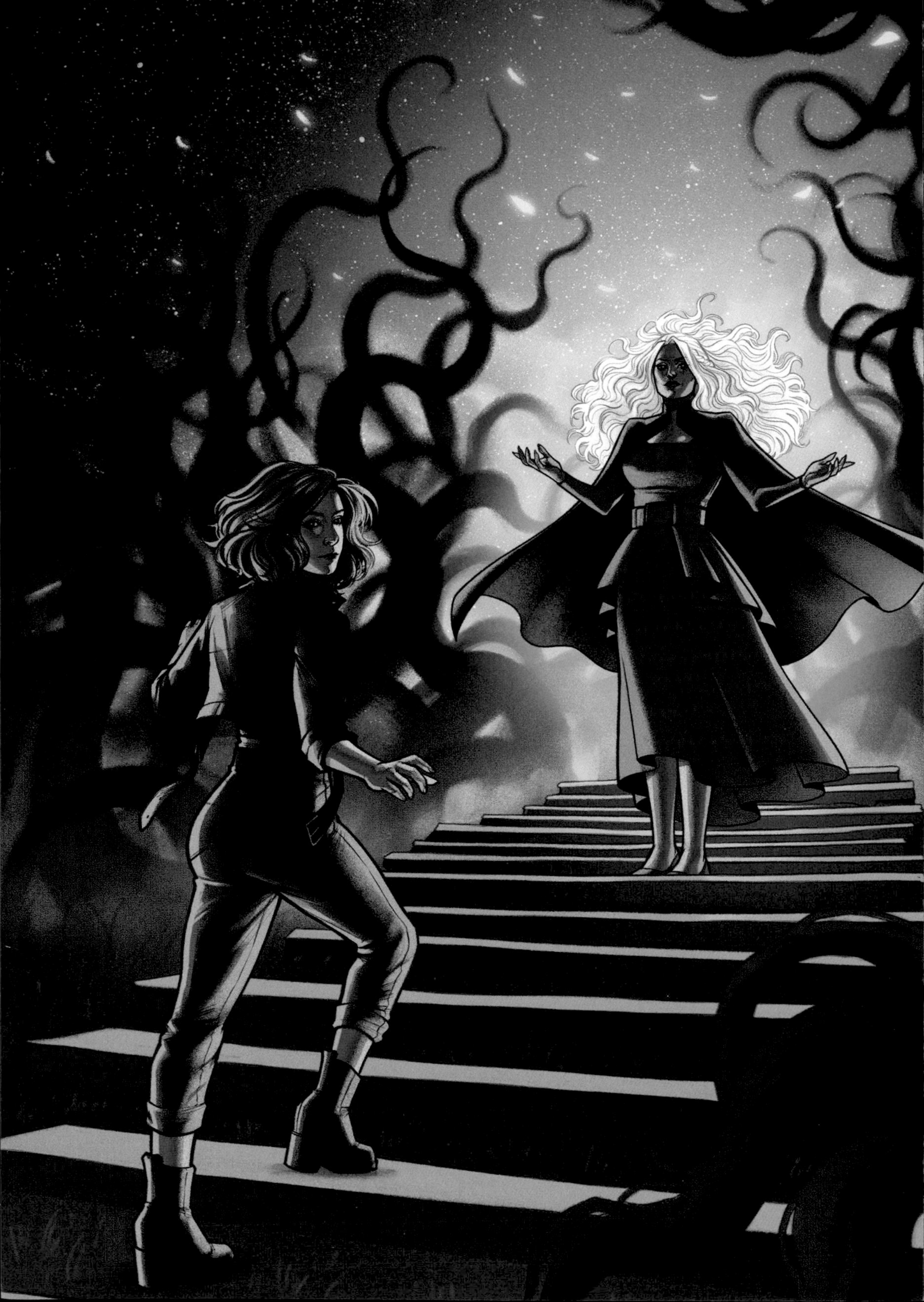

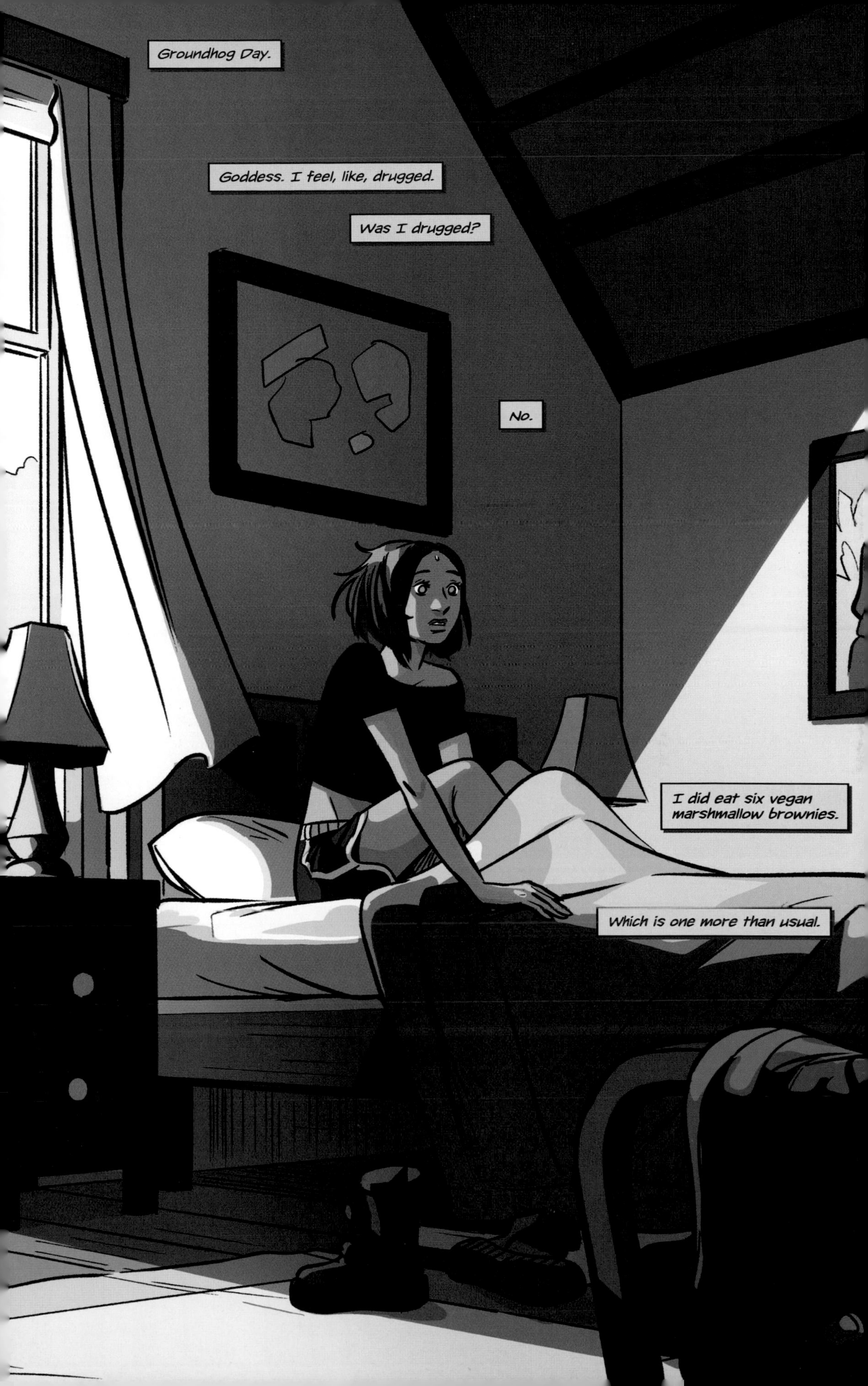
Groundhog Day.
Goddess. I feel, like, drugged.
Was I drugged?
No.
I did eat six vegan marshmallow brownies.
Which is one more than usual.

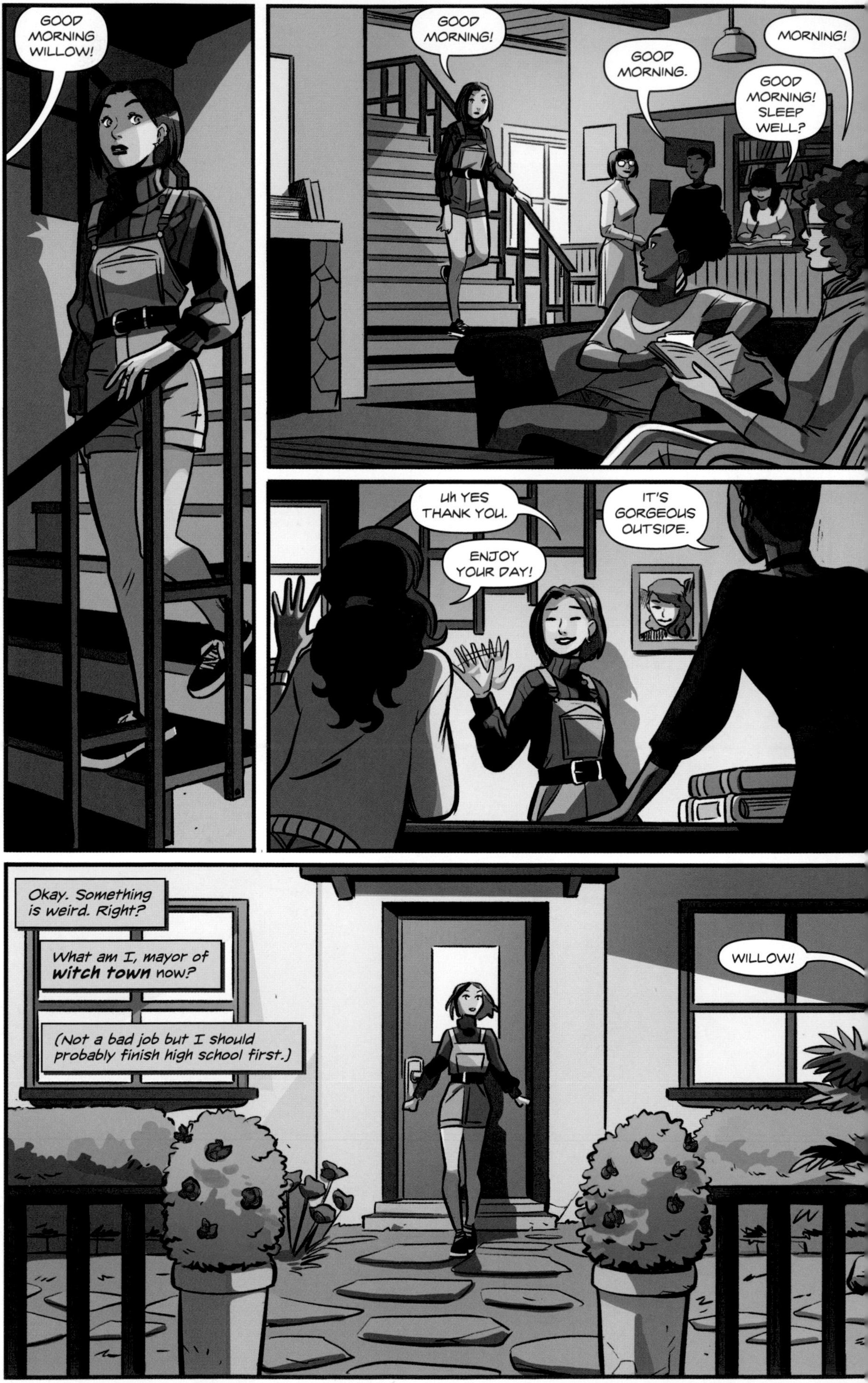
GOOD MORNING WILLOW!
GOOD MORNING!
GOOD MORNING.
MORNING!
GOOD MORNING! SLEEP WELL?
Uh YES THANK YOU.
IT'S GORGEOUS OUTSIDE.
ENJOY YOUR DAY!
Okay. Something is weird. Right?
What am I, mayor of **witch town** now?
(Not a bad job but I should probably finish high school first.)
WILLOW!

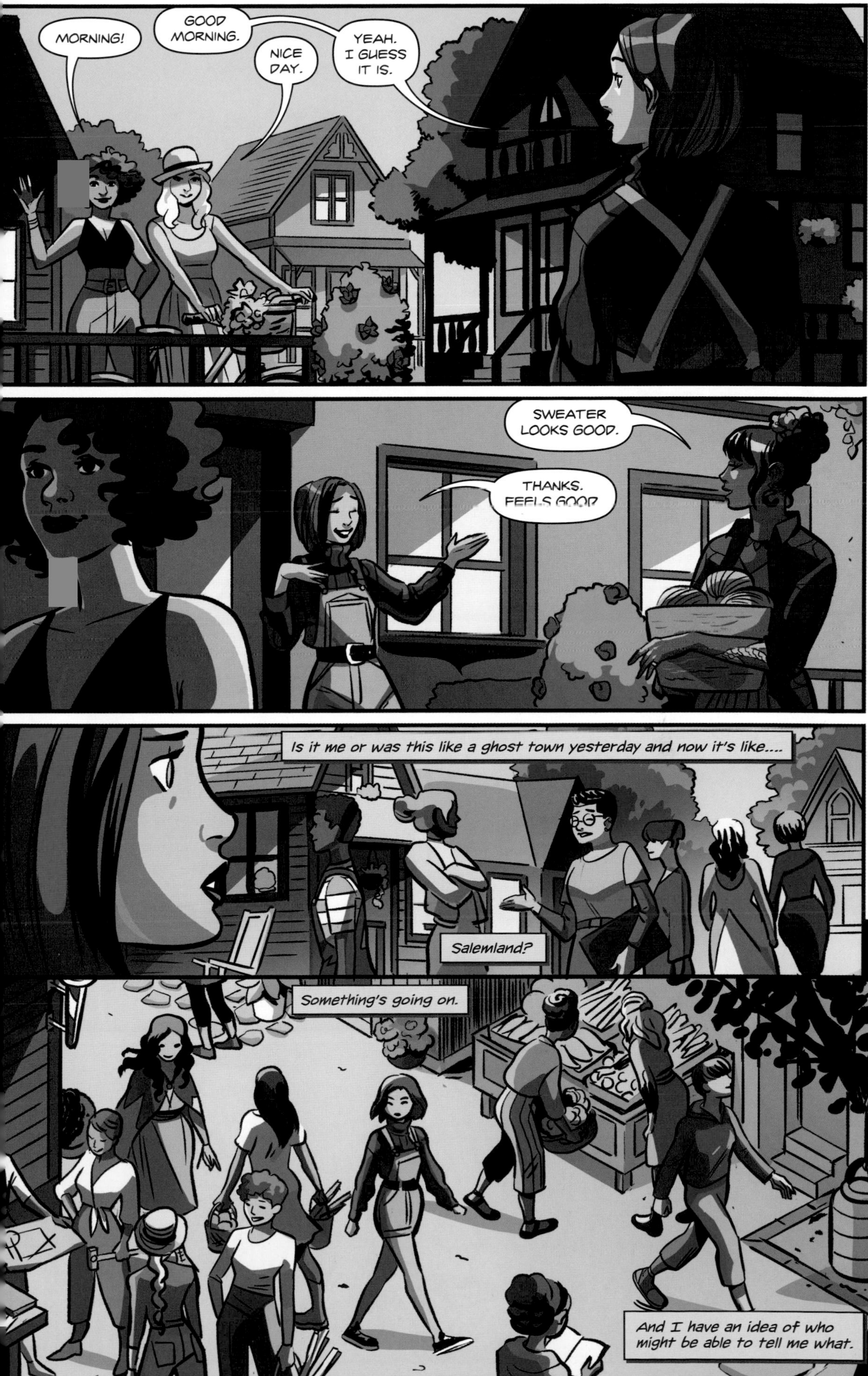
MORNING!
GOOD MORNING.
NICE DAY.
YEAH. I GUESS IT IS.
SWEATER LOOKS GOOD.
THANKS. FEELS GOOD.
Is it me or was this like a ghost town yesterday and now it's like....
Salemland?
Something's going on.
And I have an idea of who might be able to tell me what.

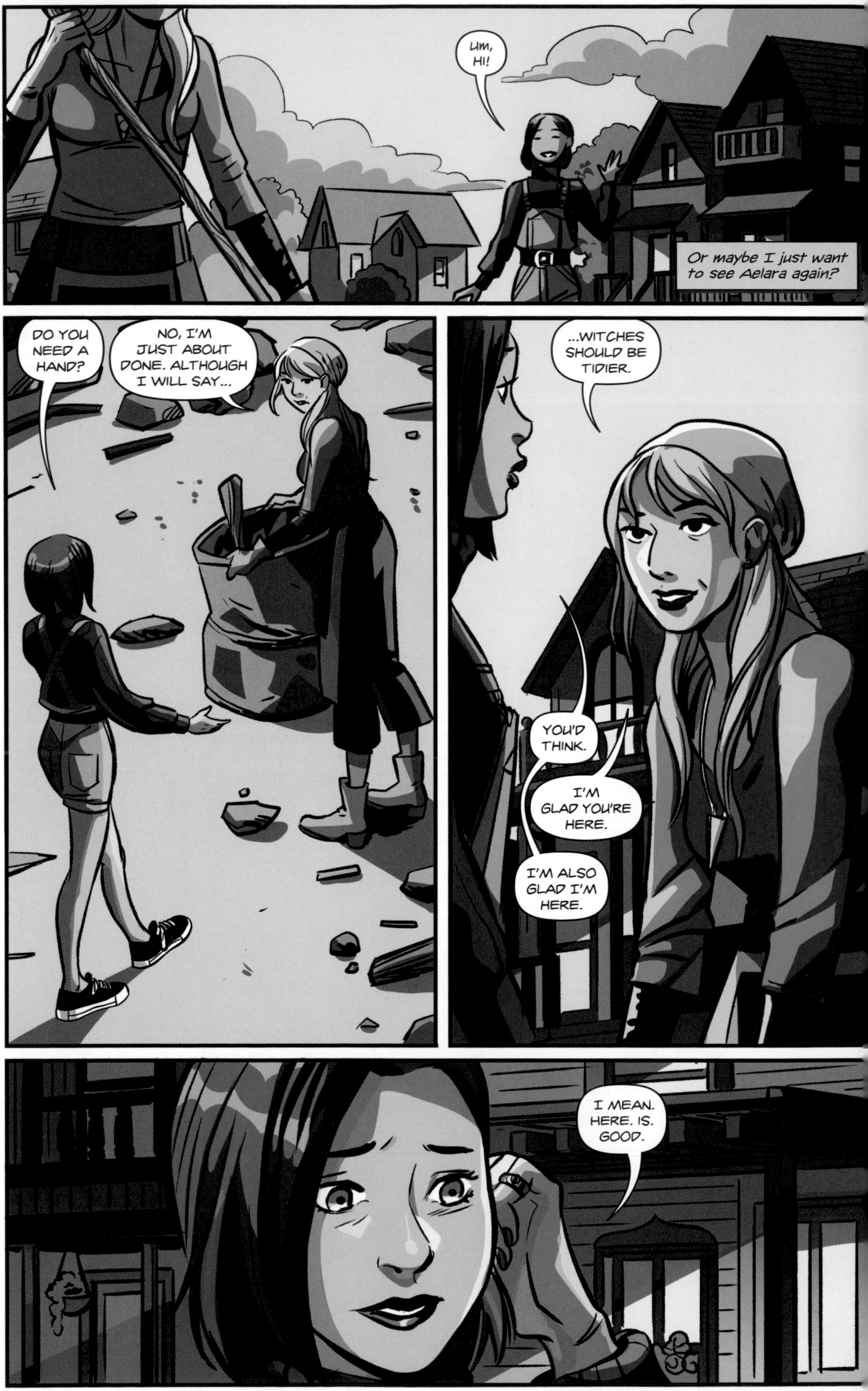
UM, HI!
Or maybe I just want to see Aelara again?
DO YOU NEED A HAND?
NO, I'M JUST ABOUT DONE. ALTHOUGH I WILL SAY...
...WITCHES SHOULD BE TIDIER.
YOU'D THINK.
I'M GLAD YOU'RE HERE.
I'M ALSO GLAD I'M HERE.
I MEAN. HERE. IS. GOOD.

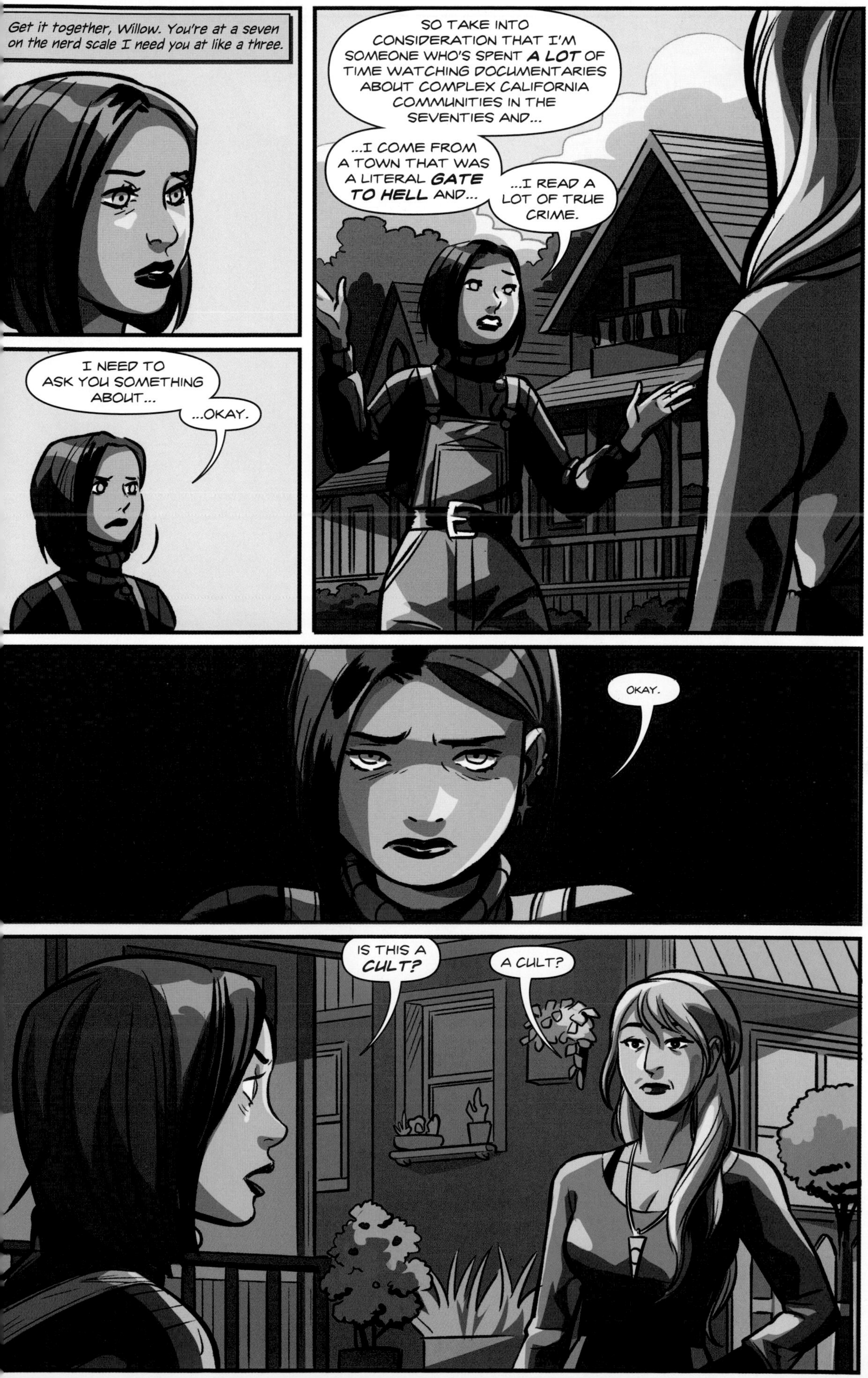
Get it together, Willow. You're at a seven on the nerd scale I need you at like a three.
I NEED TO ASK YOU SOMETHING ABOUT...
...OKAY.
SO TAKE INTO CONSIDERATION THAT I'M SOMEONE WHO'S SPENT A LOT OF TIME WATCHING DOCUMENTARIES ABOUT COMPLEX CALIFORNIA COMMUNITIES IN THE SEVENTIES AND...
...I COME FROM A TOWN THAT WAS A LITERAL GATE TO HELL AND...
...I READ A LOT OF TRUE CRIME.
OKAY.
IS THIS A CULT?
A CULT?

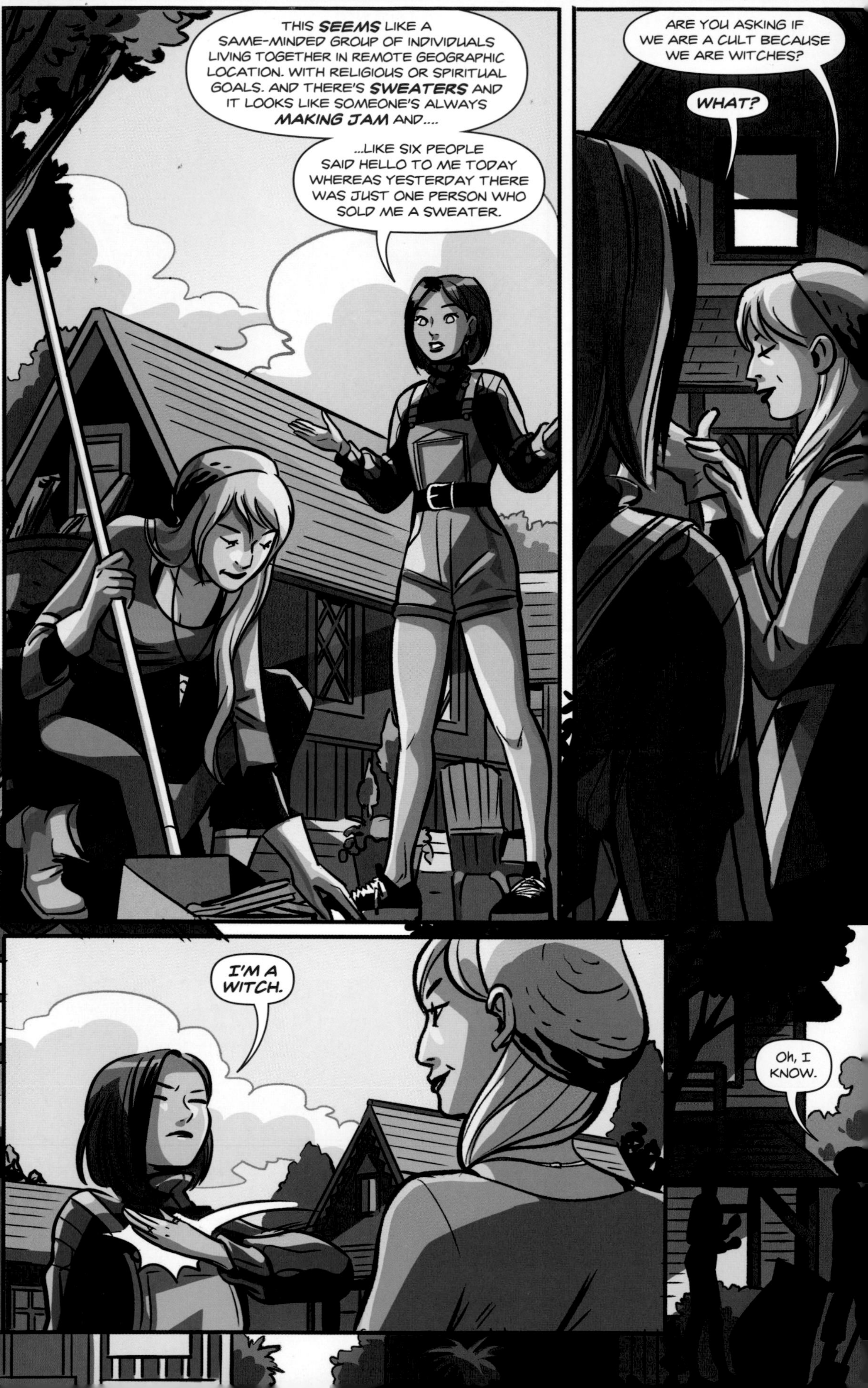
THIS SEEMS LIKE A SAME-MINDED GROUP OF INDIVIDUALS LIVING TOGETHER IN REMOTE GEOGRAPHIC LOCATION. WITH RELIGIOUS OR SPIRITUAL GOALS. AND THERE'S SWEATERS AND IT LOOKS LIKE SOMEONE'S ALWAYS MAKING JAM AND....
...LIKE SIX PEOPLE SAID HELLO TO ME TODAY WHEREAS YESTERDAY THERE WAS JUST ONE PERSON WHO SOLD ME A SWEATER.
ARE YOU ASKING IF WE ARE A CULT BECAUSE WE ARE WITCHES?
WHAT?
I'M A WITCH.
Oh, I KNOW.

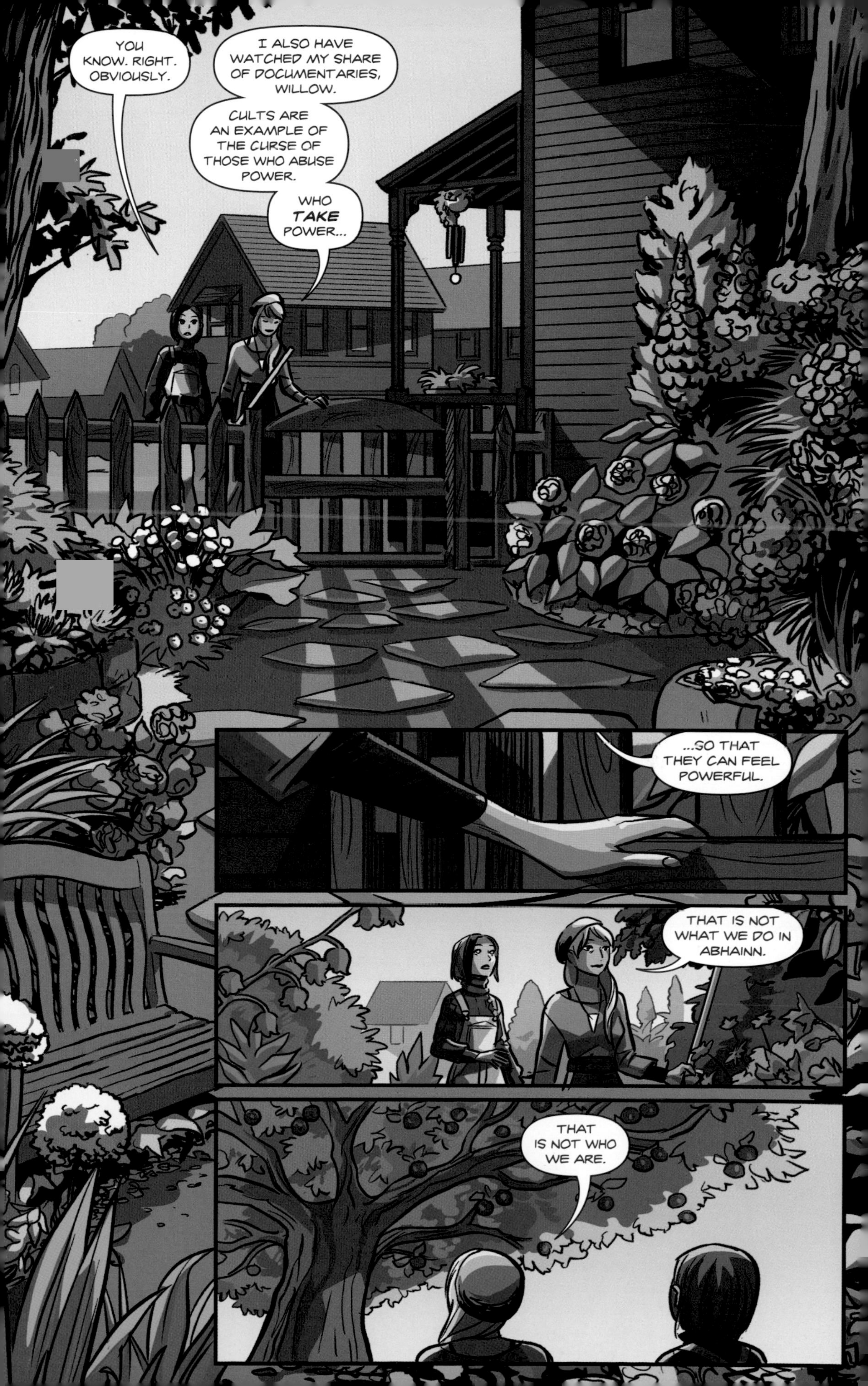
YOU KNOW. RIGHT. OBVIOUSLY.
I ALSO HAVE WATCHED MY SHARE OF DOCUMENTARIES, WILLOW.
CULTS ARE AN EXAMPLE OF THE CURSE OF THOSE WHO ABUSE POWER.
WHO *TAKE* POWER...
...SO THAT THEY CAN FEEL POWERFUL.
THAT IS NOT WHAT WE DO IN ABHAINN.
THAT IS NOT WHO WE ARE.

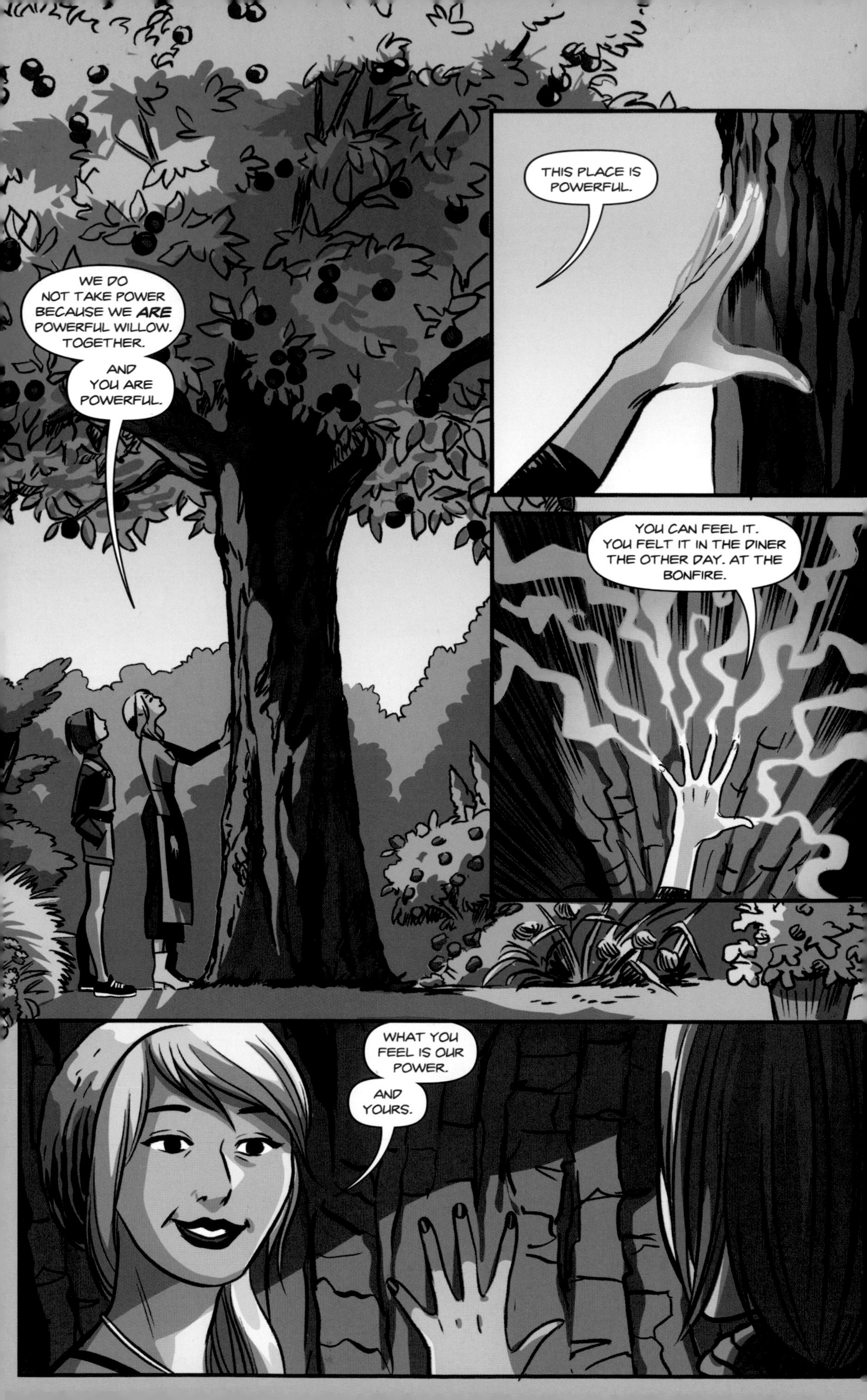
WE DO NOT TAKE POWER BECAUSE WE ***ARE*** POWERFUL WILLOW. TOGETHER.
AND YOU ARE POWERFUL.
THIS PLACE IS POWERFUL.
YOU CAN FEEL IT. YOU FELT IT IN THE DINER THE OTHER DAY. AT THE BONFIRE.
WHAT YOU FEEL IS OUR POWER.
AND YOURS.

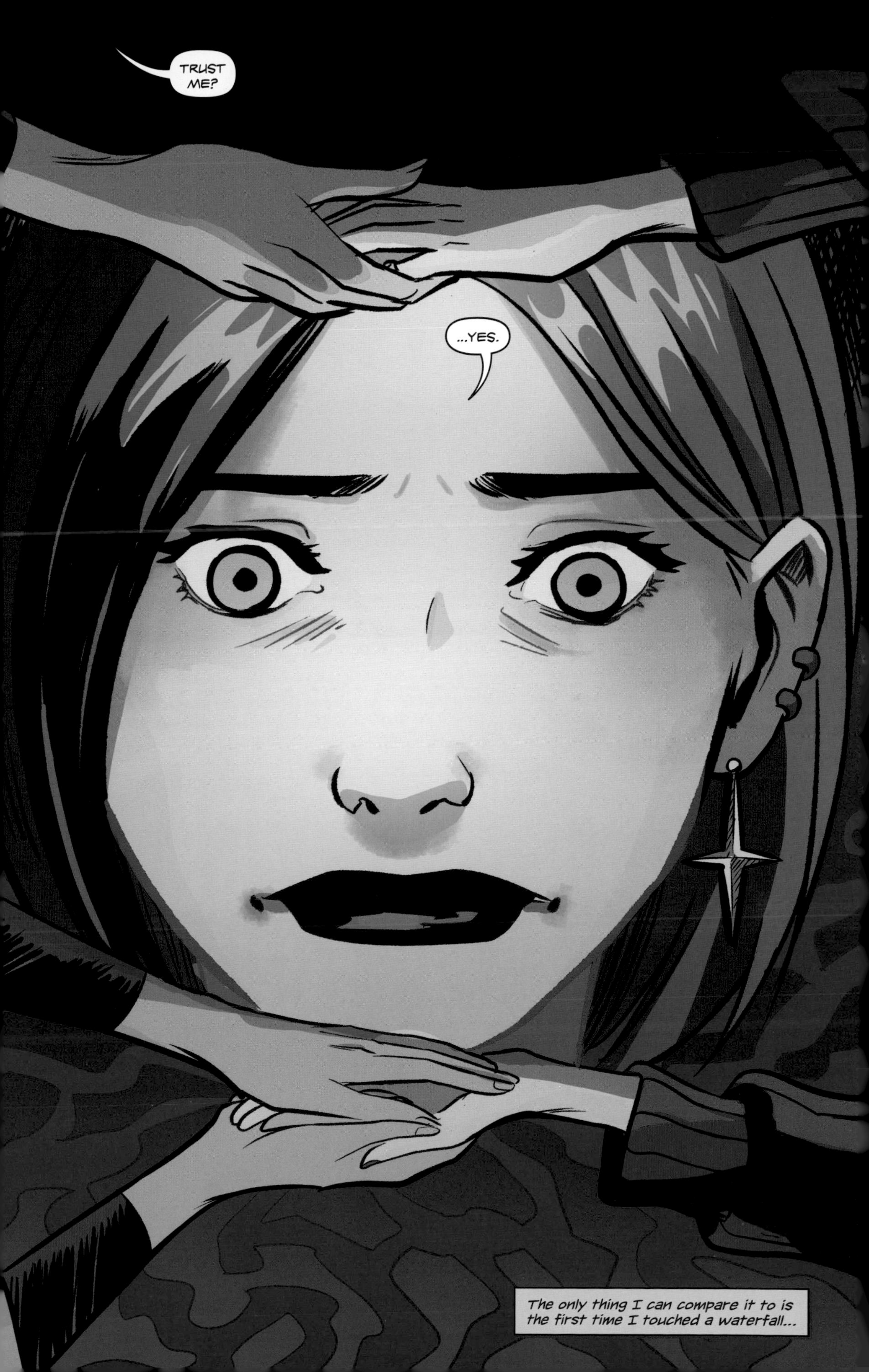
TRUST ME?
...YES.
The only thing I can compare it to is the first time I touched a waterfall...

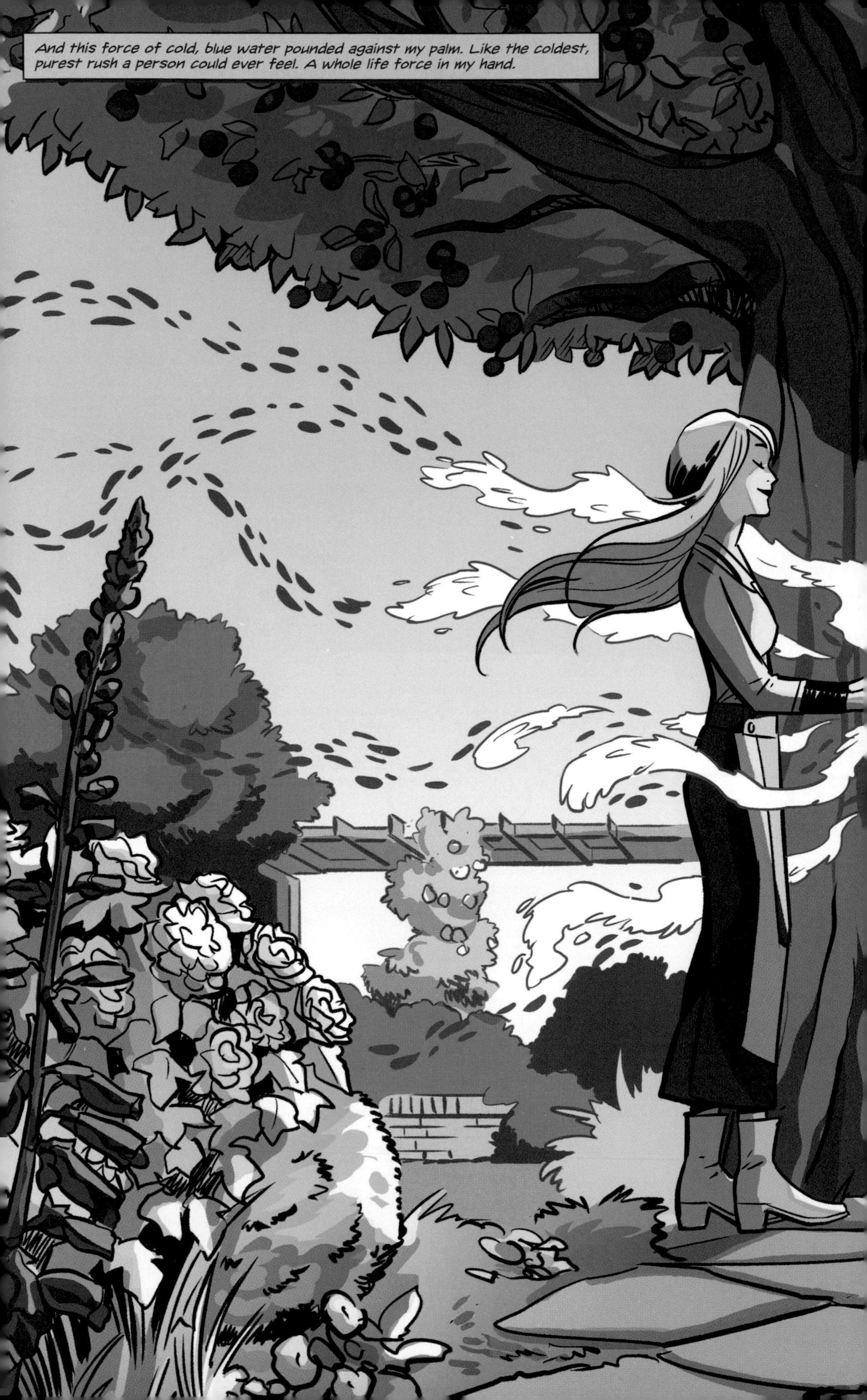
And this force of cold, blue water pounded against my palm. Like the coldest, purest rush a person could ever feel. A whole life force in my hand.

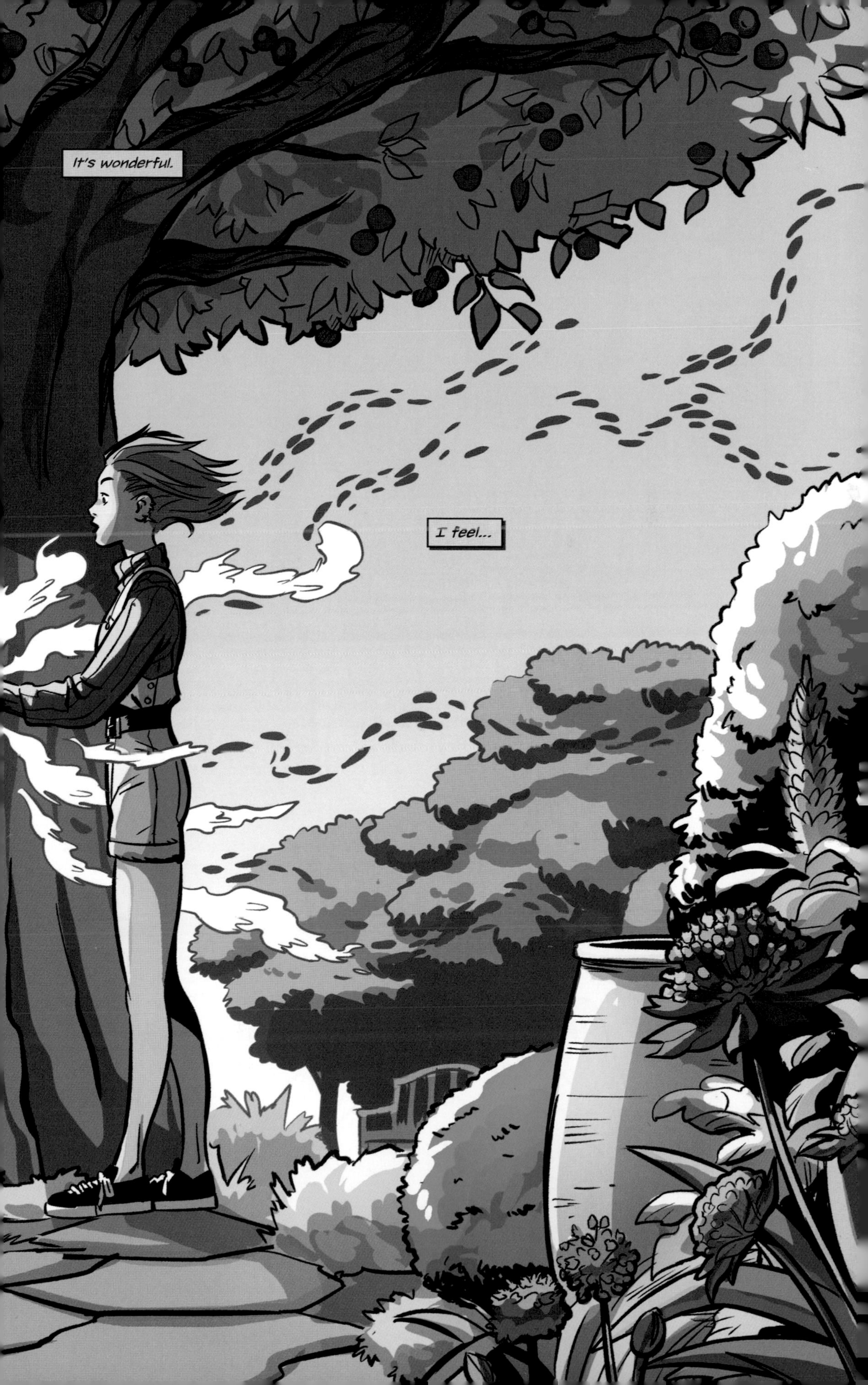
It's wonderful.
I feel...

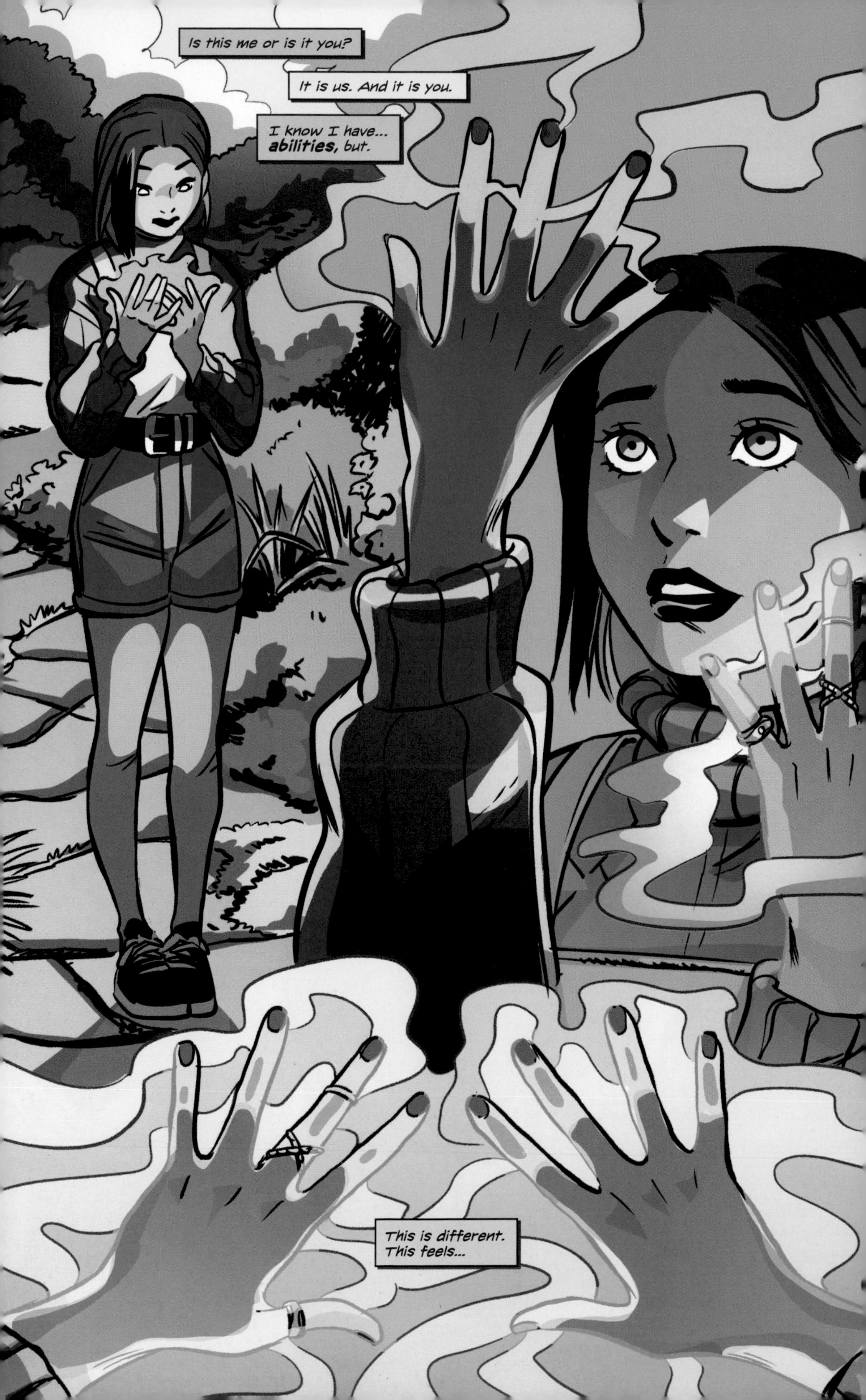
Is this me or is it you?
It is us. And it is you.
I know I have... **abilities**, but.
This is different. This feels...

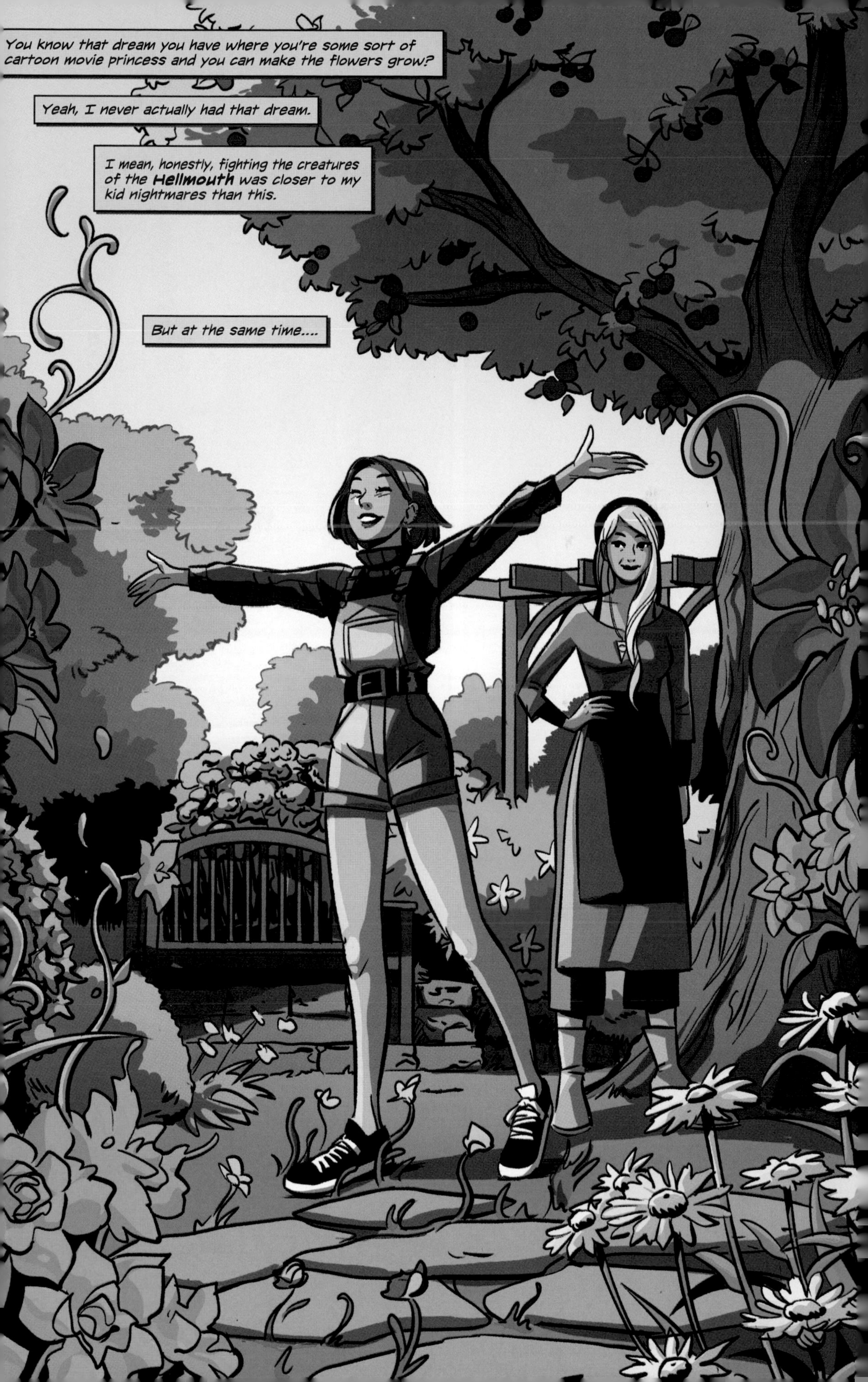
You know that dream you have where you're some sort of cartoon movie princess and you can make the flowers grow?
Yeah, I never actually had that dream.
I mean, honestly, fighting the creatures of the **Hellmouth** was closer to my kid nightmares than this.
But at the same time....

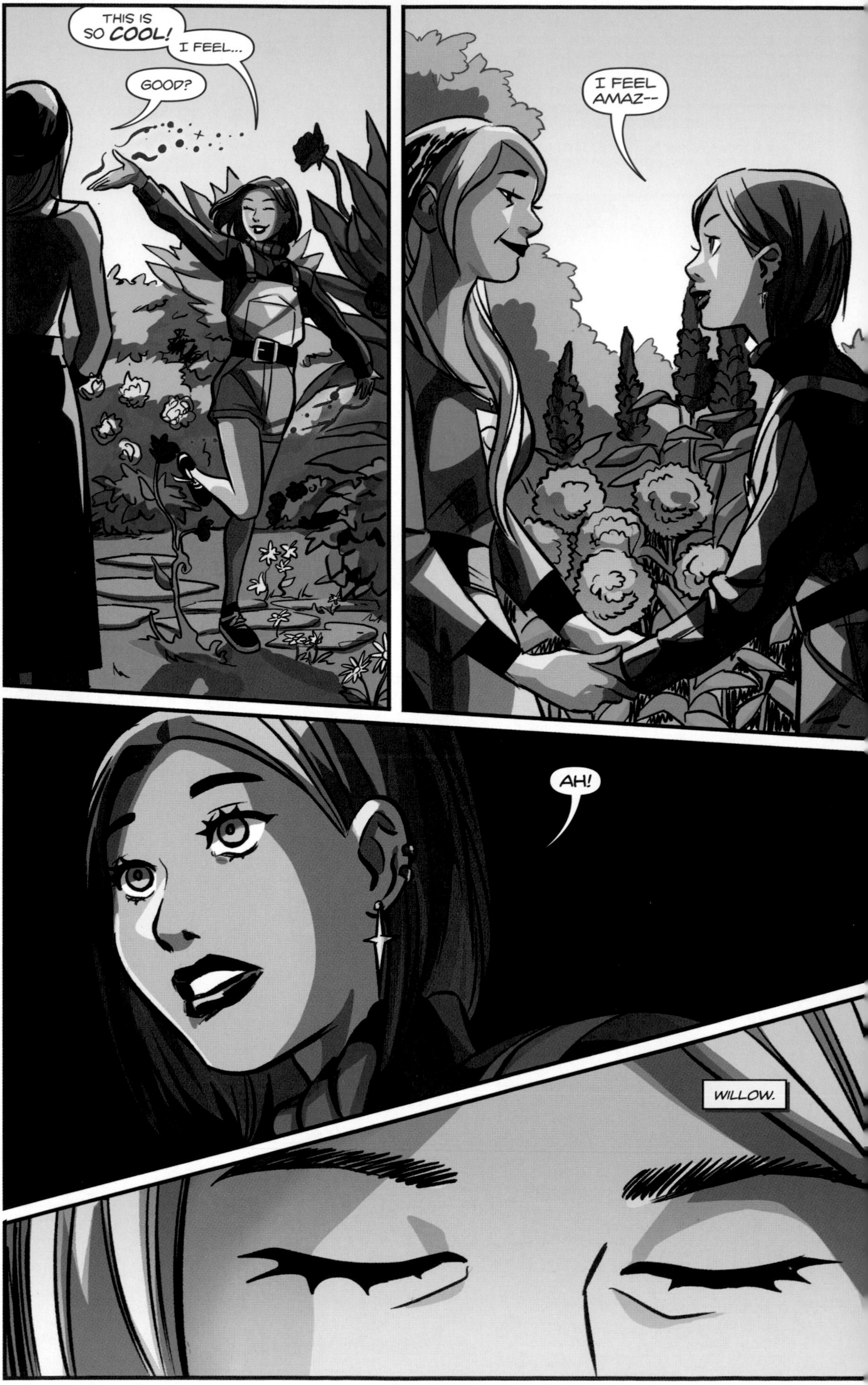
THIS IS SO COOL!
I FEEL...
GOOD?
I FEEL AMAZ--
AH!
WILLOW.

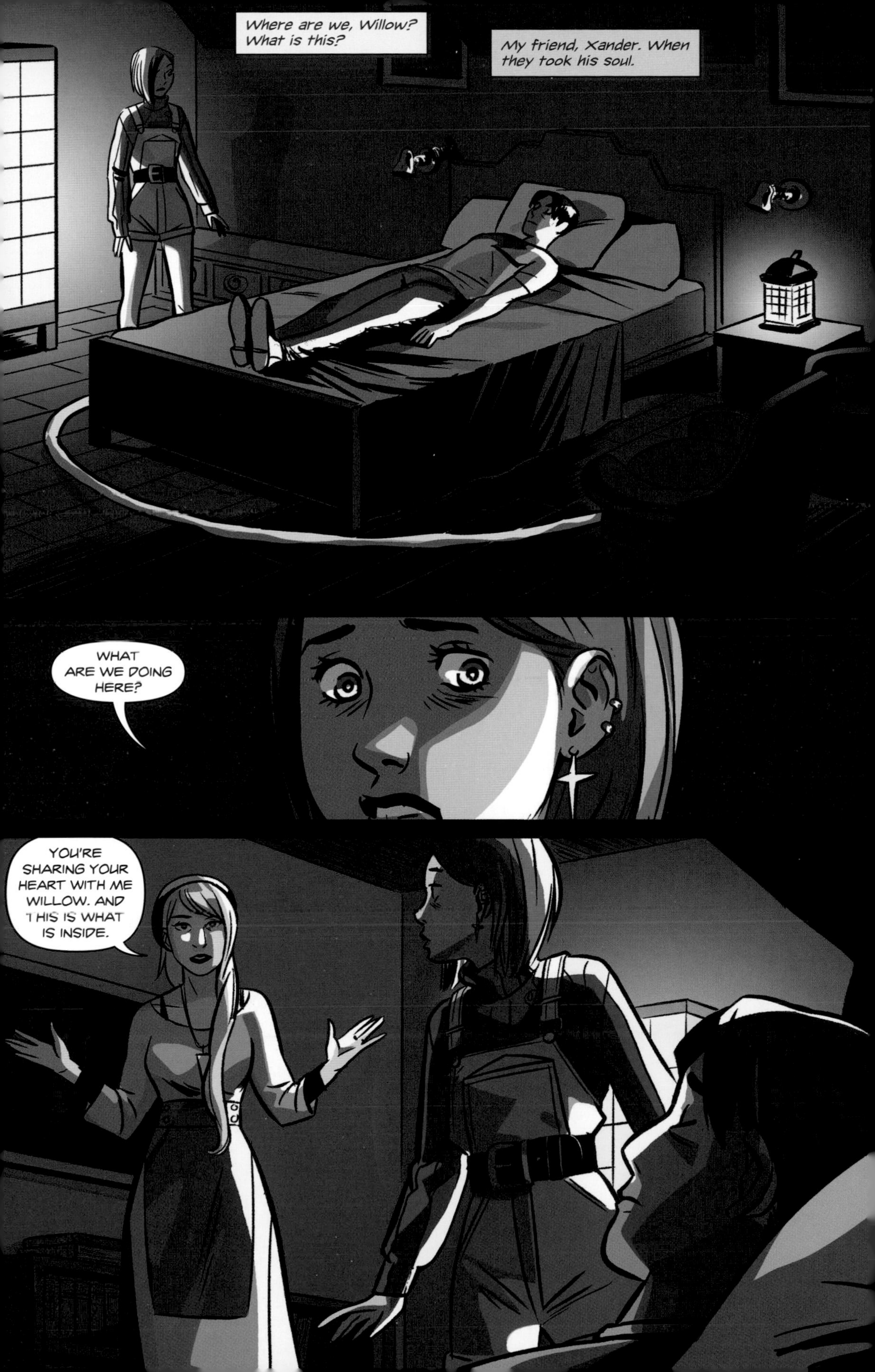
Where are we, Willow? What is this?
My friend, Xander. When they took his soul.
WHAT ARE WE DOING HERE?
YOU'RE SHARING YOUR HEART WITH ME WILLOW. AND THIS IS WHAT IS INSIDE.

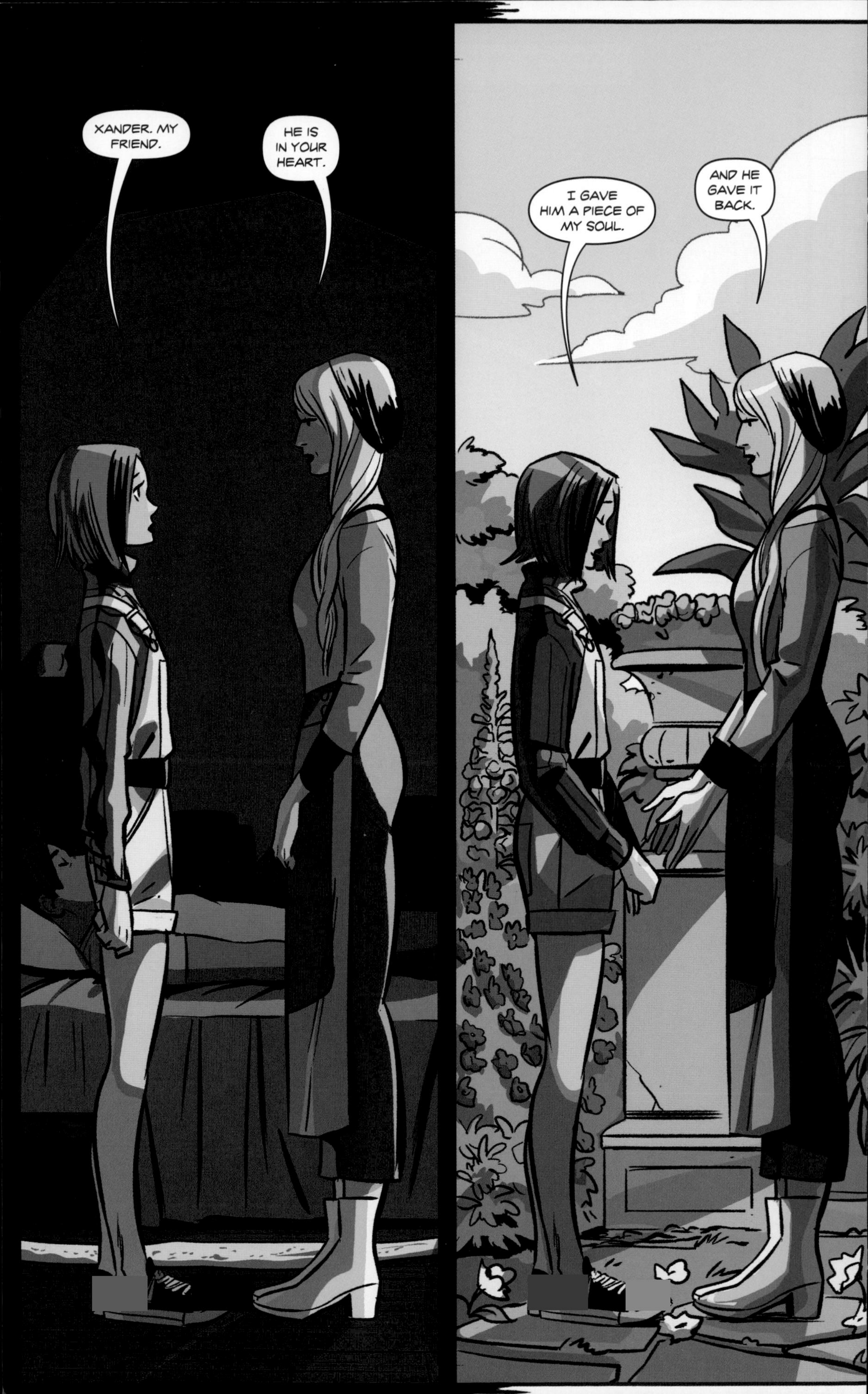
XANDER. MY FRIEND.
HE IS IN YOUR HEART.
I GAVE HIM A PIECE OF MY SOUL.
AND HE GAVE IT BACK.

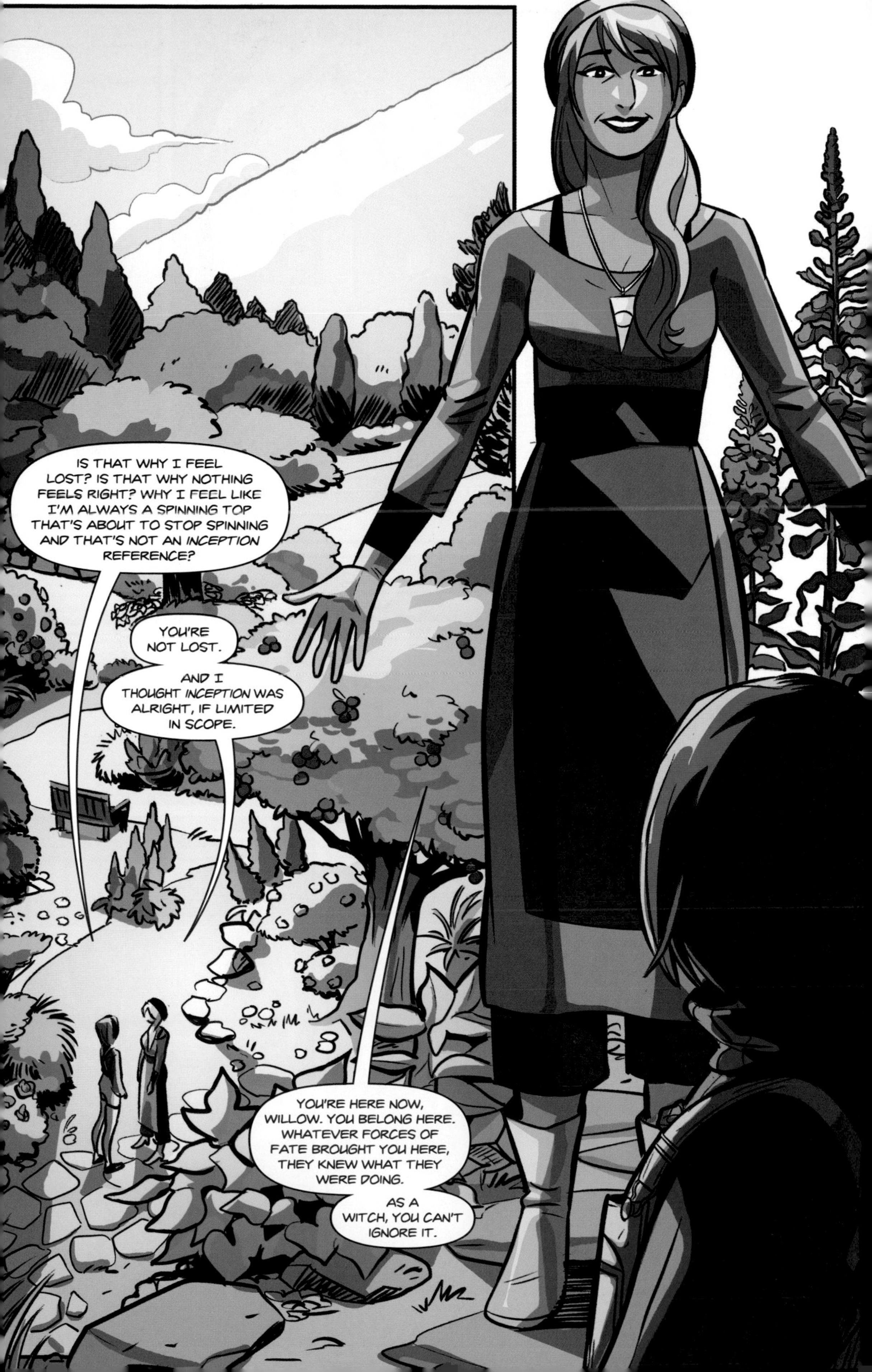
IS THAT WHY I FEEL LOST? IS THAT WHY NOTHING FEELS RIGHT? WHY I FEEL LIKE I'M ALWAYS A SPINNING TOP THAT'S ABOUT TO STOP SPINNING AND THAT'S NOT AN *INCEPTION* REFERENCE?
YOU'RE NOT LOST.
AND I THOUGHT *INCEPTION* WAS ALRIGHT, IF LIMITED IN SCOPE.
YOU'RE HERE NOW, WILLOW. YOU BELONG HERE. WHATEVER FORCES OF FATE BROUGHT YOU HERE, THEY KNEW WHAT THEY WERE DOING.
AS A WITCH, YOU CAN'T IGNORE IT.

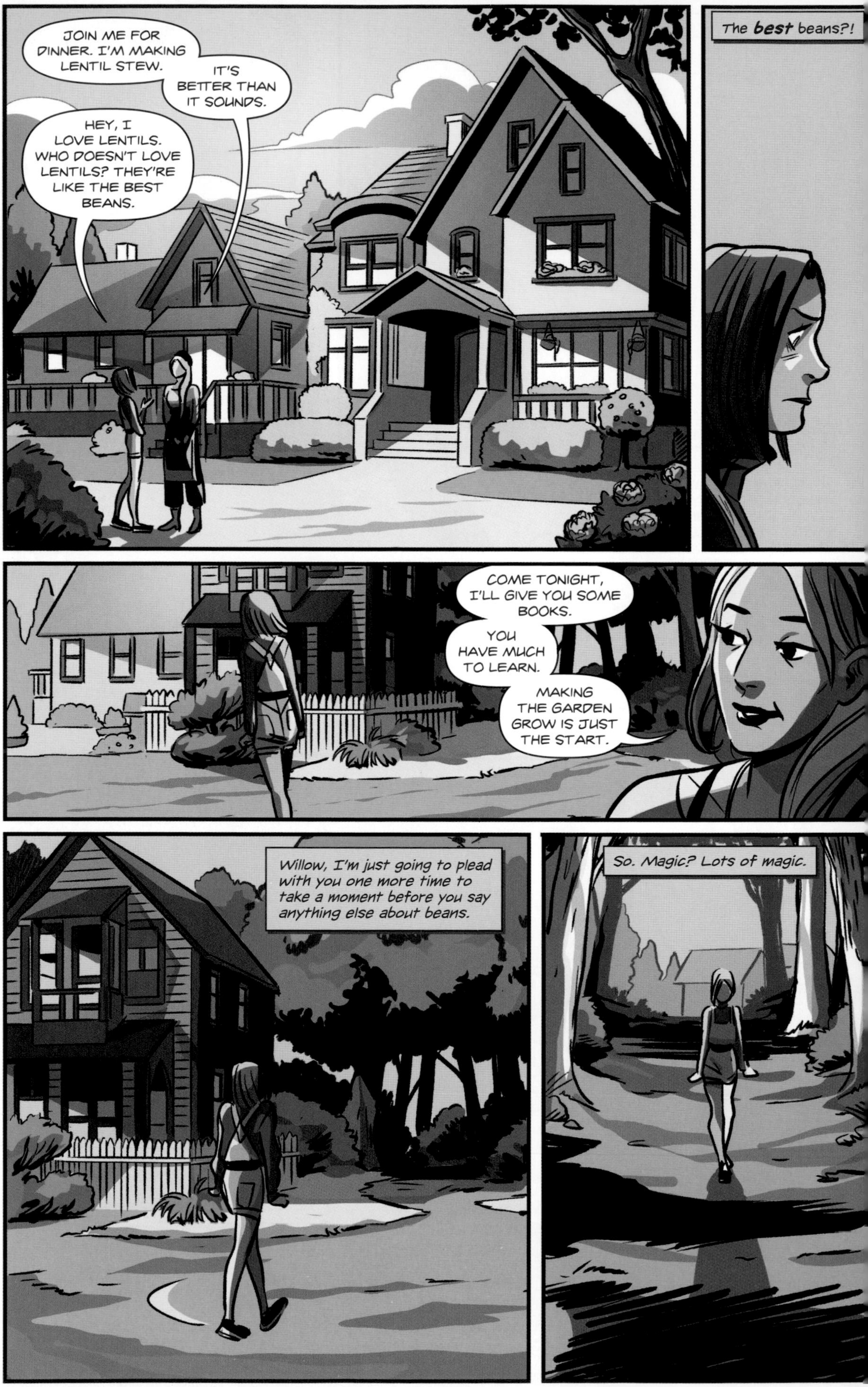
JOIN ME FOR DINNER. I'M MAKING LENTIL STEW.
IT'S BETTER THAN IT SOUNDS.
HEY, I LOVE LENTILS. WHO DOESN'T LOVE LENTILS? THEY'RE LIKE THE BEST BEANS.
The **best** beans?!
COME TONIGHT, I'LL GIVE YOU SOME BOOKS.
YOU HAVE MUCH TO LEARN.
MAKING THE GARDEN GROW IS JUST THE START.
Willow, I'm just going to plead with you one more time to take a moment before you say anything else about beans.
So. Magic? Lots of magic.

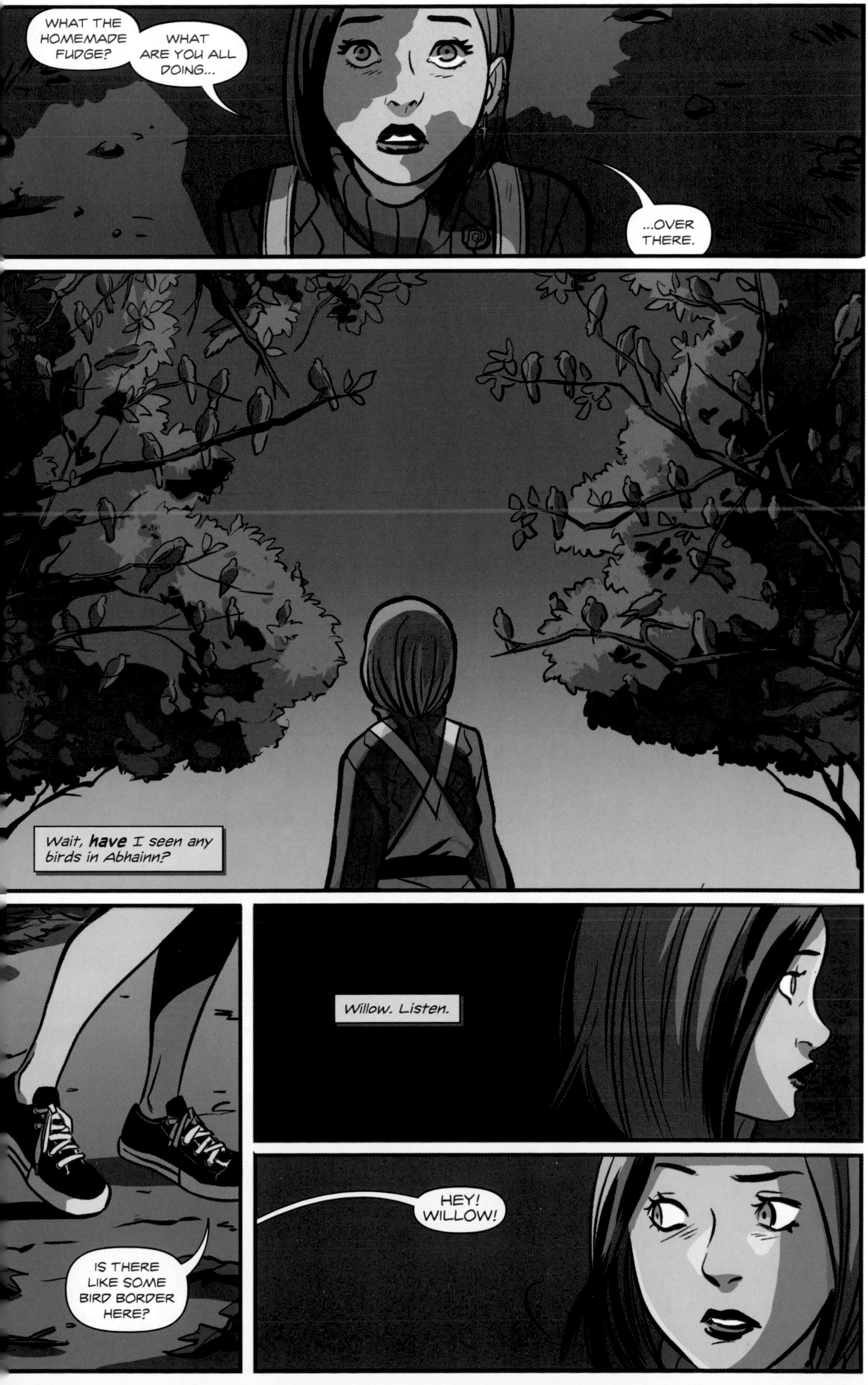
WHAT THE HOMEMADE FUDGE?
WHAT ARE YOU ALL DOING...
...OVER THERE.
Wait, **have** I seen any birds in Abhainn?
IS THERE LIKE SOME BIRD BORDER HERE?
Willow. Listen.
HEY! WILLOW!

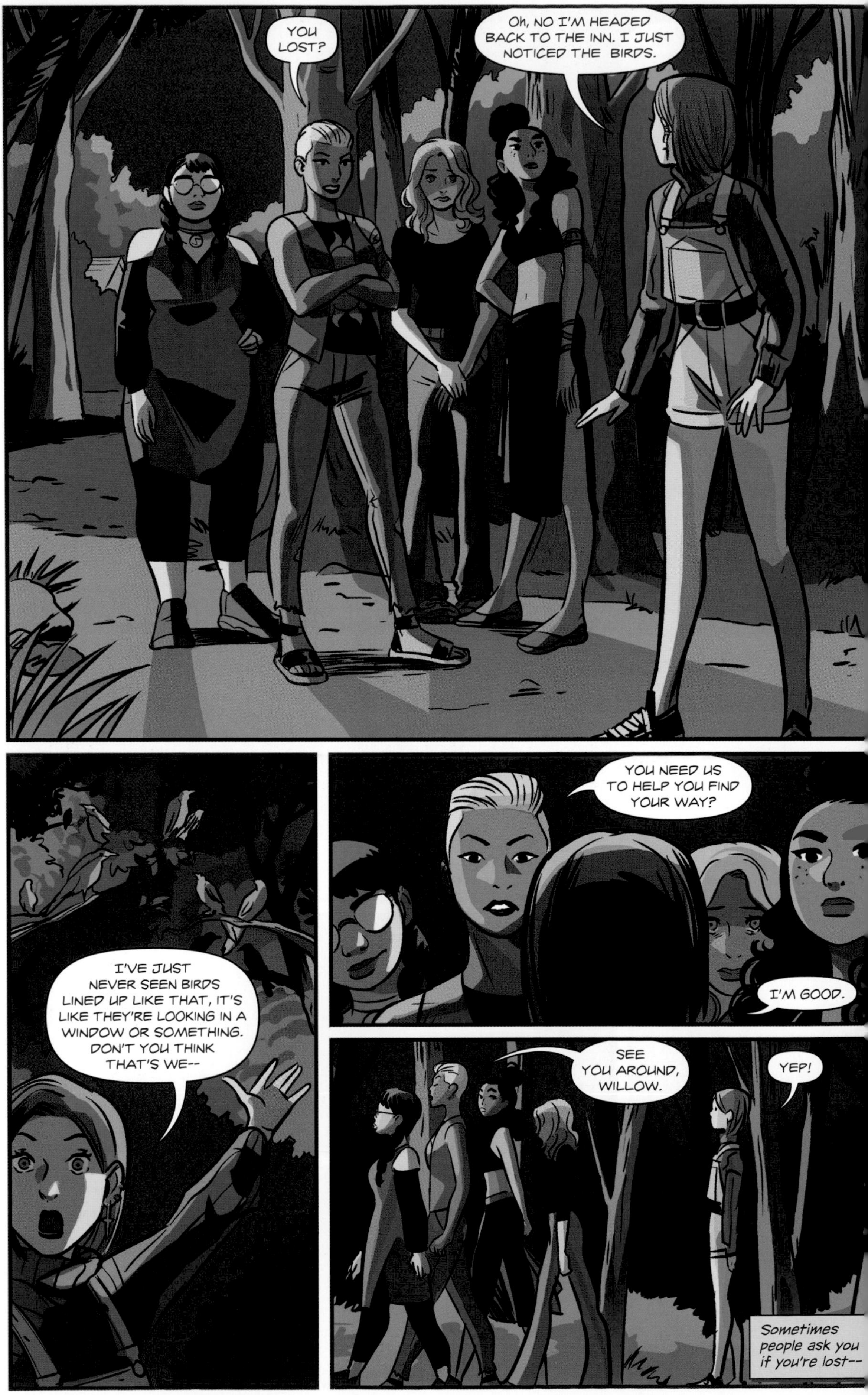
YOU LOST?
Oh, NO I'M HEADED BACK TO THE INN. I JUST NOTICED THE BIRDS.
I'VE JUST NEVER SEEN BIRDS LINED UP LIKE THAT, IT'S LIKE THEY'RE LOOKING IN A WINDOW OR SOMETHING. DON'T YOU THINK THAT'S WE--
YOU NEED US TO HELP YOU FIND YOUR WAY?
I'M GOOD.
SEE YOU AROUND, WILLOW.
YEP!
Sometimes people ask you if you're lost--

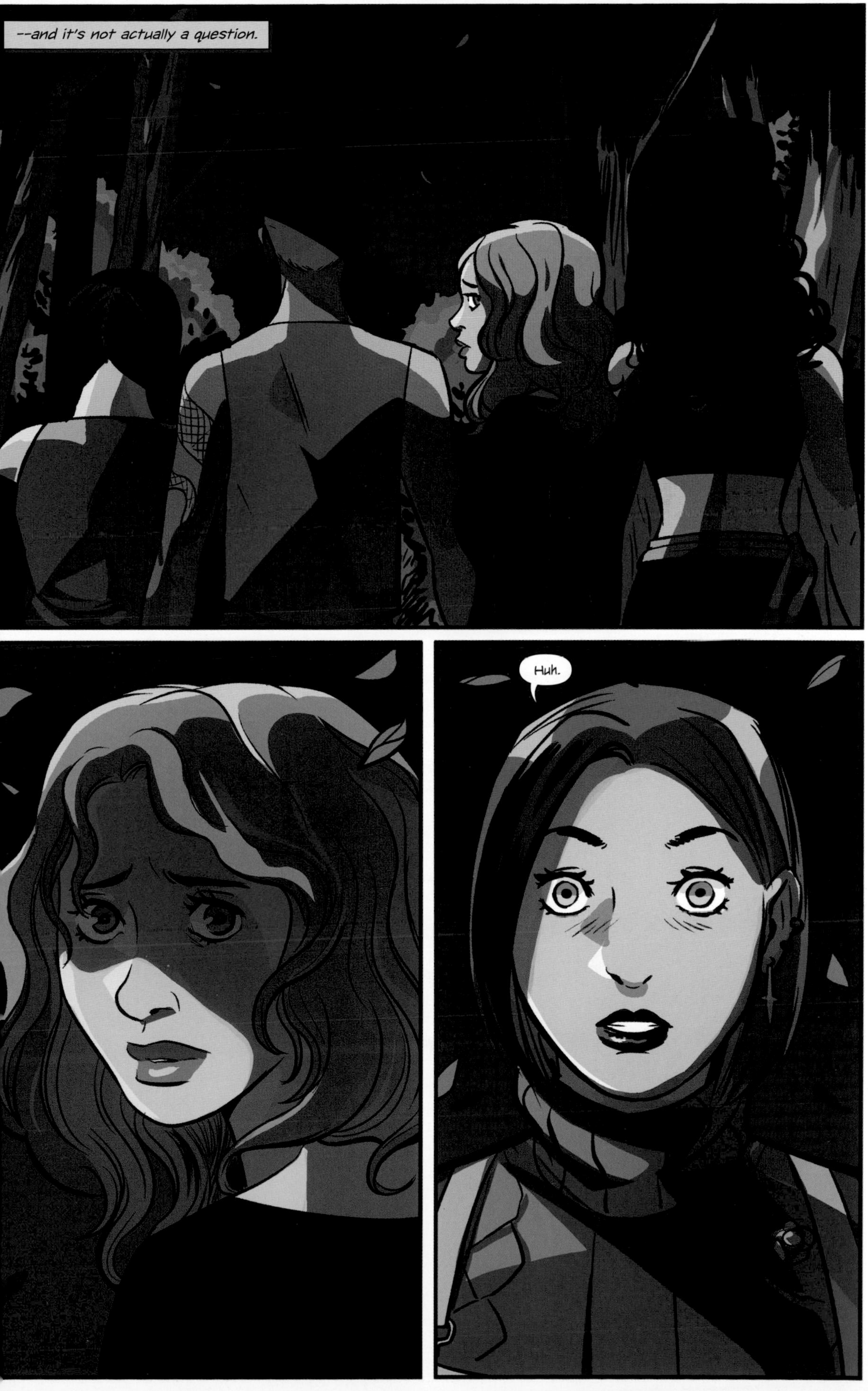
--and it's not actually a question.
Huh.

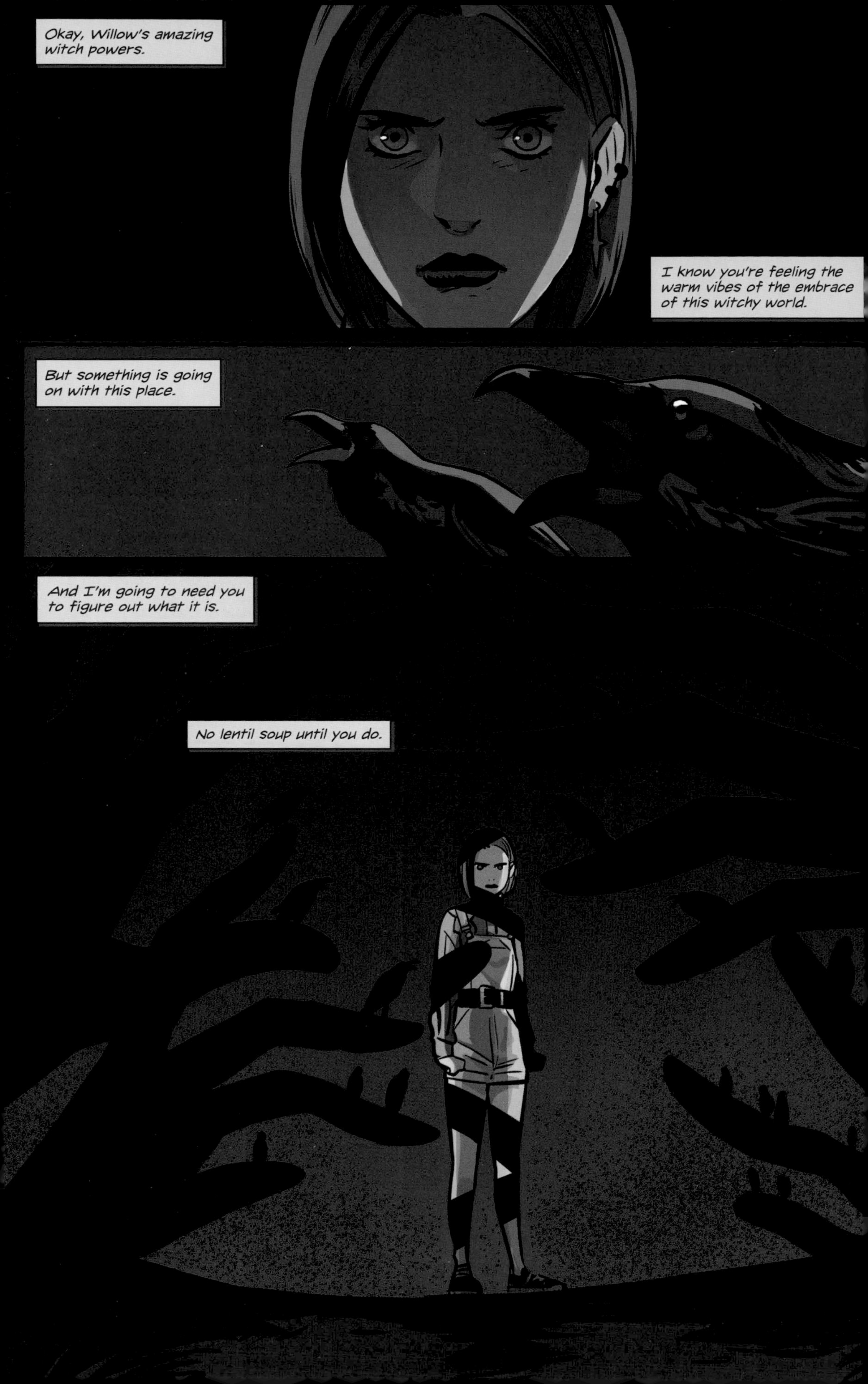
Okay, Willow's amazing witch powers.
I know you're feeling the warm vibes of the embrace of this witchy world.
But something is going on with this place.
And I'm going to need you to figure out what it is.
No lentil soup until you do.

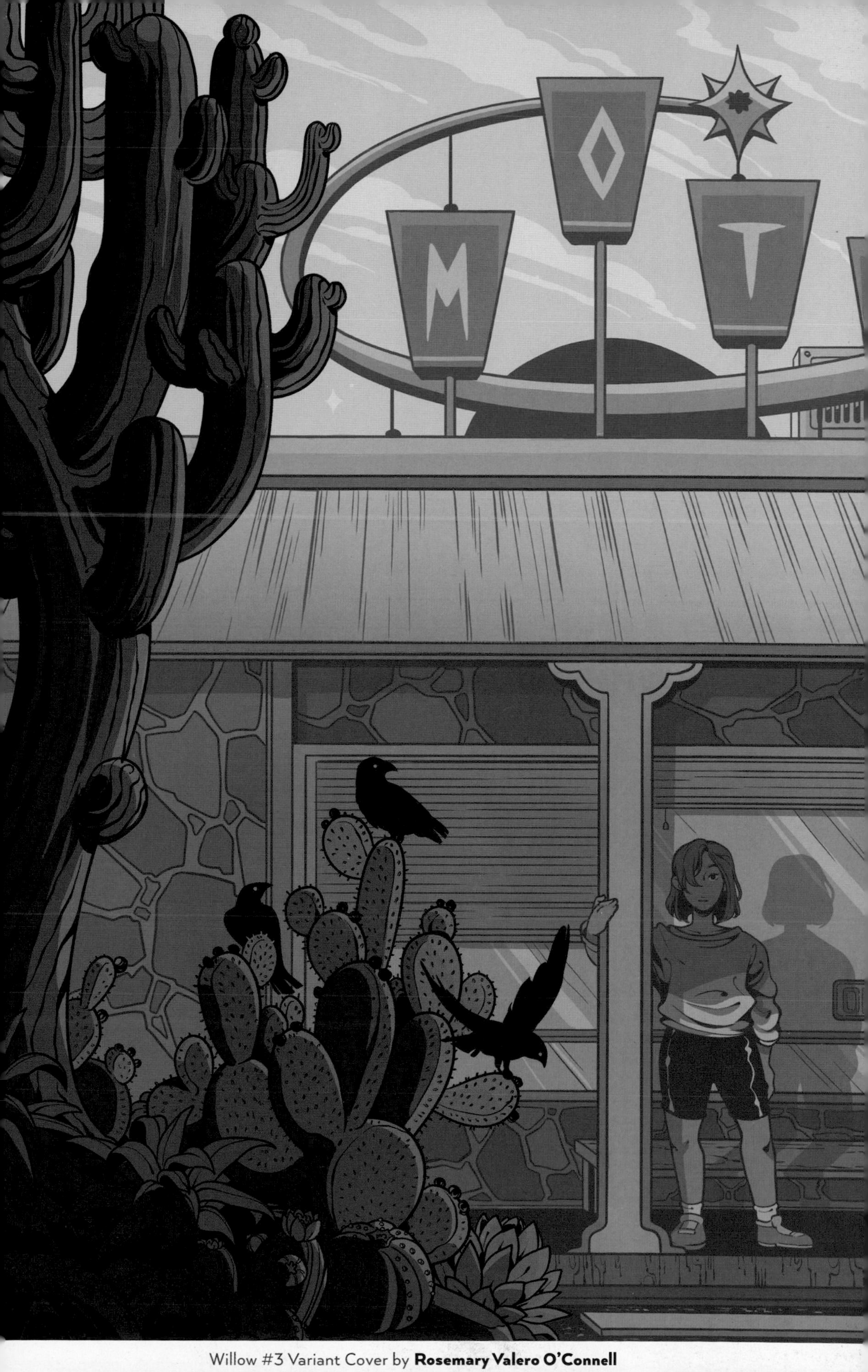
M
T

Willow #3 Variant Cover by **Rosemary Valero O'Connell**

CHAPTER
FOUR

Willow #4 Main Cover by **Jen Bartel**

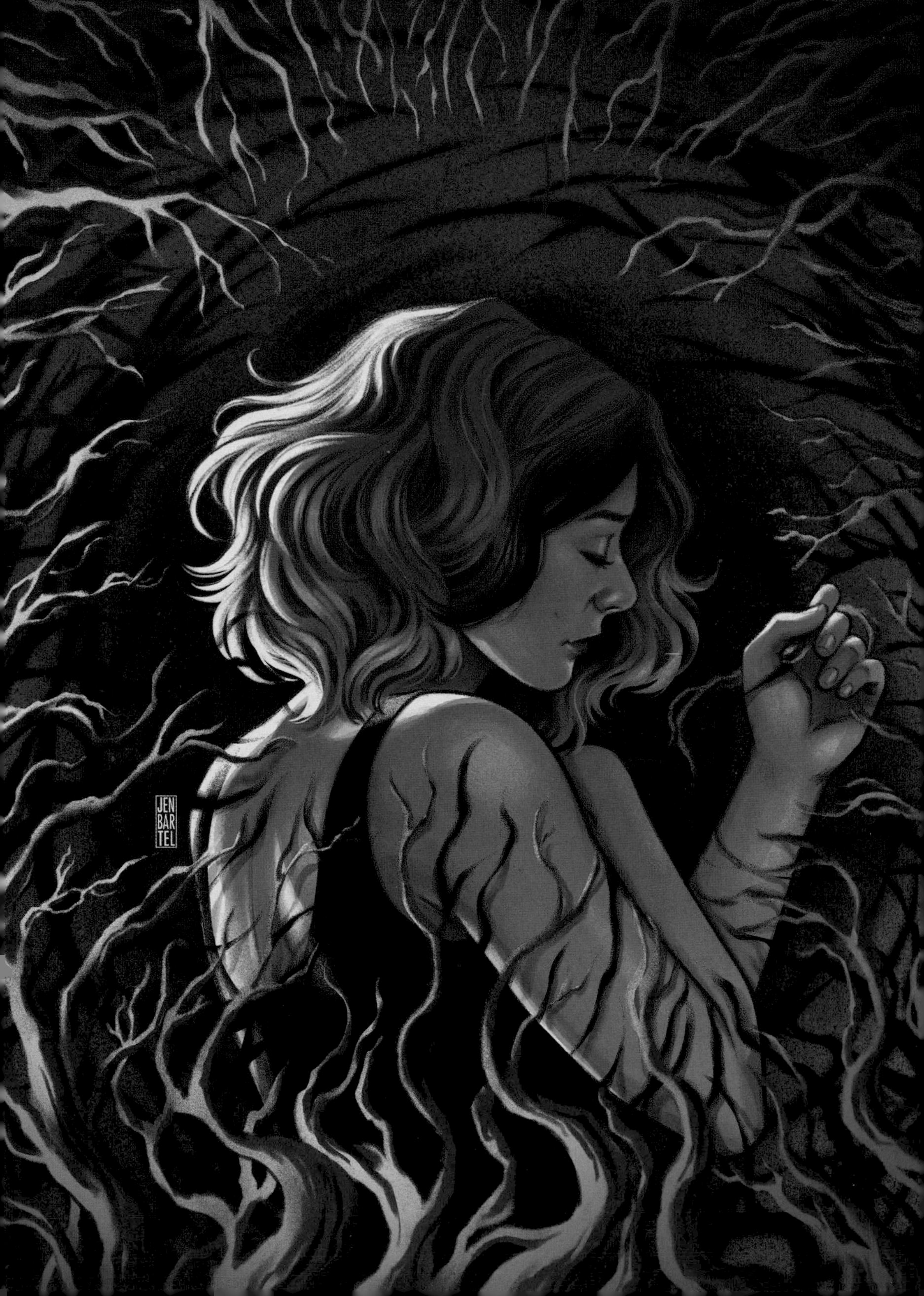
JEN BAR TEL

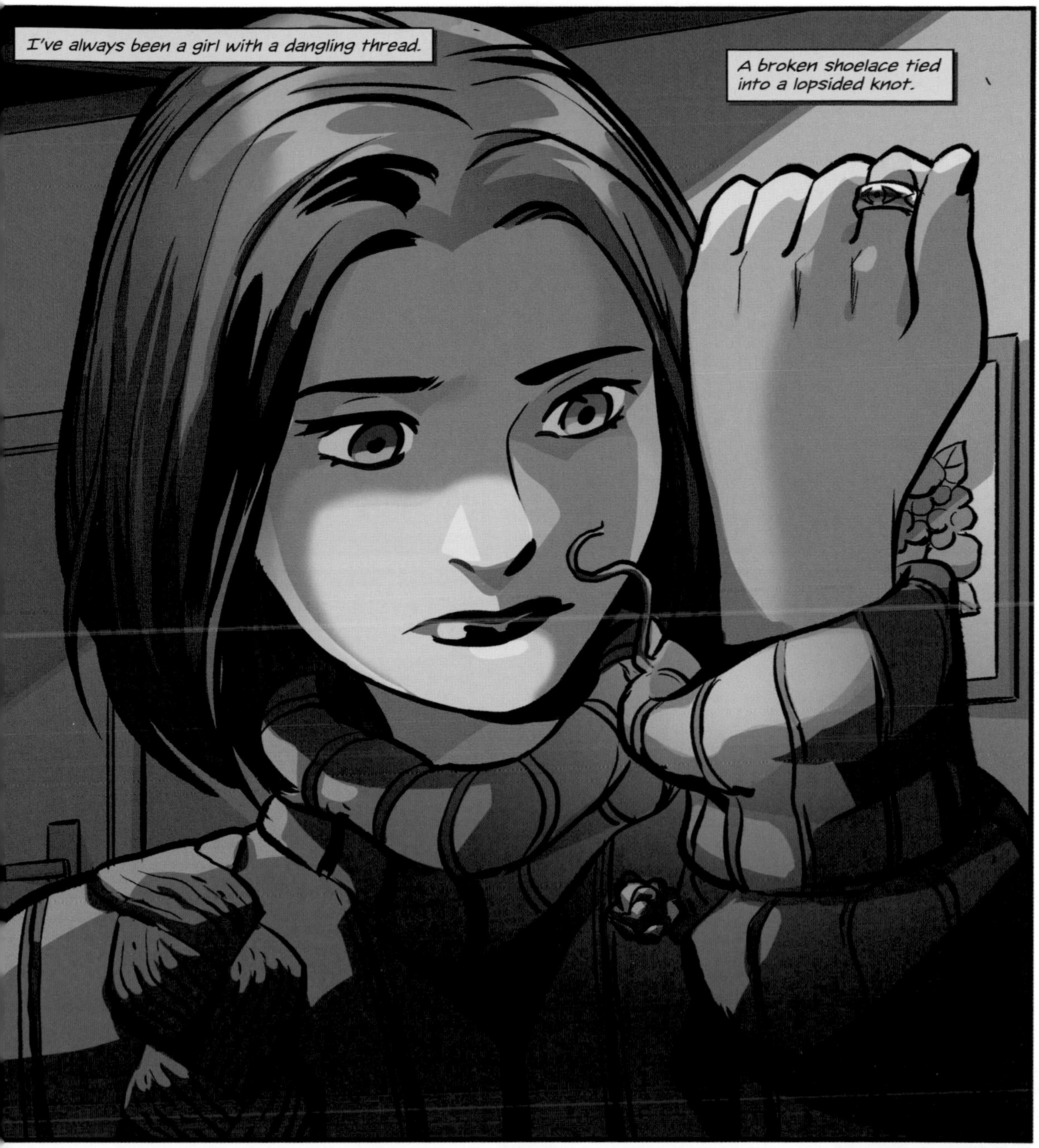
I've always been a girl with a dangling thread.
A broken shoelace tied into a lopsided knot.

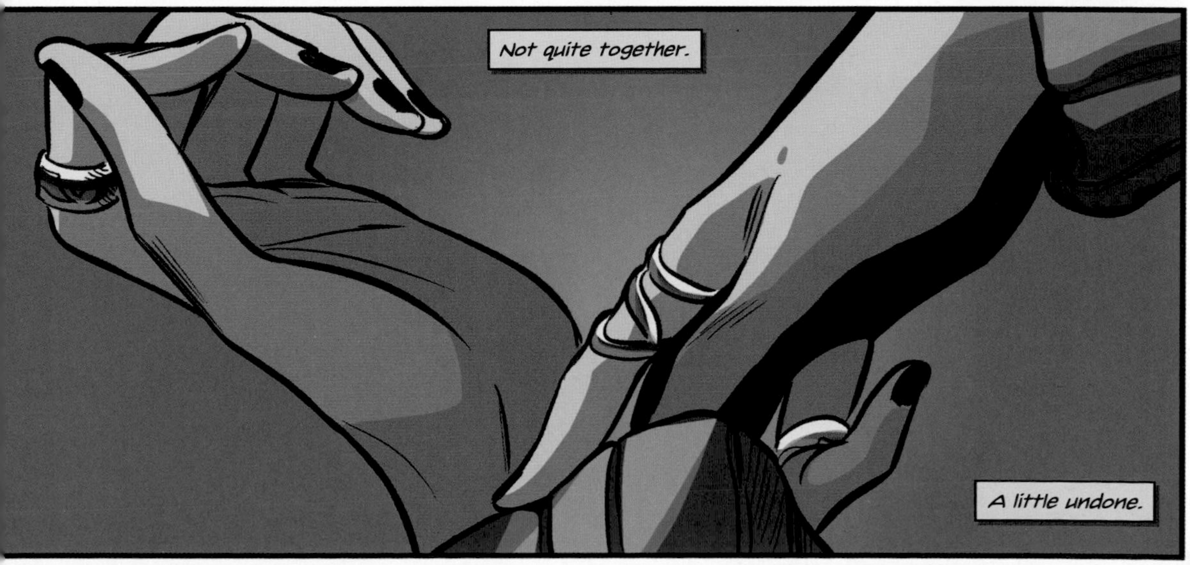
Not quite together.
A little undone.

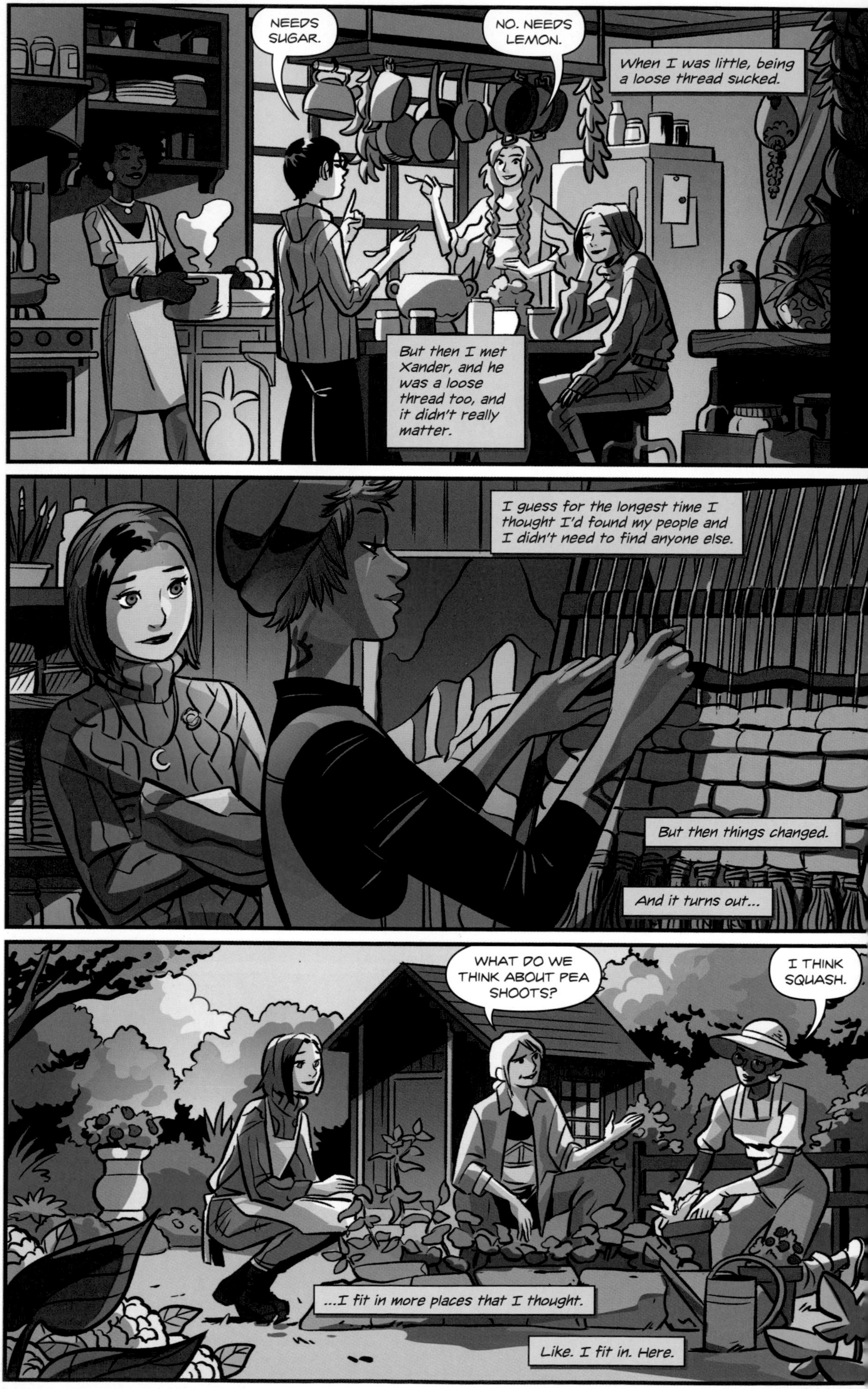
NEEDS SUGAR.
NO. NEEDS LEMON.
When I was little, being a loose thread sucked.
But then I met Xander, and he was a loose thread too, and it didn't really matter.
I guess for the longest time I thought I'd found my people and I didn't need to find anyone else.
But then things changed.
And it turns out...
WHAT DO WE THINK ABOUT PEA SHOOTS?
I THINK SQUASH.
...I fit in more places that I thought.
Like. I fit in. Here.

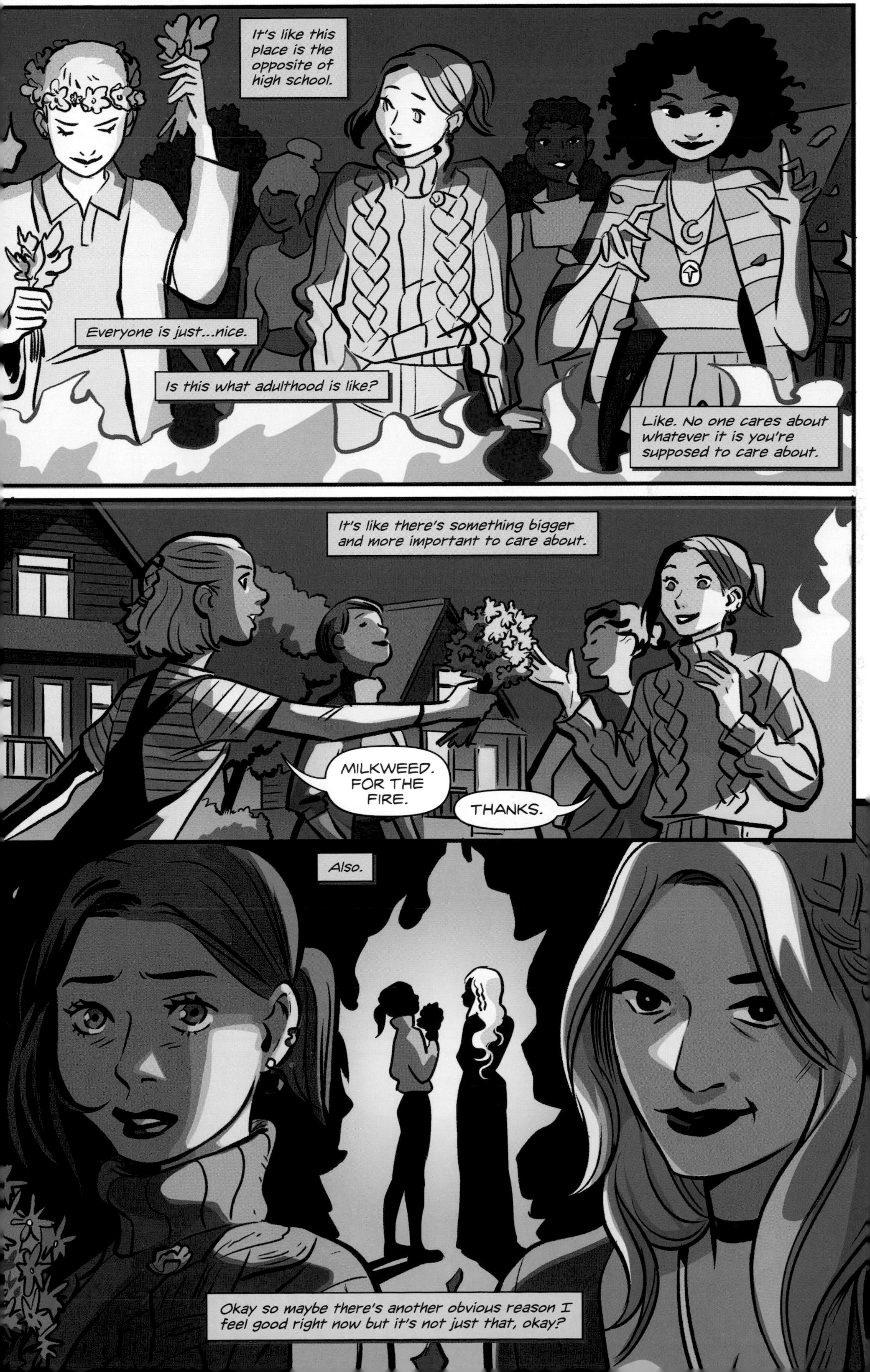

It's like this place is the opposite of high school.
Everyone is just...nice.
Is this what adulthood is like?
Like. No one cares about whatever it is you're supposed to care about.
It's like there's something bigger and more important to care about.
MILKWEED. FOR THE FIRE.
THANKS.
Also.
Okay so maybe there's another obvious reason I feel good right now but it's not just that, okay?

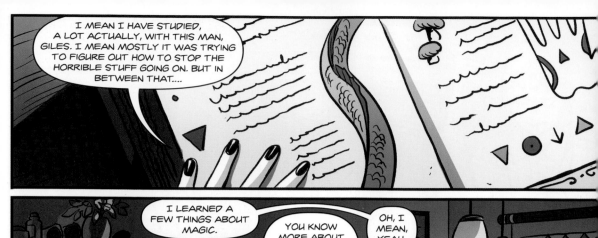

I MEAN I HAVE STUDIED, A LOT ACTUALLY, WITH THIS MAN, GILES. I MEAN MOSTLY IT WAS TRYING TO FIGURE OUT HOW TO STOP THE HORRIBLE STUFF GOING ON. BUT IN BETWEEN THAT....

I LEARNED A FEW THINGS ABOUT MAGIC.

YOU KNOW MORE ABOUT WELSH AND IRISH WICCAN LORE THAN ANYONE I'VE EVER MET.

OH, I MEAN, YEAH.

I'M MY MEDIEVAL TRIVIA TEAM'S TOP SCHOLAR, ON CASTLES AND TAPESTRIES.

SO YOU'RE LIKE ROYALTY.

LIKE A SCHOLAR BUT NERDIER.

I'D LOVE TO READ MORE ABOUT THE HISTORY OF THIS PLACE.

IT'S NOT IN ANY BOOK YOU'D FIND IN THE OUTSIDE WORLD.

WHAT'S THAT BOOK? THE BIG ONE.

THAT'S AGRICULTURAL INCANTATIONS.

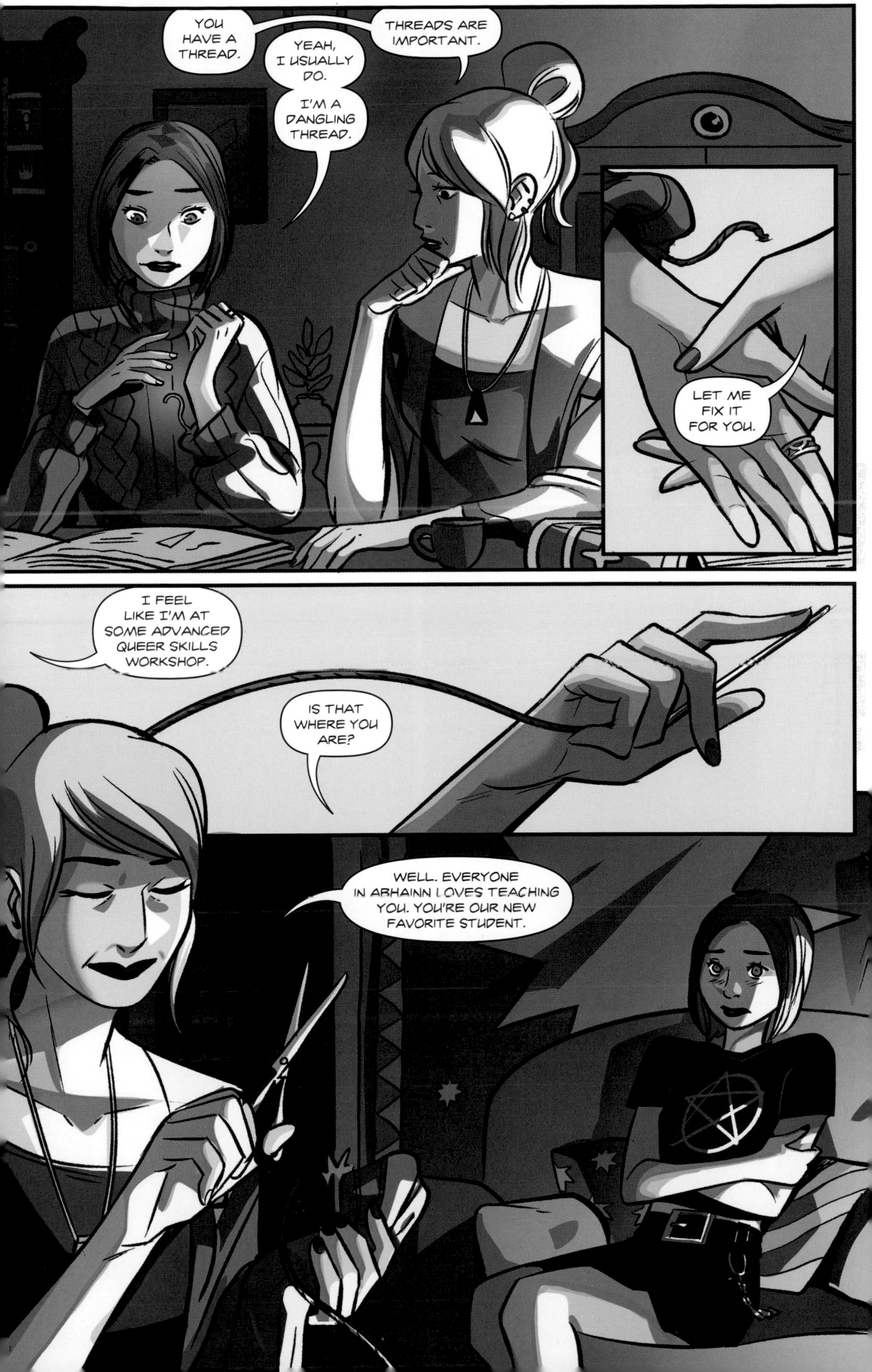
YOU HAVE A THREAD.
YEAH, I USUALLY DO.
THREADS ARE IMPORTANT.
I'M A DANGLING THREAD.
LET ME FIX IT FOR YOU.
I FEEL LIKE I'M AT SOME ADVANCED QUEER SKILLS WORKSHOP.
IS THAT WHERE YOU ARE?
WELL. EVERYONE IN ARHAINN LOVES TEACHING YOU. YOU'RE OUR NEW FAVORITE STUDENT.

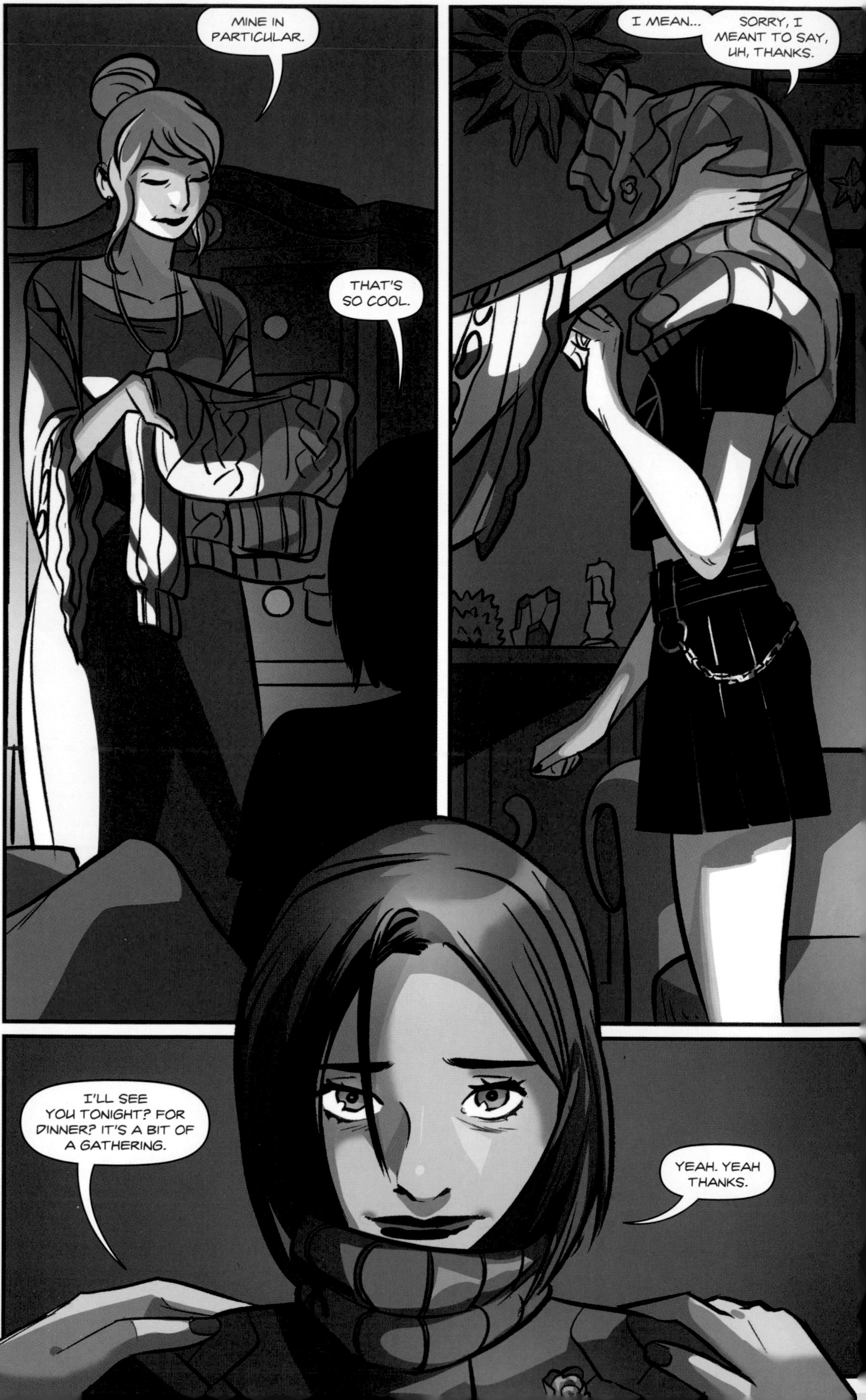
MINE IN PARTICULAR.
THAT'S SO COOL.
I MEAN...
SORRY, I MEANT TO SAY, UH, THANKS.
I'LL SEE YOU TONIGHT? FOR DINNER? IT'S A BIT OF A GATHERING.
YEAH. YEAH THANKS.

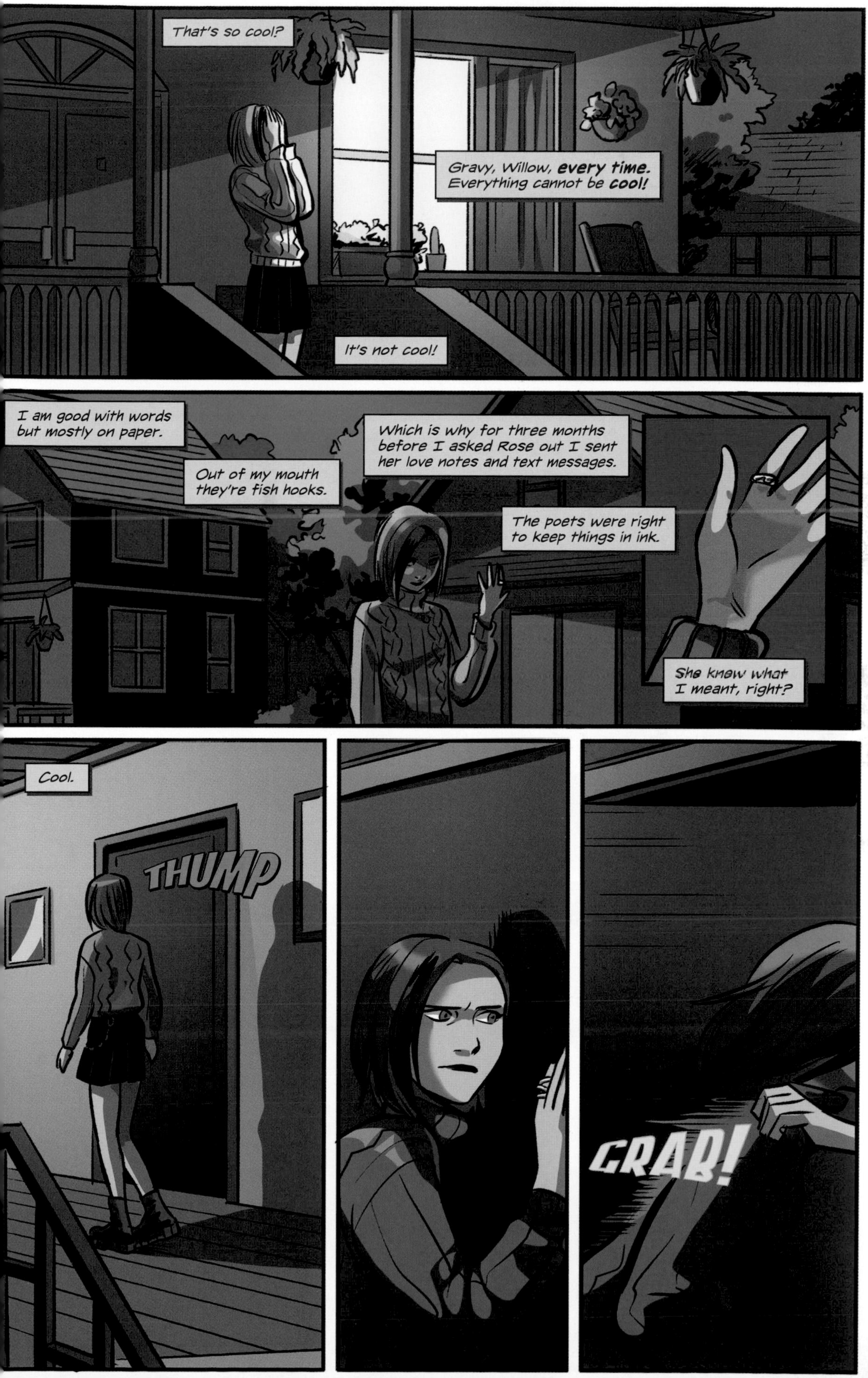
That's so cool?
Gravy, Willow, every time. Everything cannot be cool!
It's not cool!
I am good with words but mostly on paper.
Out of my mouth they're fish hooks.
Which is why for three months before I asked Rose out I sent her love notes and text messages.
The poets were right to keep things in ink.
She knew what I meant, right?
Cool.
THUMP
GRAB!

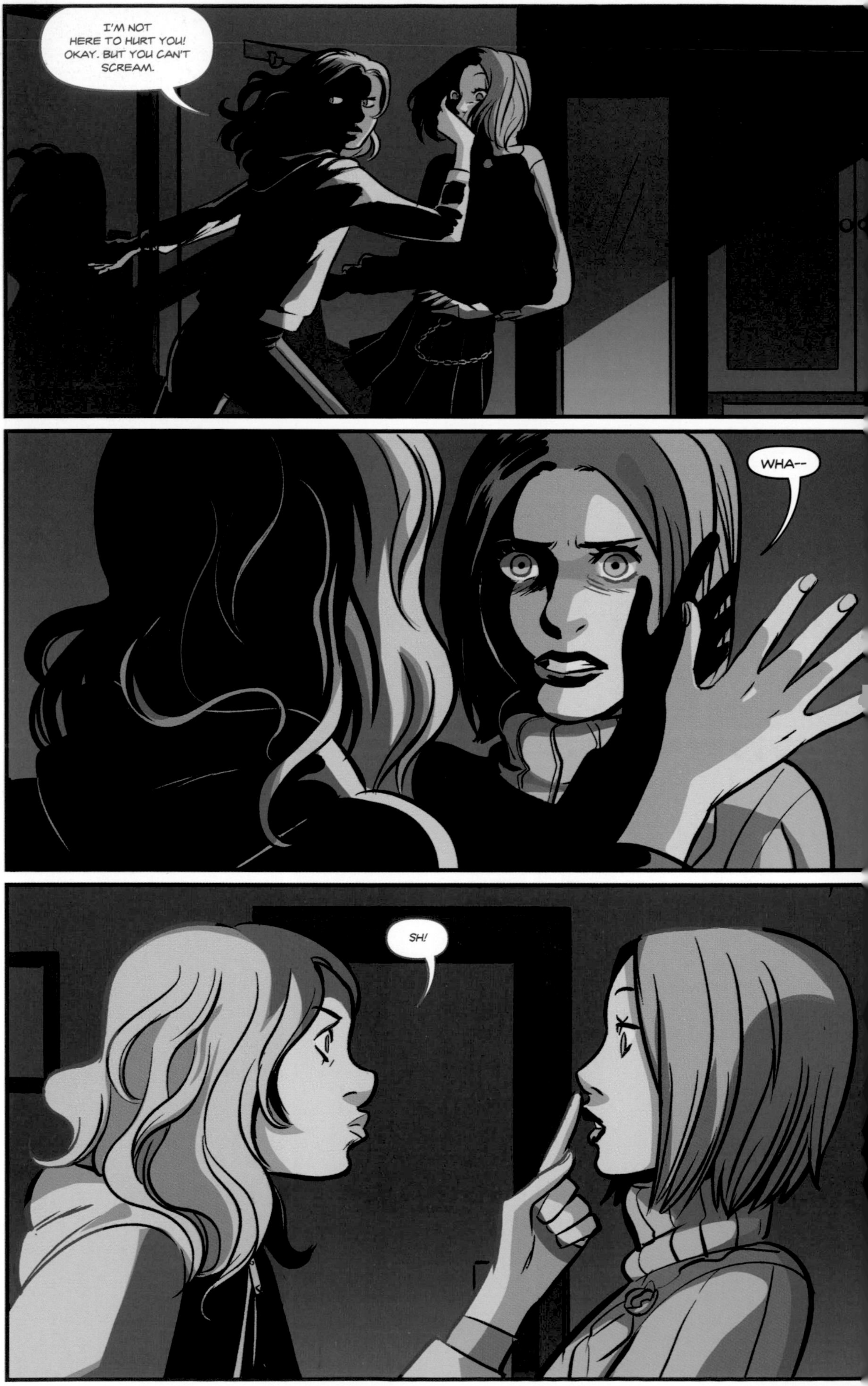
I'M NOT HERE TO HURT YOU! OKAY. BUT YOU CAN'T SCREAM.
WHA--
SH!

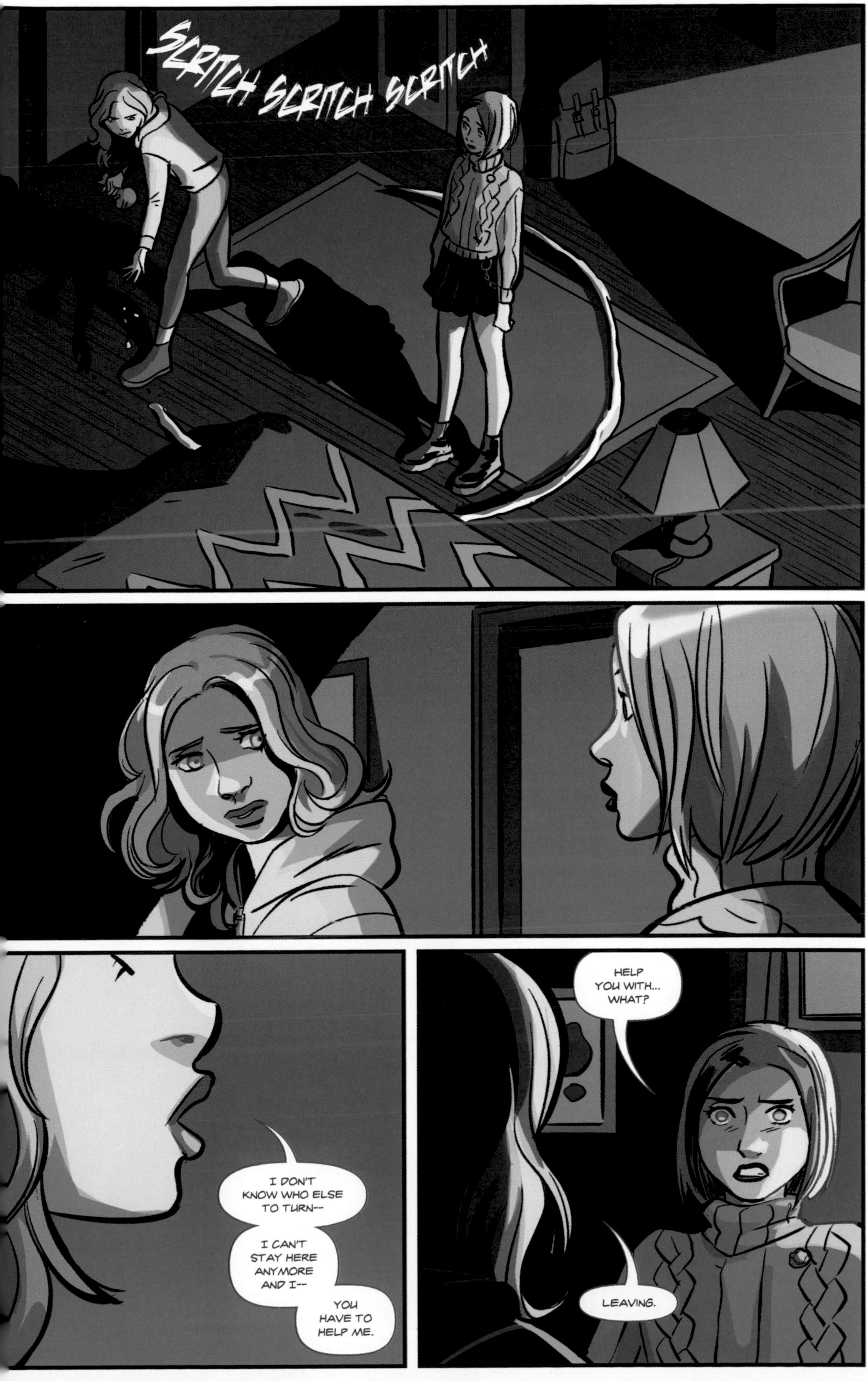
SCRITCH SCRITCH SCRITCH
I DON'T KNOW WHO ELSE TO TURN--
I CAN'T STAY HERE ANYMORE AND I--
YOU HAVE TO HELP ME.
HELP YOU WITH... WHAT?
LEAVING.

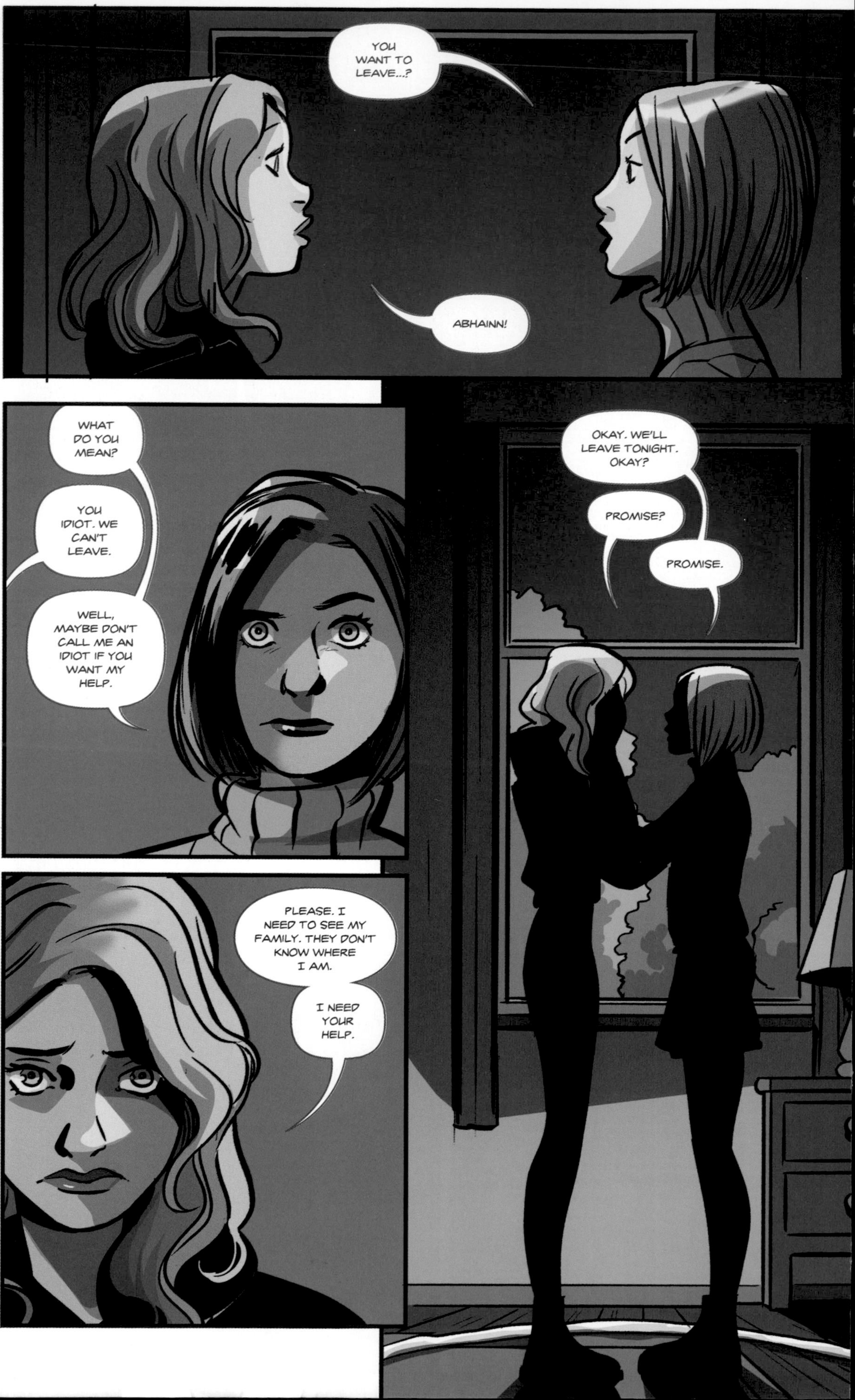
YOU WANT TO LEAVE...?
ABHAINN!
WHAT DO YOU MEAN?
YOU IDIOT. WE CAN'T LEAVE.
WELL, MAYBE DON'T CALL ME AN IDIOT IF YOU WANT MY HELP.
PLEASE. I NEED TO SEE MY FAMILY. THEY DON'T KNOW WHERE I AM.
I NEED YOUR HELP.
OKAY. WE'LL LEAVE TONIGHT. OKAY?
PROMISE?
PROMISE.

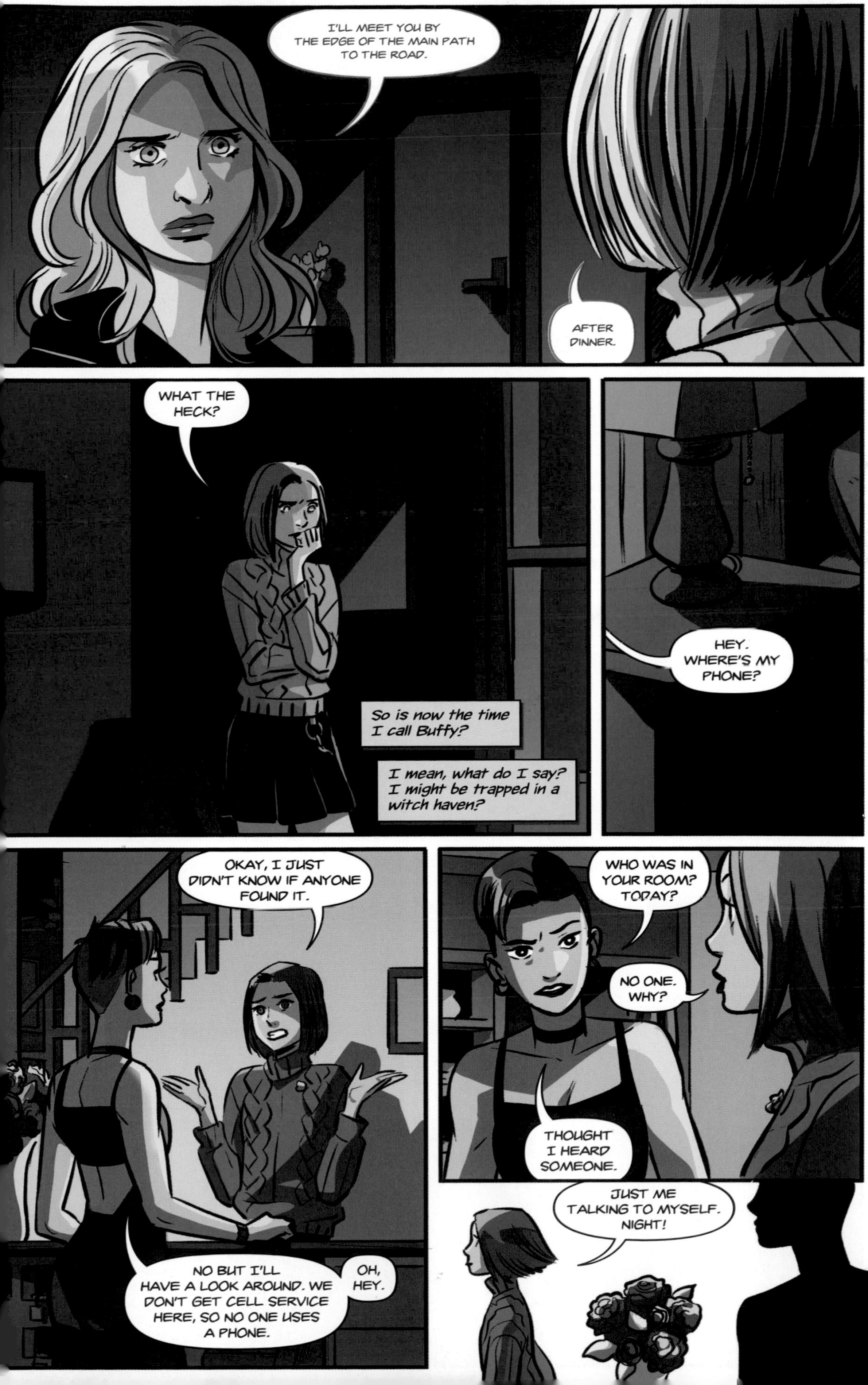
I'LL MEET YOU BY THE EDGE OF THE MAIN PATH TO THE ROAD.
AFTER DINNER.
WHAT THE HECK?
So is now the time I call Buffy?
I mean, what do I say? I might be trapped in a witch haven?
HEY. WHERE'S MY PHONE?
OKAY, I JUST DIDN'T KNOW IF ANYONE FOUND IT.
NO BUT I'LL HAVE A LOOK AROUND. WE DON'T GET CELL SERVICE HERE, SO NO ONE USES A PHONE.
OH, HEY.
WHO WAS IN YOUR ROOM? TODAY?
NO ONE. WHY?
THOUGHT I HEARD SOMEONE.
JUST ME TALKING TO MYSELF. NIGHT!

I LOVE THAT MOVIE! IT'S MY FAV WITCH MOVIE!

YET AGAIN WRITTEN BY PEOPLE WHO HAVE NO IDEA WHAT THEY'RE TALKING ABOUT.

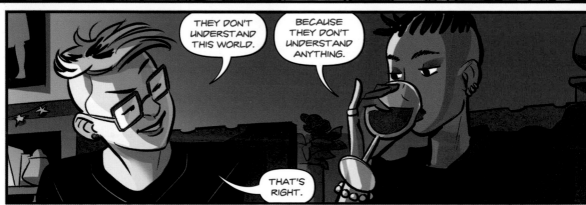

THEY DON'T UNDERSTAND THIS WORLD.

BECAUSE THEY DON'T UNDERSTAND ANYTHING.

THAT'S RIGHT.

ISN'T IT BETTER IF THEY DON'T?

WE ARE SAFER HIDDEN. SAFER HERE IF THEY FORGET US.

ISN'T THAT THE MOVIE WHERE THEY WEAR ALL THE PLEATHER?

YOU KNOW IT.

I LOVED EVERYTHING I READ ABOUT WITCHES WHEN I WAS GROWING UP.

I MEAN, IT WAS WHAT LET ME KNOW THAT THIS WORLD EXISTED, YOU KNOW?

THAT SOMETHING OTHER THAN WHAT I WAS IN WAS POSSIBLE. THAT THERE WAS AN ESCAPE.

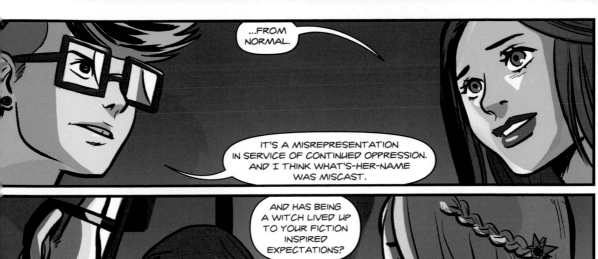

...FROM NORMAL.

IT'S A MISREPRESENTATION IN SERVICE OF CONTINUED OPPRESSION. AND I THINK WHAT'S-HER-NAME WAS MISCAST.

AND HAS BEING A WITCH LIVED UP TO YOUR FICTION INSPIRED EXPECTATIONS?

OH, I MEAN, IT'S BEEN WAY MORE COMPLICATED THAN I THOUGHT IT WOULD BE.

LIKE, INTENSE, BUT...

...I DON'T THINK I WOULD STILL BE ALIVE IF IT WASN'T FOR BEING A WITCH.

WE ARE WITCHES. AS WITCHES WE STAND.

TOGETHER.

TO NEW FRIENDS.

HEAR HEAR.

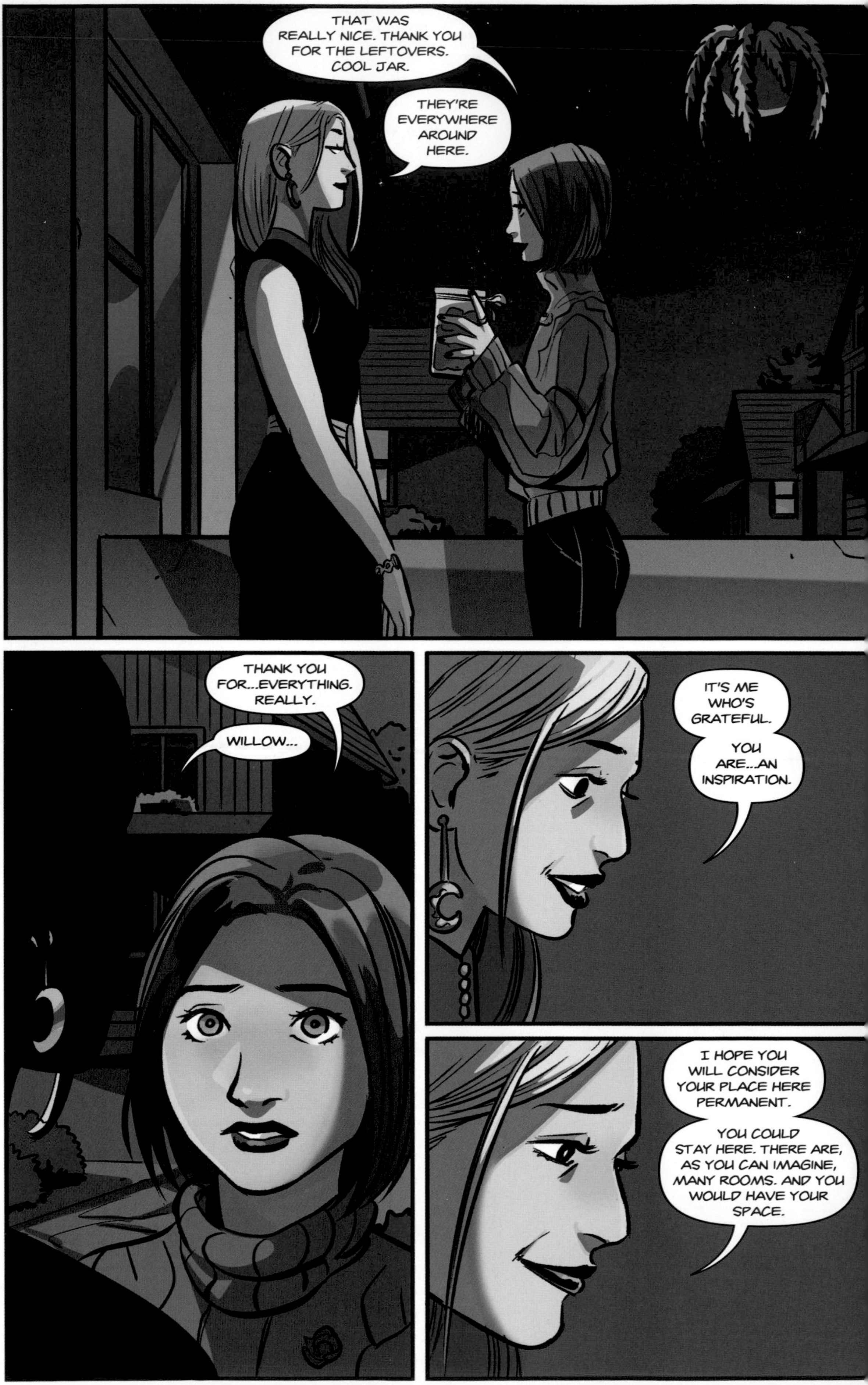
THAT WAS REALLY NICE. THANK YOU FOR THE LEFTOVERS. COOL JAR.
THEY'RE EVERYWHERE AROUND HERE.
THANK YOU FOR...EVERYTHING. REALLY.
WILLOW...
IT'S ME WHO'S GRATEFUL.
YOU ARE...AN INSPIRATION.
I HOPE YOU WILL CONSIDER YOUR PLACE HERE PERMANENT.
YOU COULD STAY HERE. THERE ARE, AS YOU CAN IMAGINE, MANY ROOMS. AND YOU WOULD HAVE YOUR SPACE.

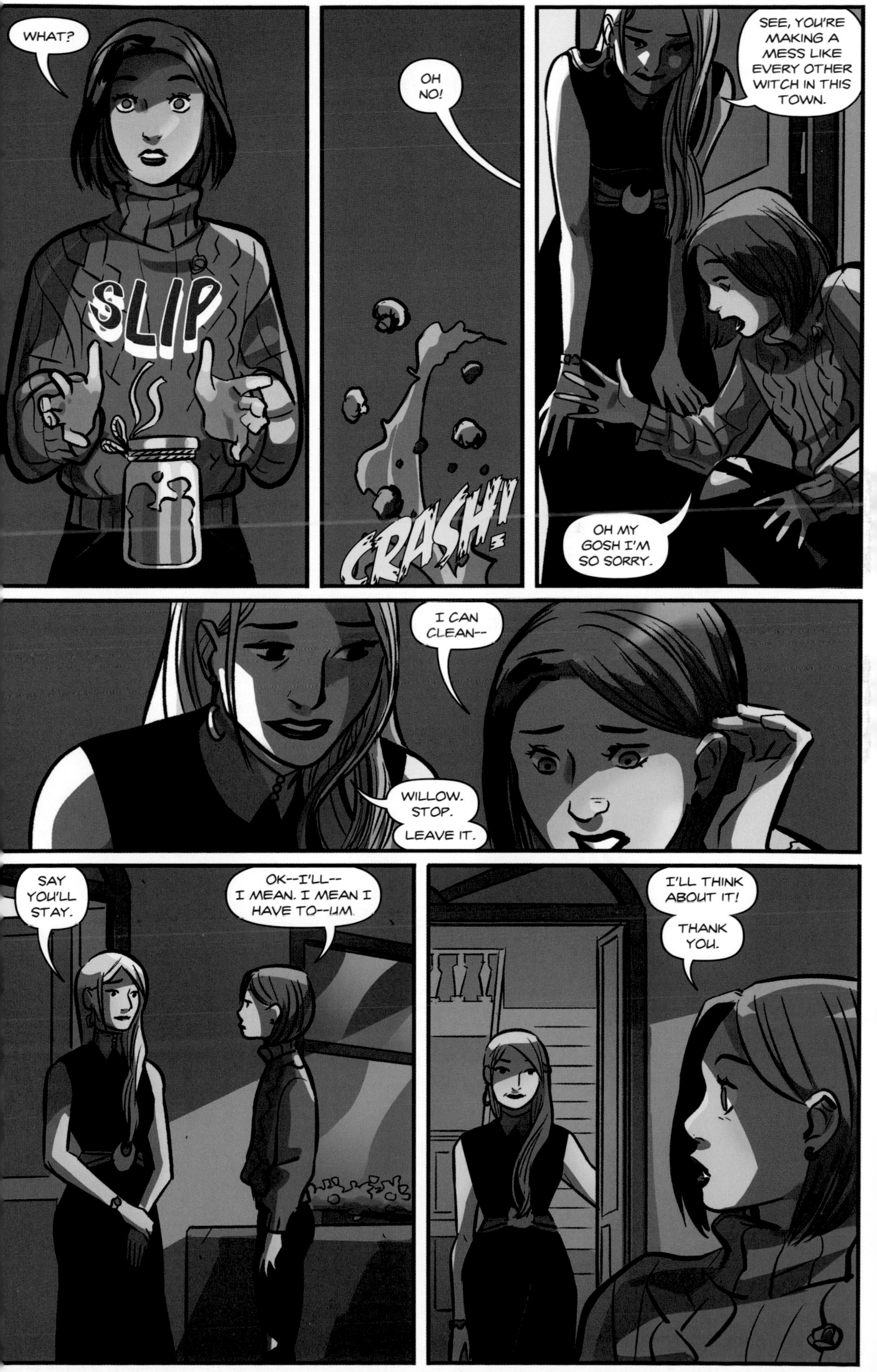
WHAT?
SLIP
OH NO!
CRASH!
SEE, YOU'RE MAKING A MESS LIKE EVERY OTHER WITCH IN THIS TOWN.
OH MY GOSH I'M SO SORRY.
I CAN CLEAN--
WILLOW. STOP.
LEAVE IT.
SAY YOU'LL STAY.
OK--I'LL-- I MEAN. I MEAN I HAVE TO--UM.
I'LL THINK ABOUT IT!
THANK YOU.

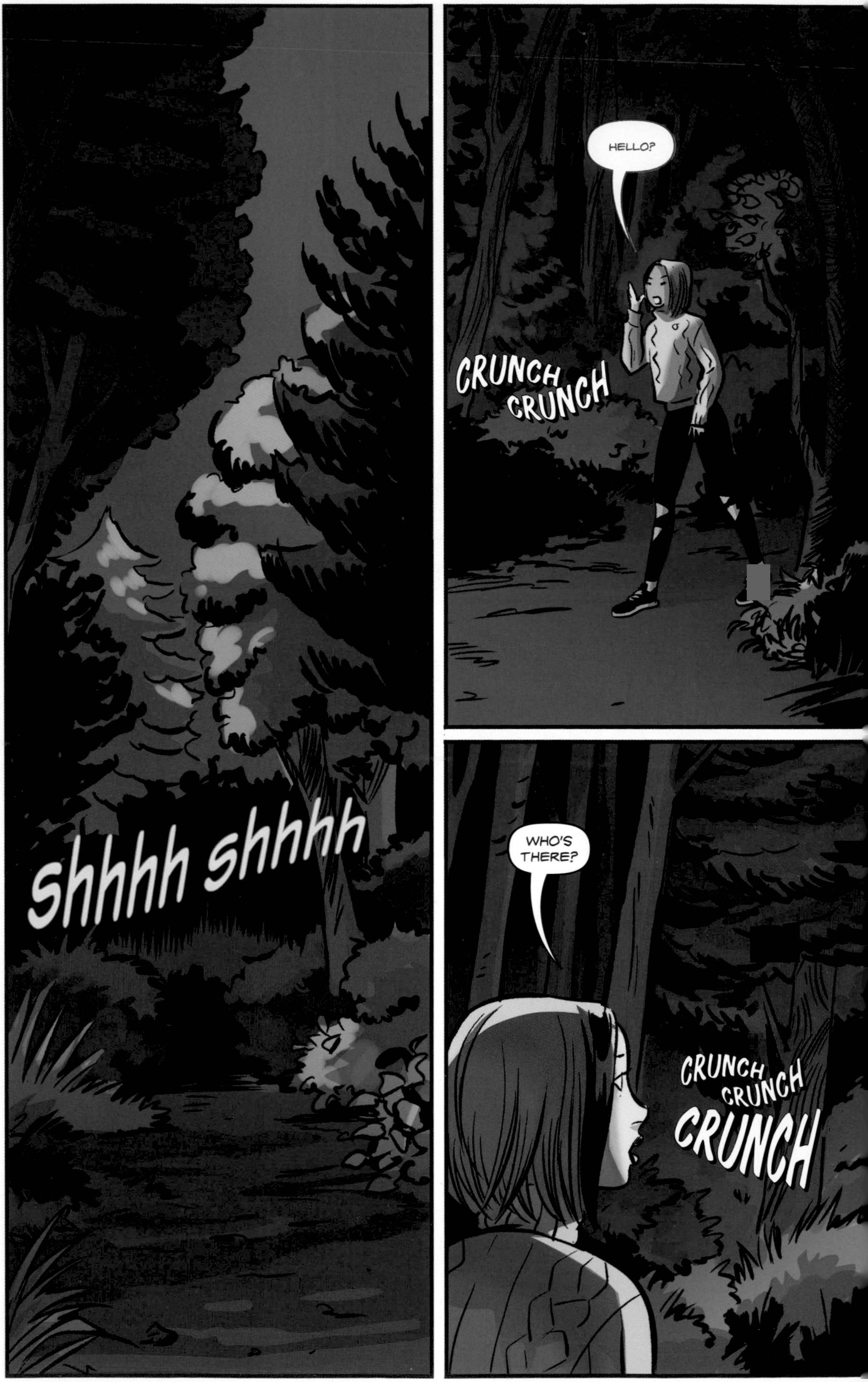
shhhh shhhh
HELLO?
CRUNCH CRUNCH
WHO'S THERE?
CRUNCH CRUNCH CRUNCH

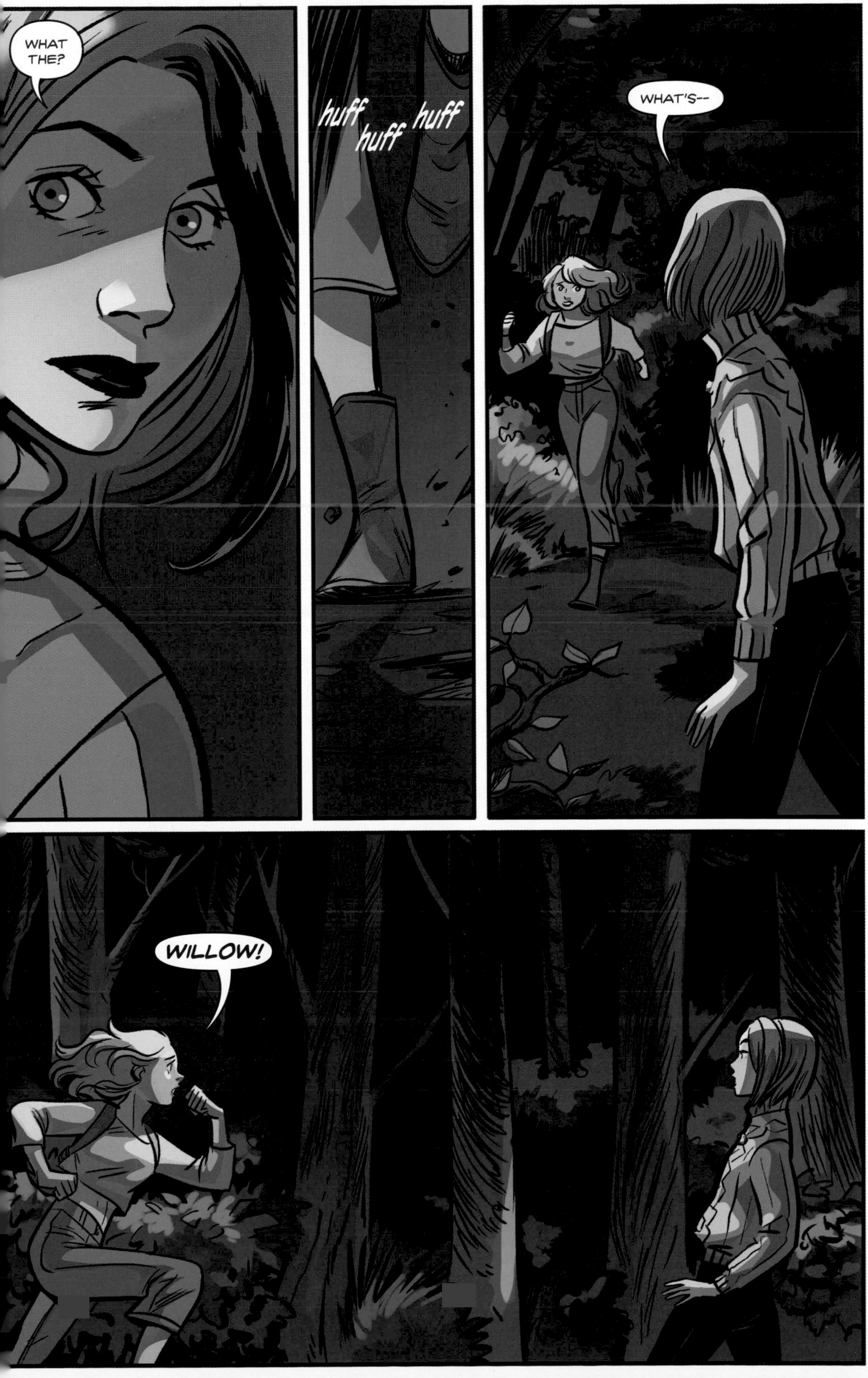

WHAT THE?
huff huff huff
WHAT'S--
WILLOW!

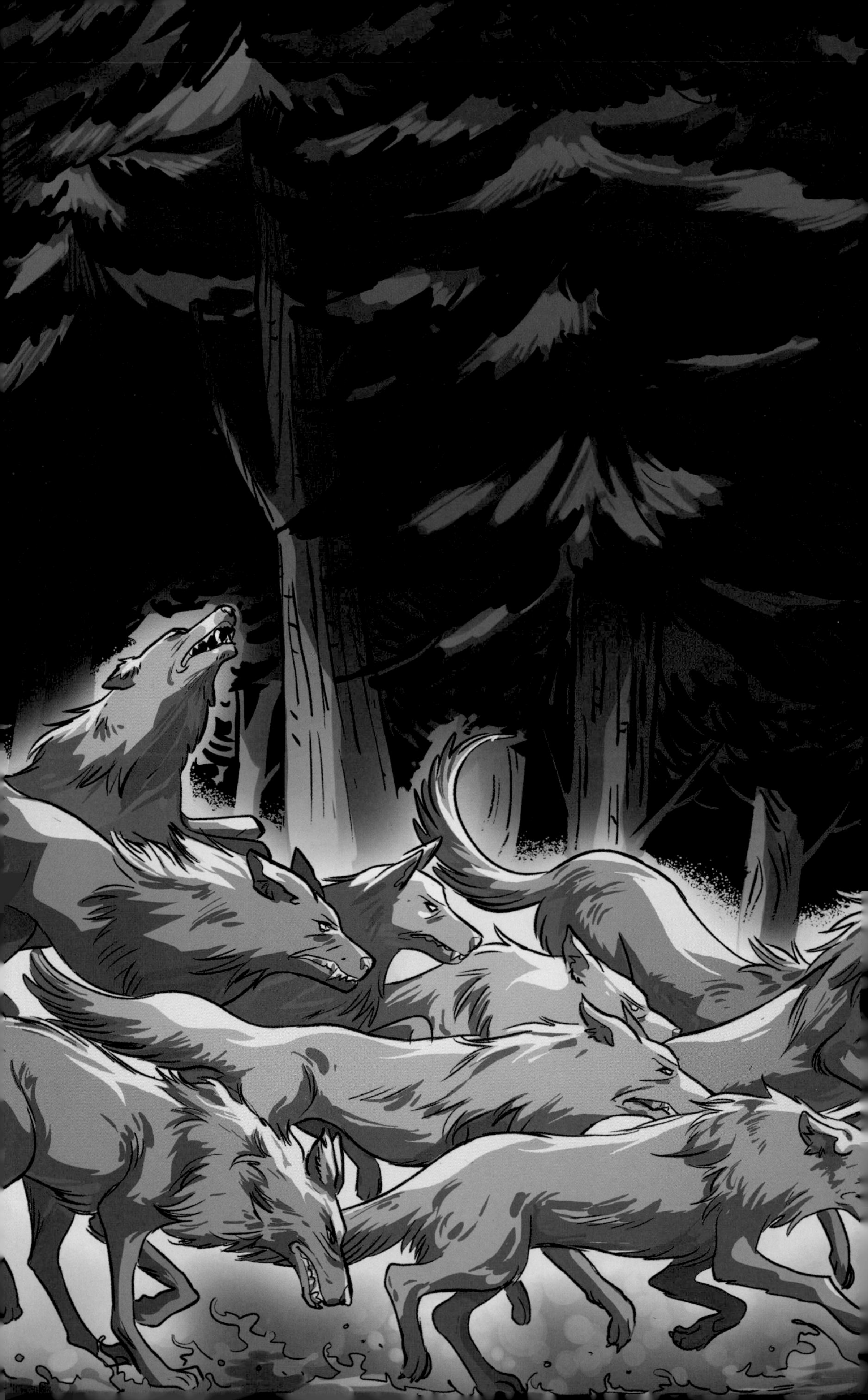

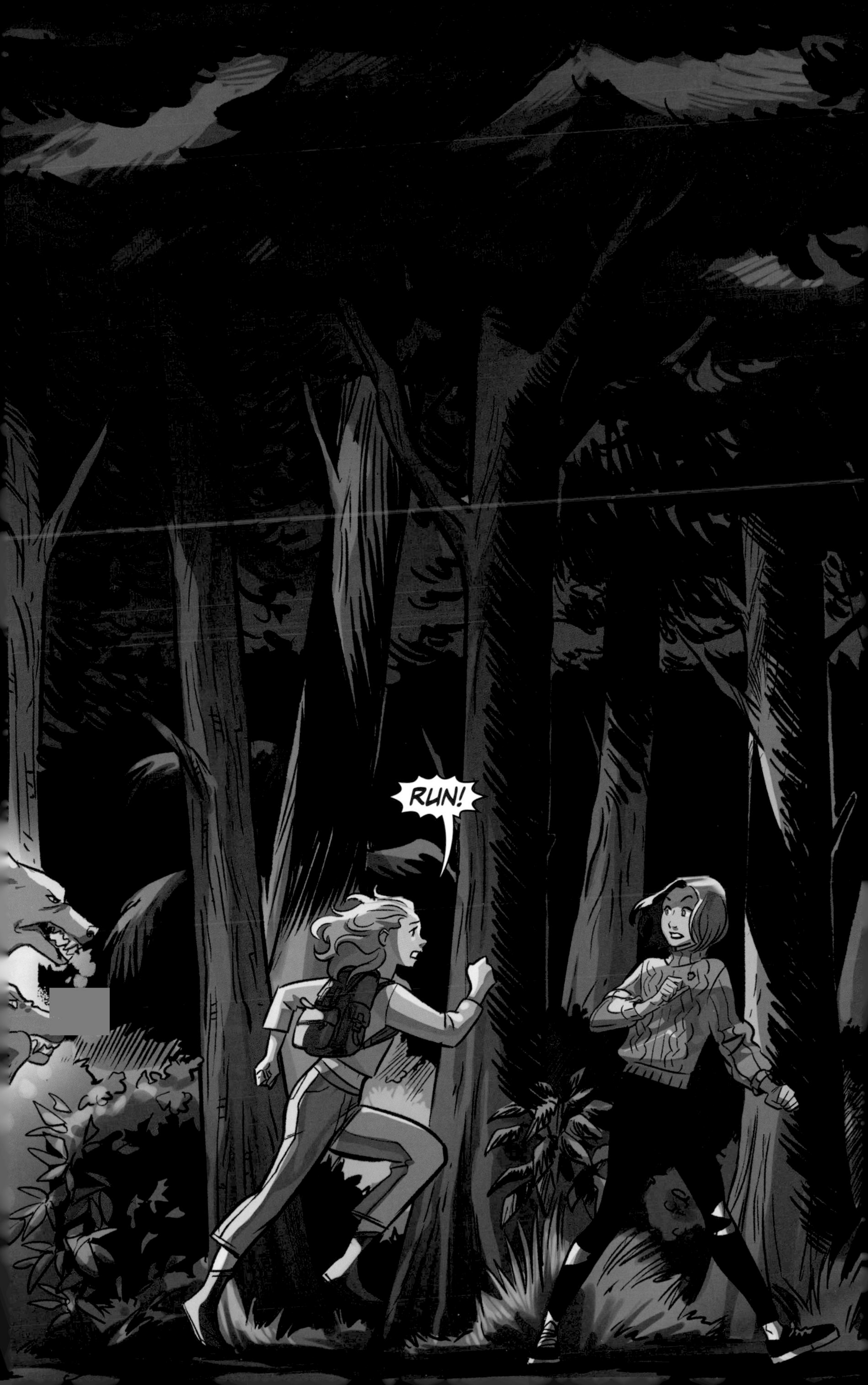
RUN!

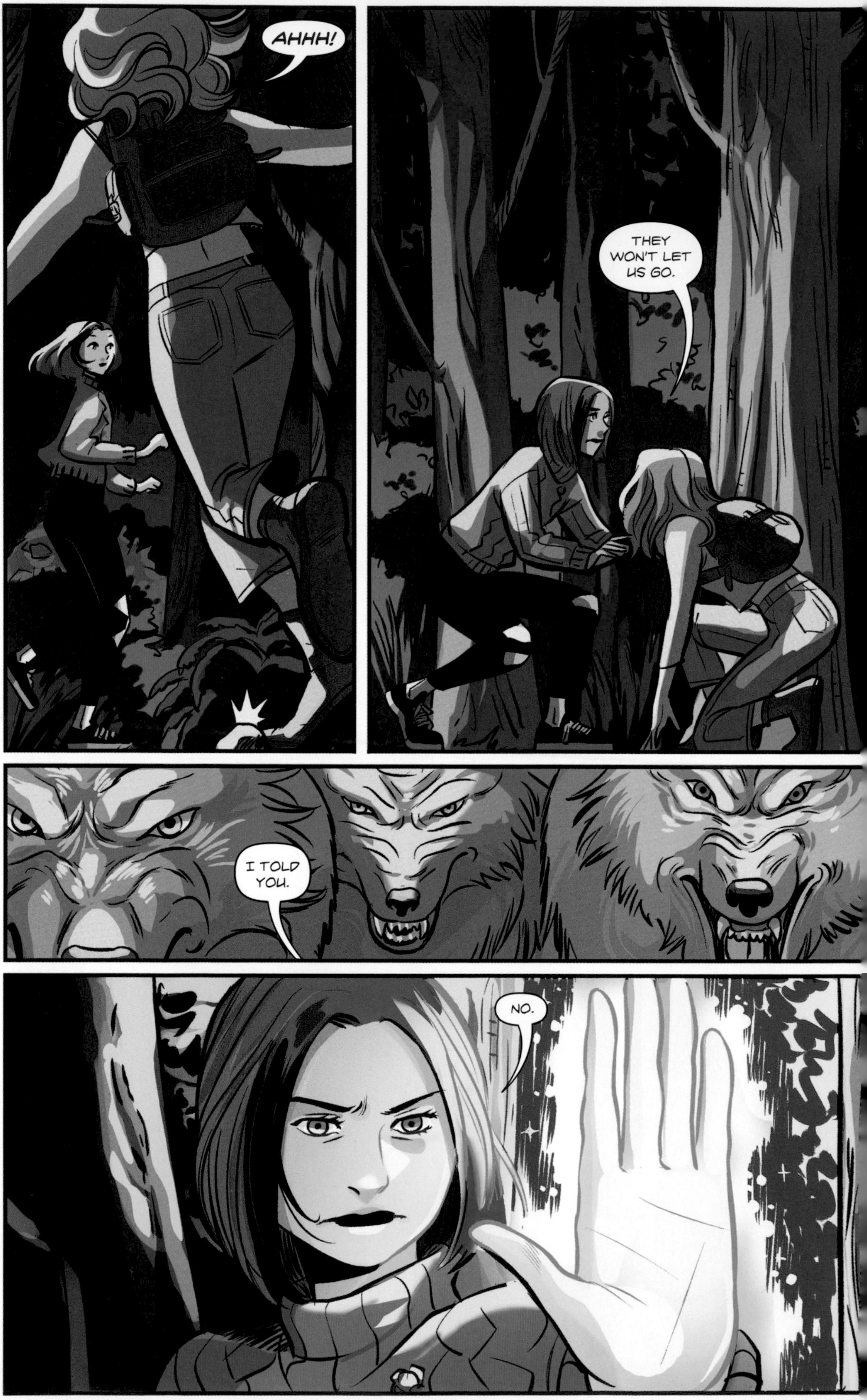
AHHH!
THEY WON'T LET US GO.
I TOLD YOU.
NO.

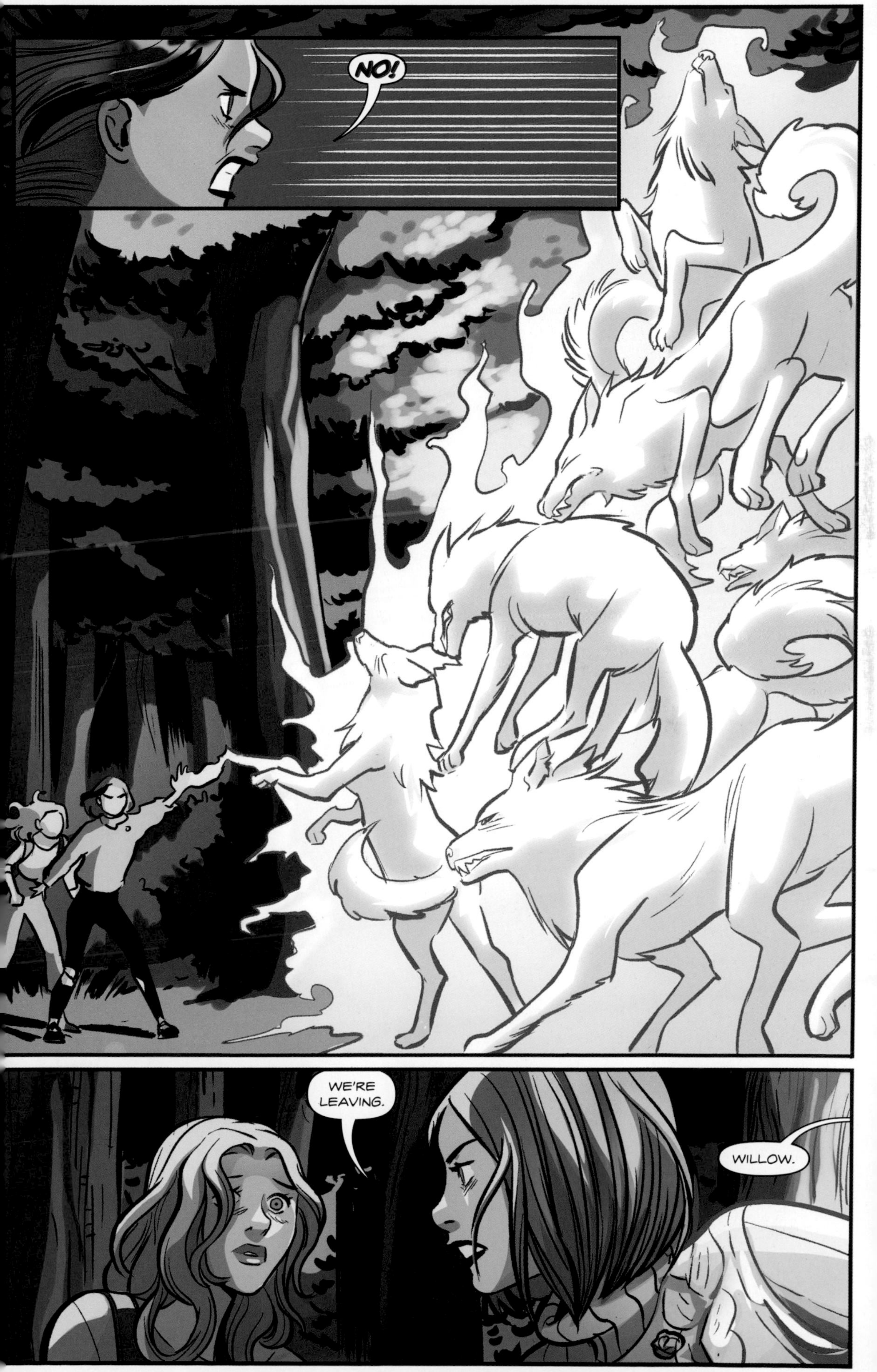
NO!
WE'RE LEAVING.
WILLOW.

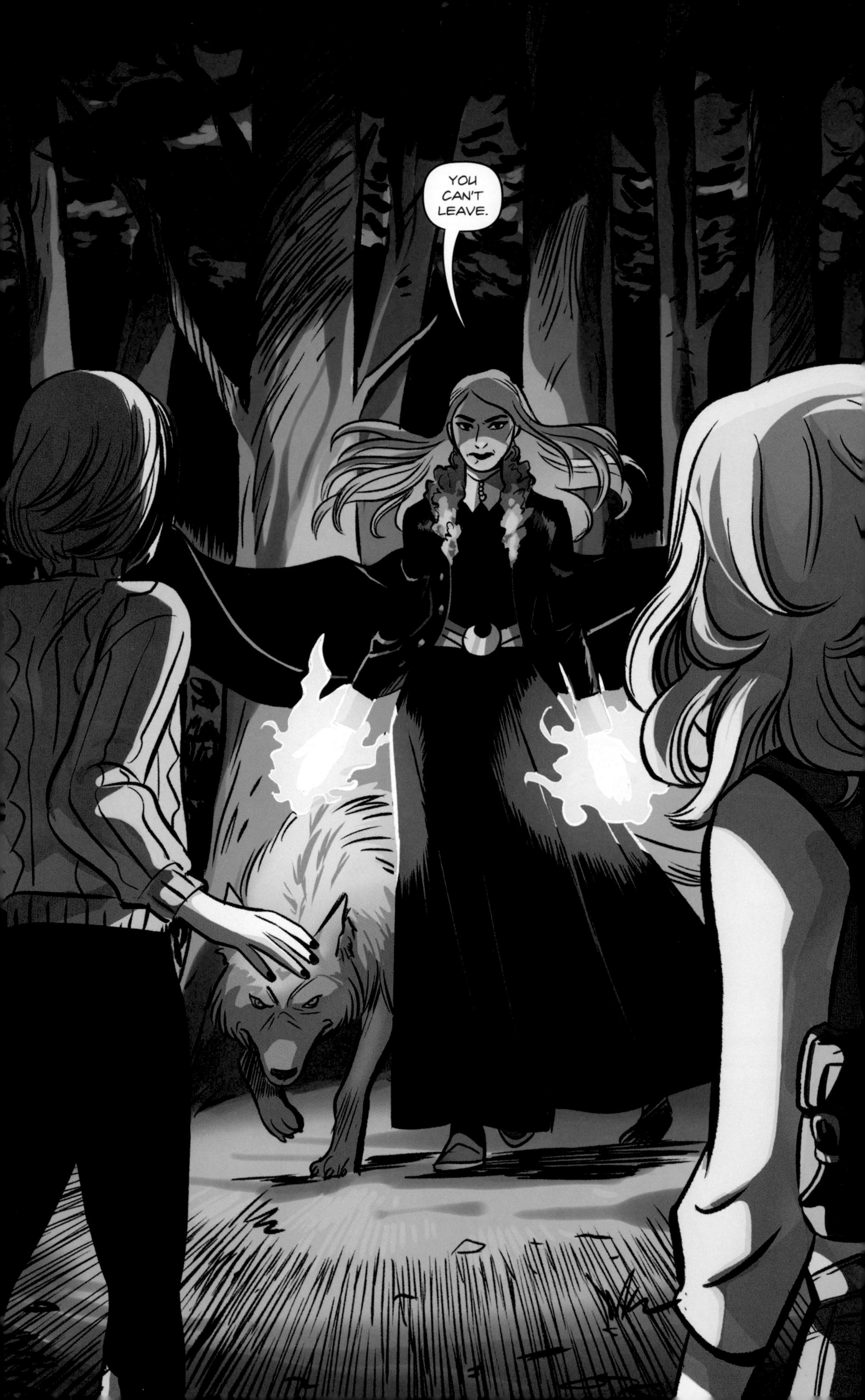
YOU CAN'T LEAVE.

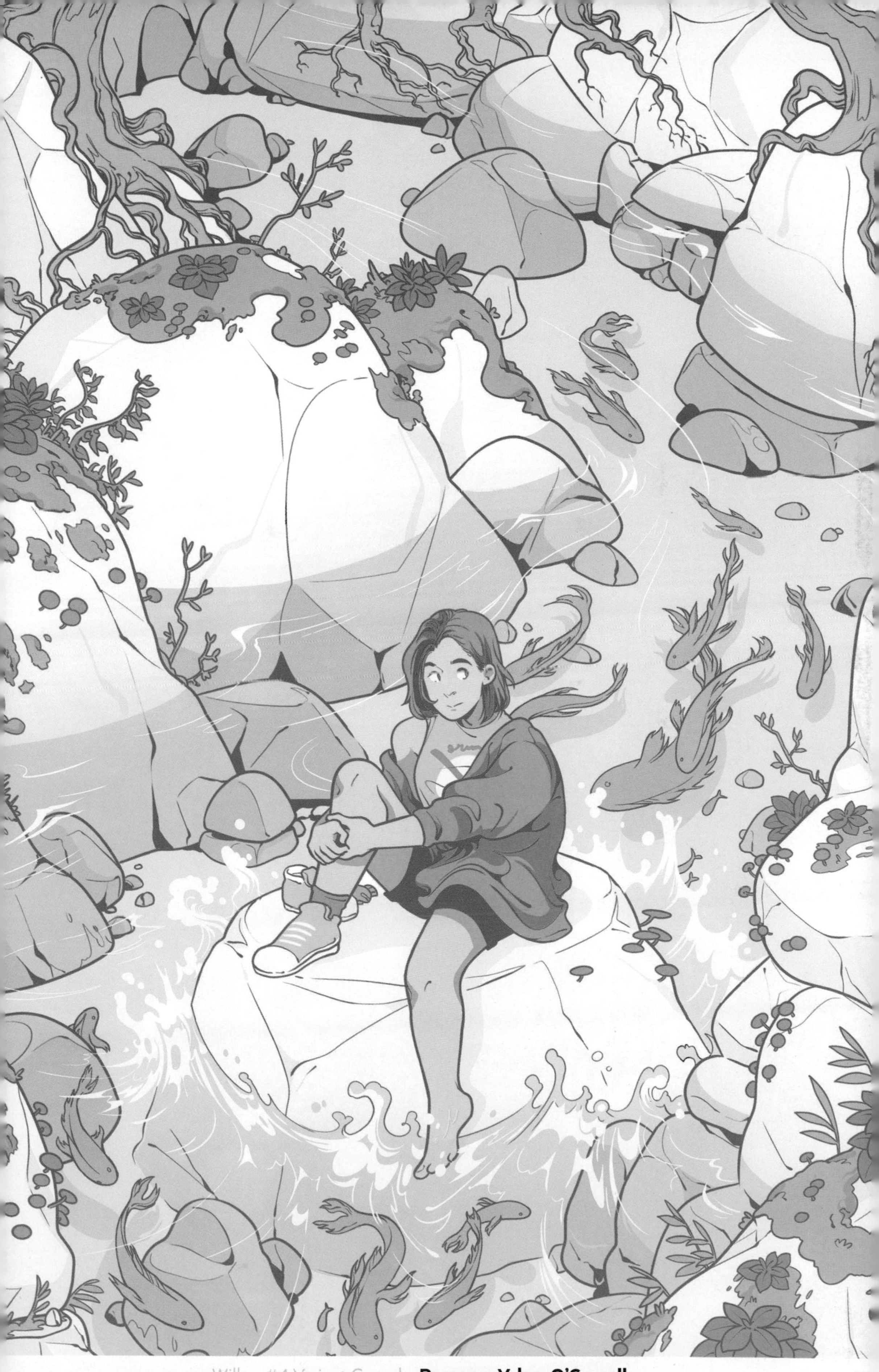

Willow #4 Variant Cover by **Rosemary Valero O'Connell**

CHAPTER FIVE

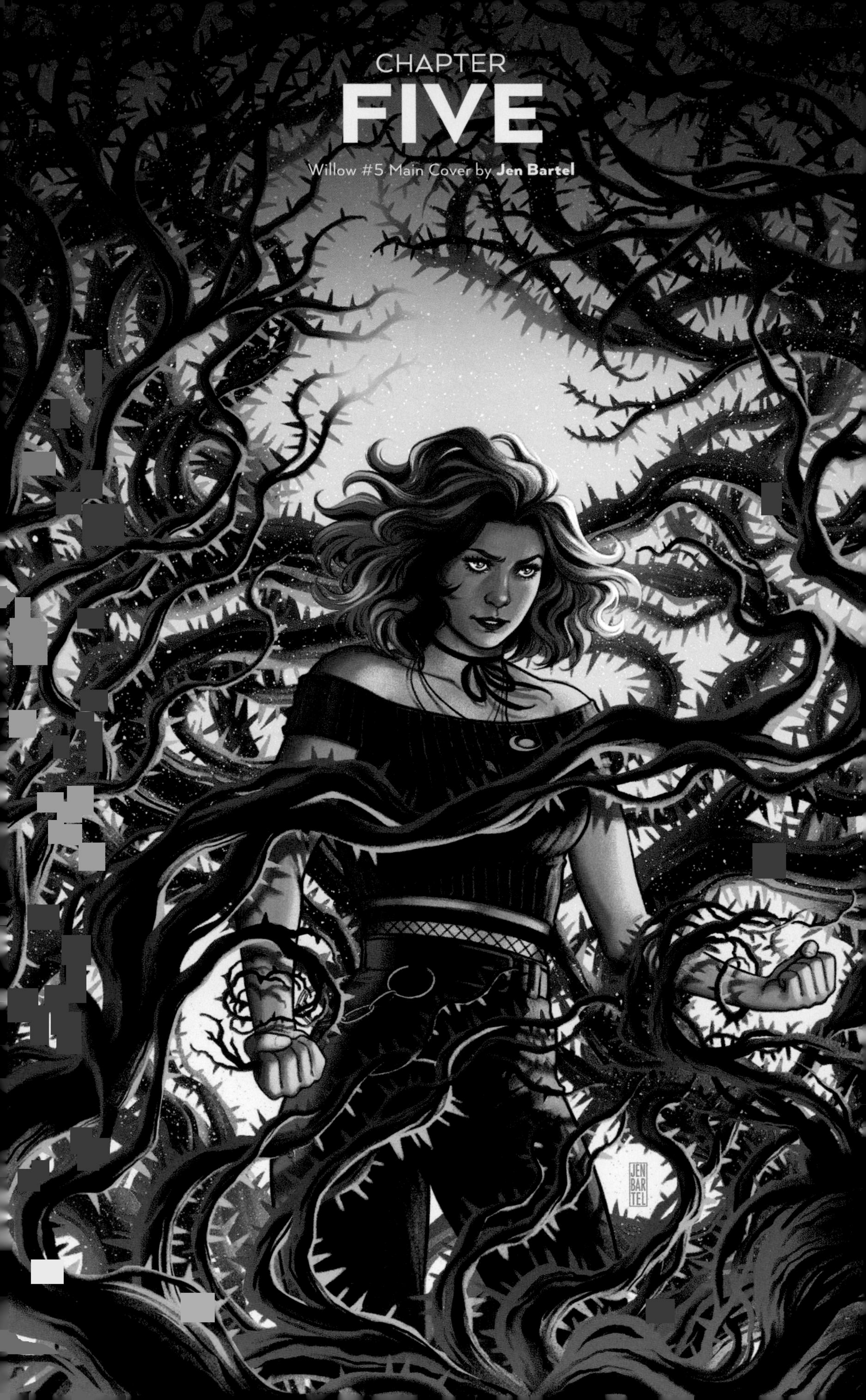
JEN BARTEL

Willow #5 Main Cover by **Jen Bartel**

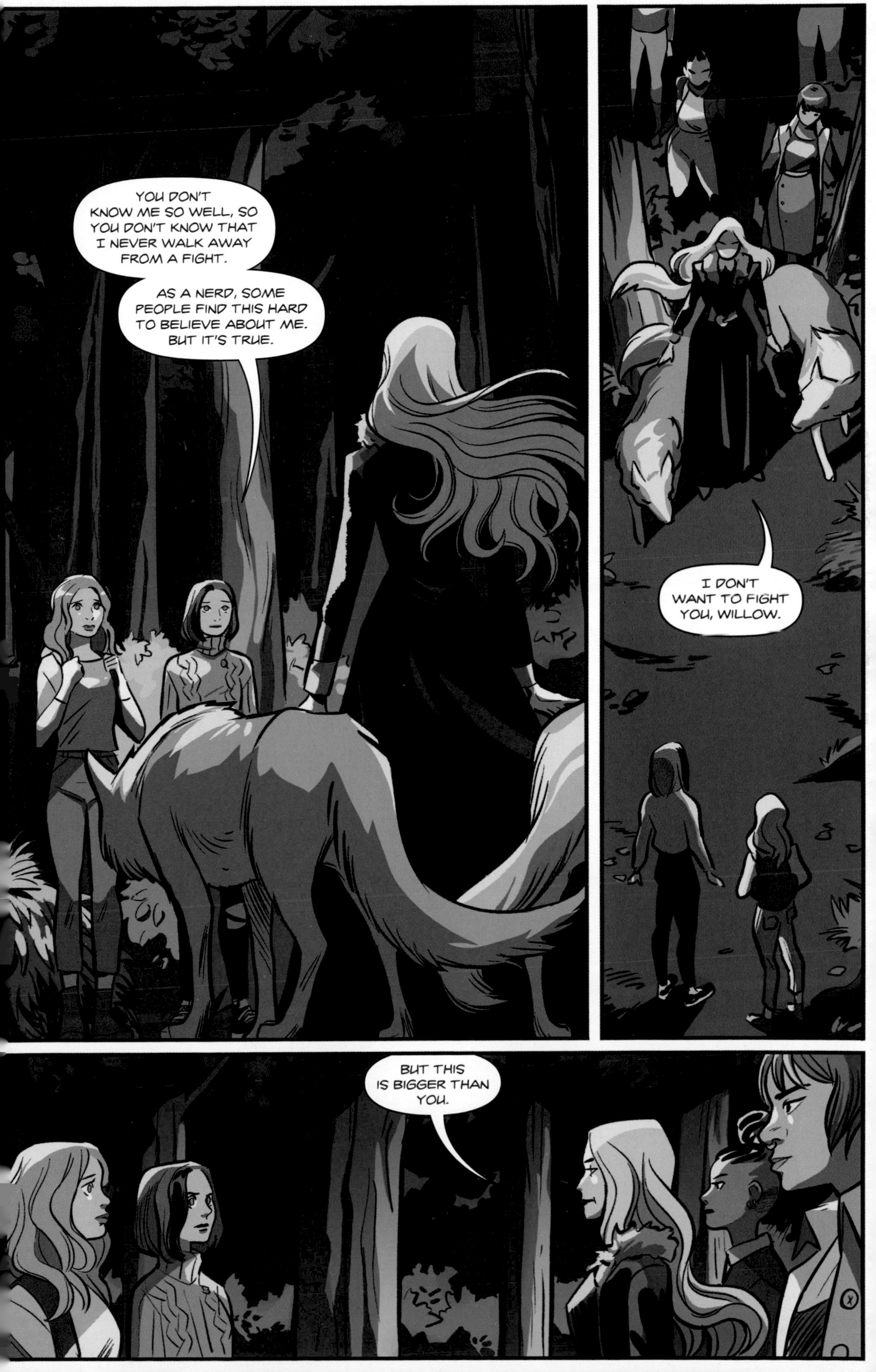
YOU DON'T KNOW ME SO WELL, SO YOU DON'T KNOW THAT I NEVER WALK AWAY FROM A FIGHT.
AS A NERD, SOME PEOPLE FIND THIS HARD TO BELIEVE ABOUT ME. BUT IT'S TRUE.
I DON'T WANT TO FIGHT YOU, WILLOW.
BUT THIS IS BIGGER THAN YOU.

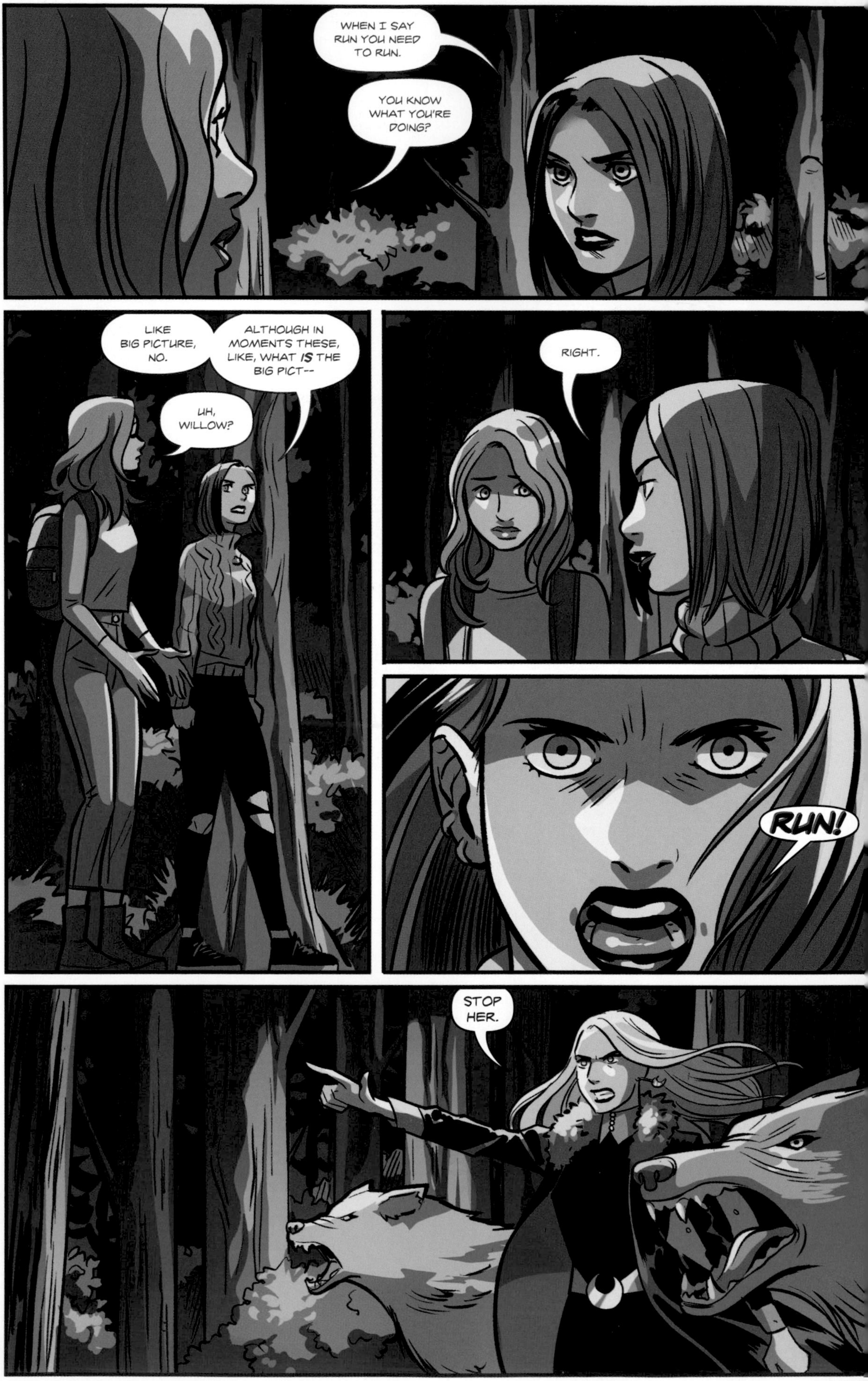
WHEN I SAY RUN YOU NEED TO RUN.
YOU KNOW WHAT YOU'RE DOING?
LIKE BIG PICTURE, NO.
ALTHOUGH IN MOMENTS THESE, LIKE, WHAT *IS* THE BIG PICT--
UH, WILLOW?
RIGHT.
RUN!
STOP HER.

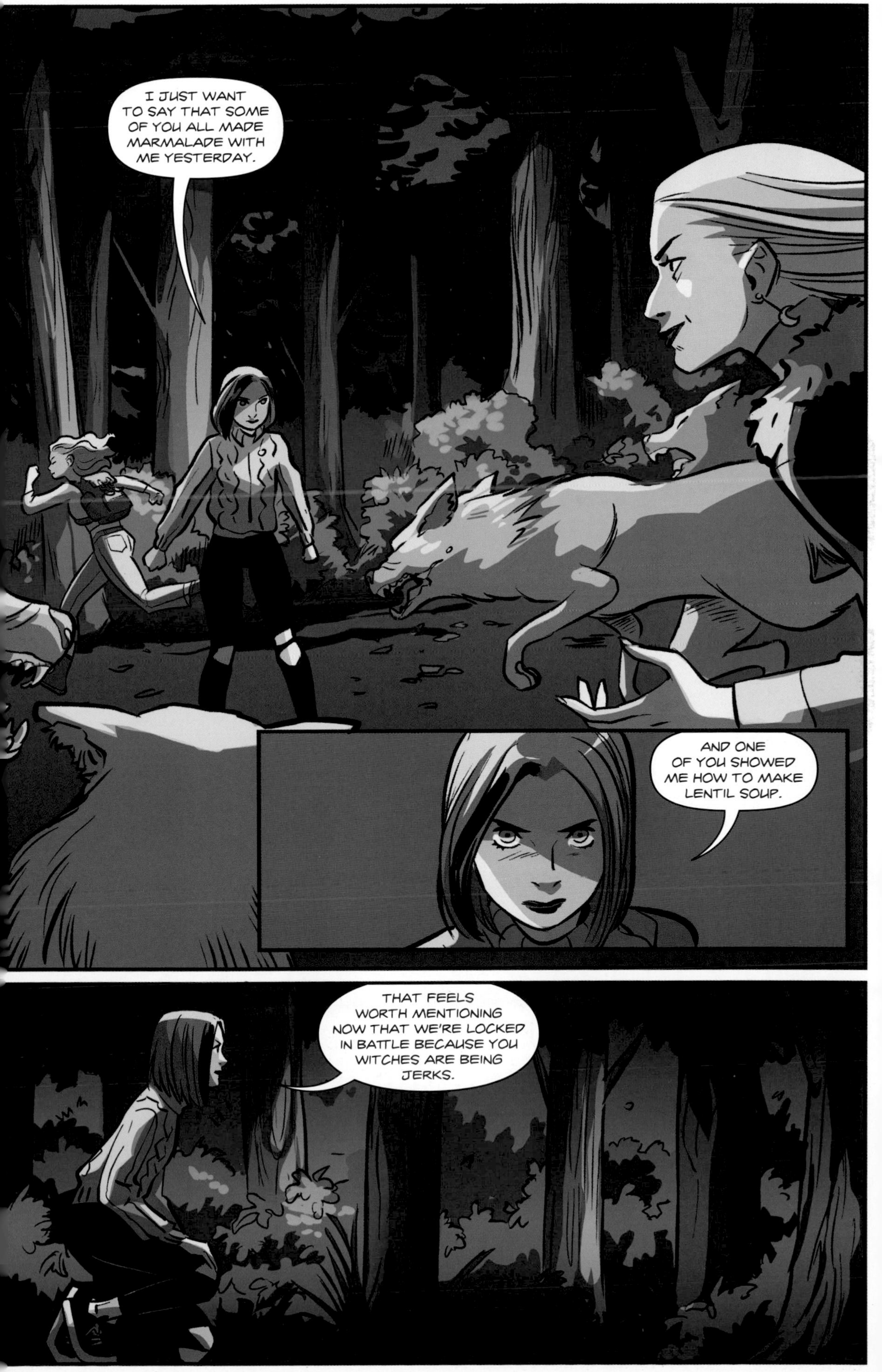
I JUST WANT TO SAY THAT SOME OF YOU ALL MADE MARMALADE WITH ME YESTERDAY.
AND ONE OF YOU SHOWED ME HOW TO MAKE LENTIL SOUP.
THAT FEELS WORTH MENTIONING NOW THAT WE'RE LOCKED IN BATTLE BECAUSE YOU WITCHES ARE BEING JERKS.

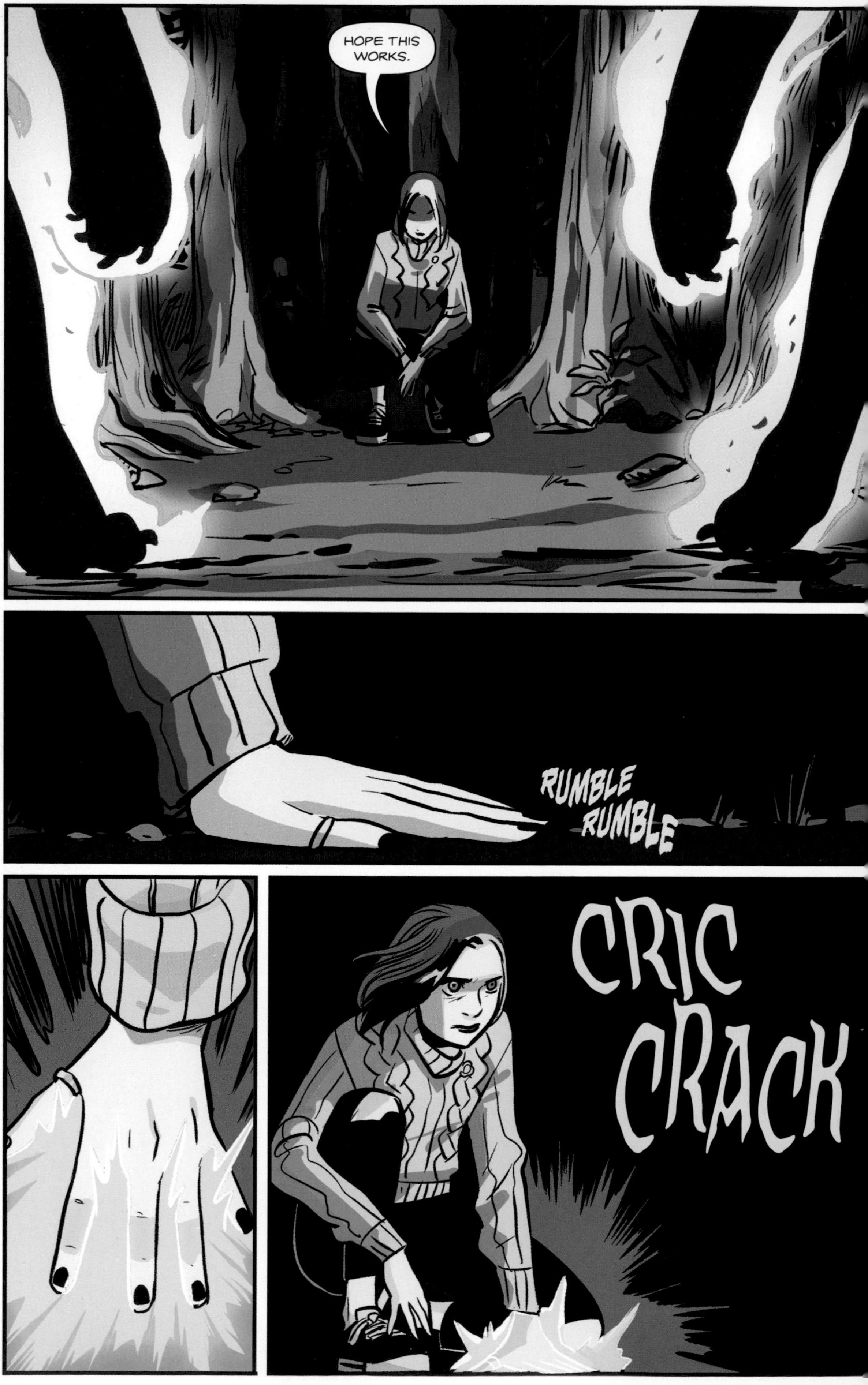
HOPE THIS WORKS.
RUMBLE RUMBLE
CRIC CRACK

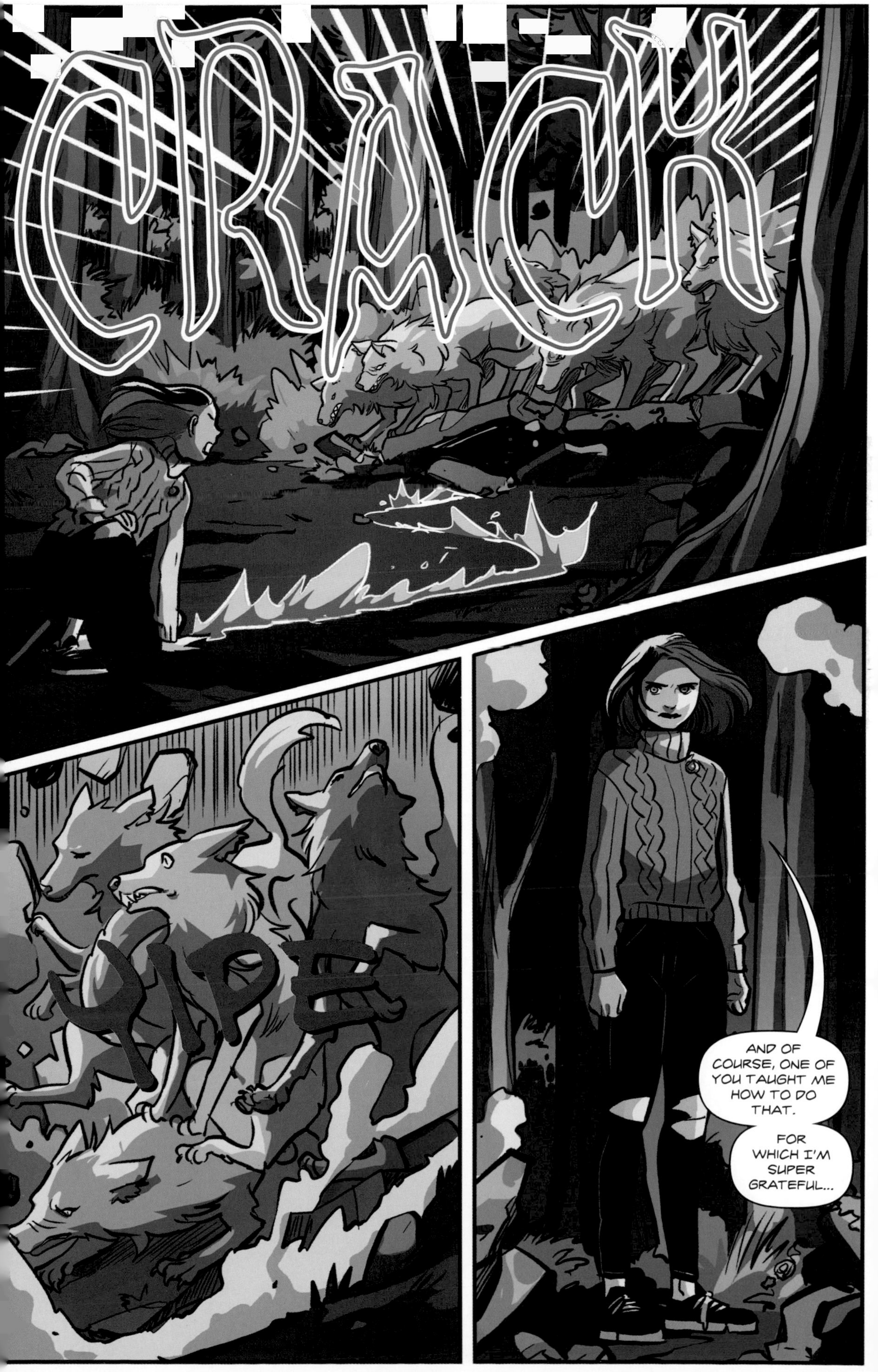
CRACK
YIPE
AND OF COURSE, ONE OF YOU TAUGHT ME HOW TO DO THAT.
FOR WHICH I'M SUPER GRATEFUL...

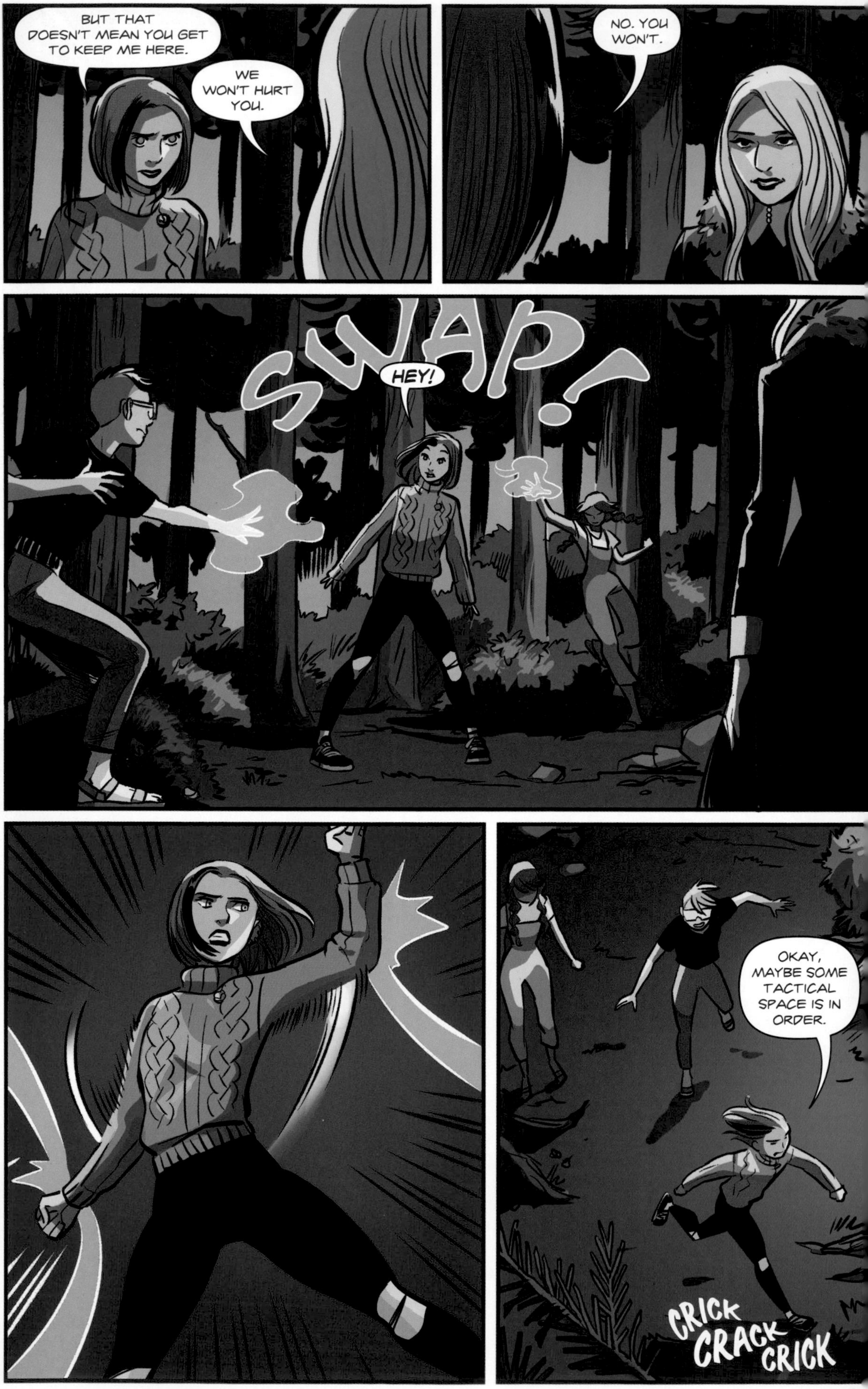
BUT THAT DOESN'T MEAN YOU GET TO KEEP ME HERE.
WE WON'T HURT YOU.
NO. YOU WON'T.
SWAP!
HEY!
OKAY, MAYBE SOME TACTICAL SPACE IS IN ORDER.
CRICK CRACK CRICK

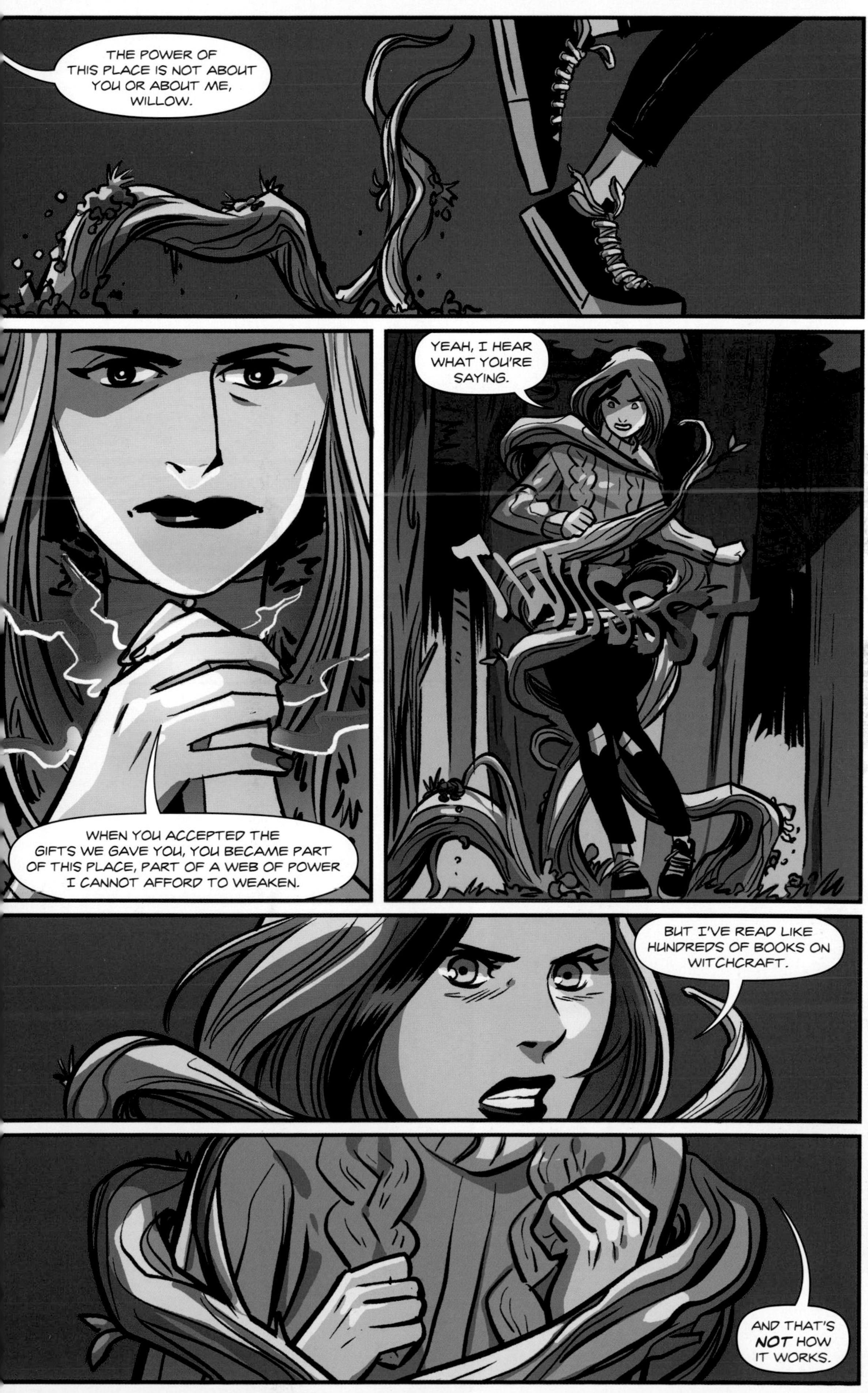
THE POWER OF THIS PLACE IS NOT ABOUT YOU OR ABOUT ME, WILLOW.
WHEN YOU ACCEPTED THE GIFTS WE GAVE YOU, YOU BECAME PART OF THIS PLACE, PART OF A WEB OF POWER I CANNOT AFFORD TO WEAKEN.
YEAH, I HEAR WHAT YOU'RE SAYING.
THWSSST
BUT I'VE READ LIKE HUNDREDS OF BOOKS ON WITCHCRAFT.
AND THAT'S **NOT** HOW IT WORKS.

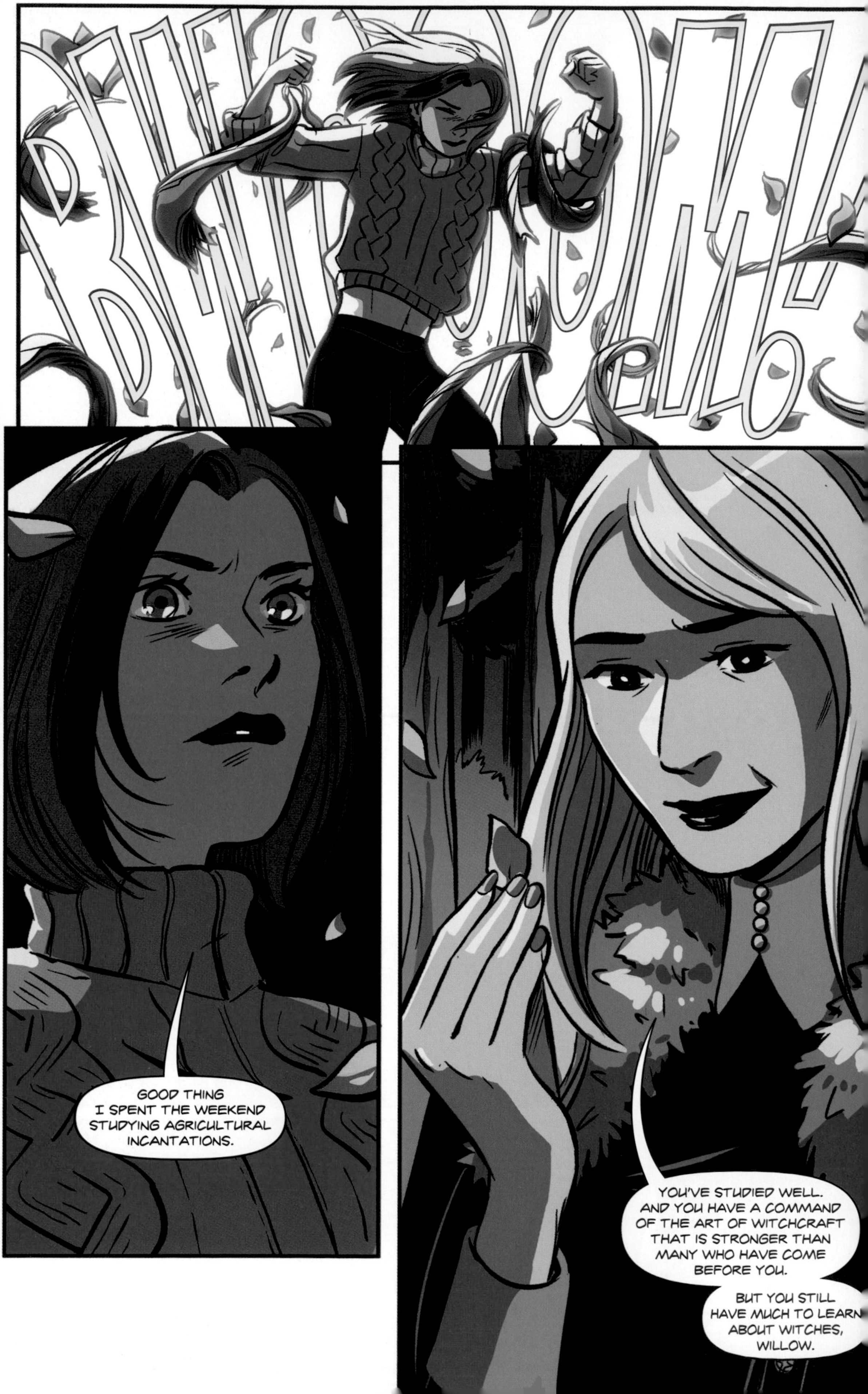
GOOD THING I SPENT THE WEEKEND STUDYING AGRICULTURAL INCANTATIONS.
YOU'VE STUDIED WELL. AND YOU HAVE A COMMAND OF THE ART OF WITCHCRAFT THAT IS STRONGER THAN MANY WHO HAVE COME BEFORE YOU.
BUT YOU STILL HAVE MUCH TO LEARN ABOUT WITCHES, WILLOW.

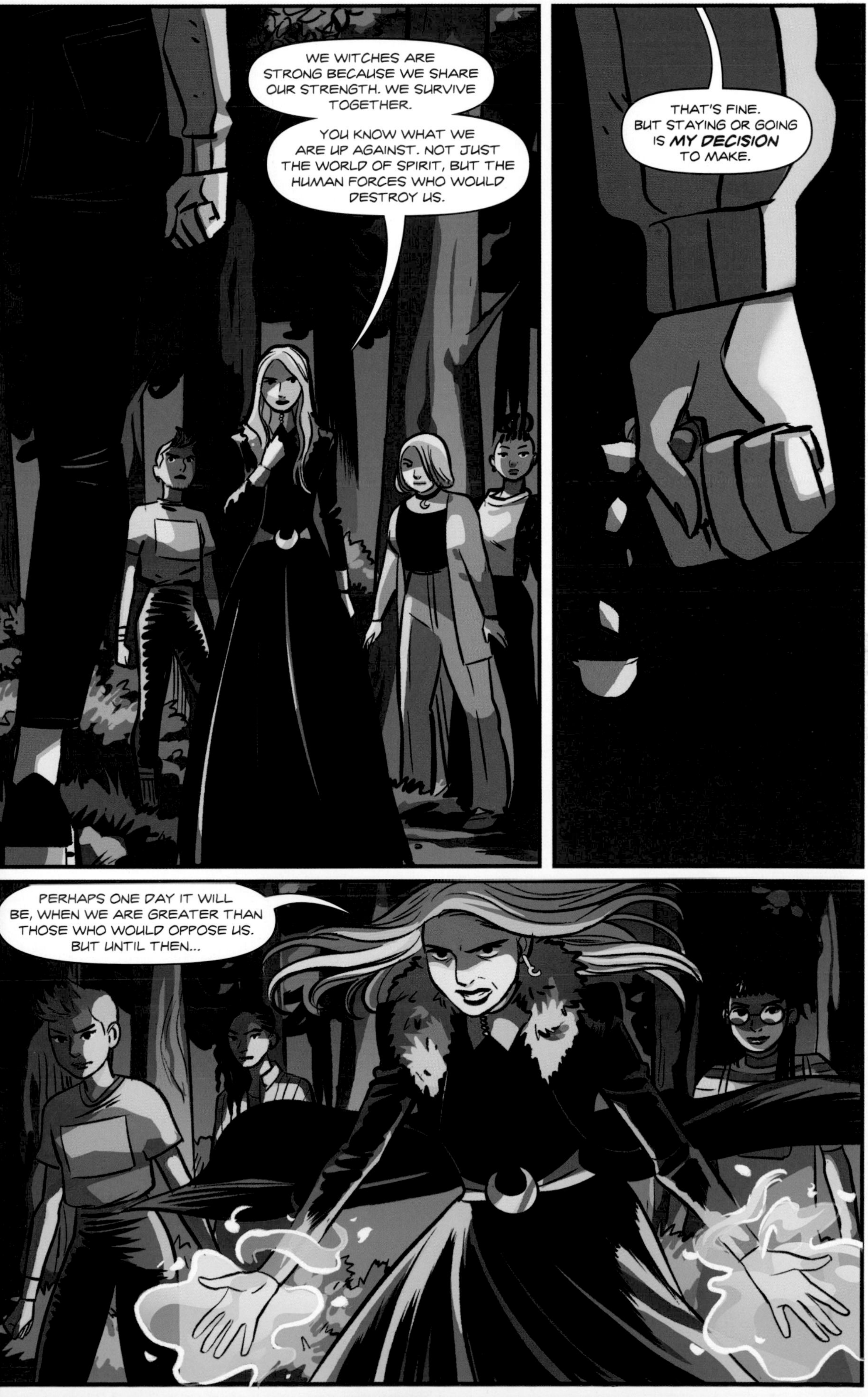
WE WITCHES ARE STRONG BECAUSE WE SHARE OUR STRENGTH. WE SURVIVE TOGETHER.
YOU KNOW WHAT WE ARE UP AGAINST. NOT JUST THE WORLD OF SPIRIT, BUT THE HUMAN FORCES WHO WOULD DESTROY US.
THAT'S FINE. BUT STAYING OR GOING IS ***MY DECISION*** TO MAKE.
PERHAPS ONE DAY IT WILL BE, WHEN WE ARE GREATER THAN THOSE WHO WOULD OPPOSE US. BUT UNTIL THEN...

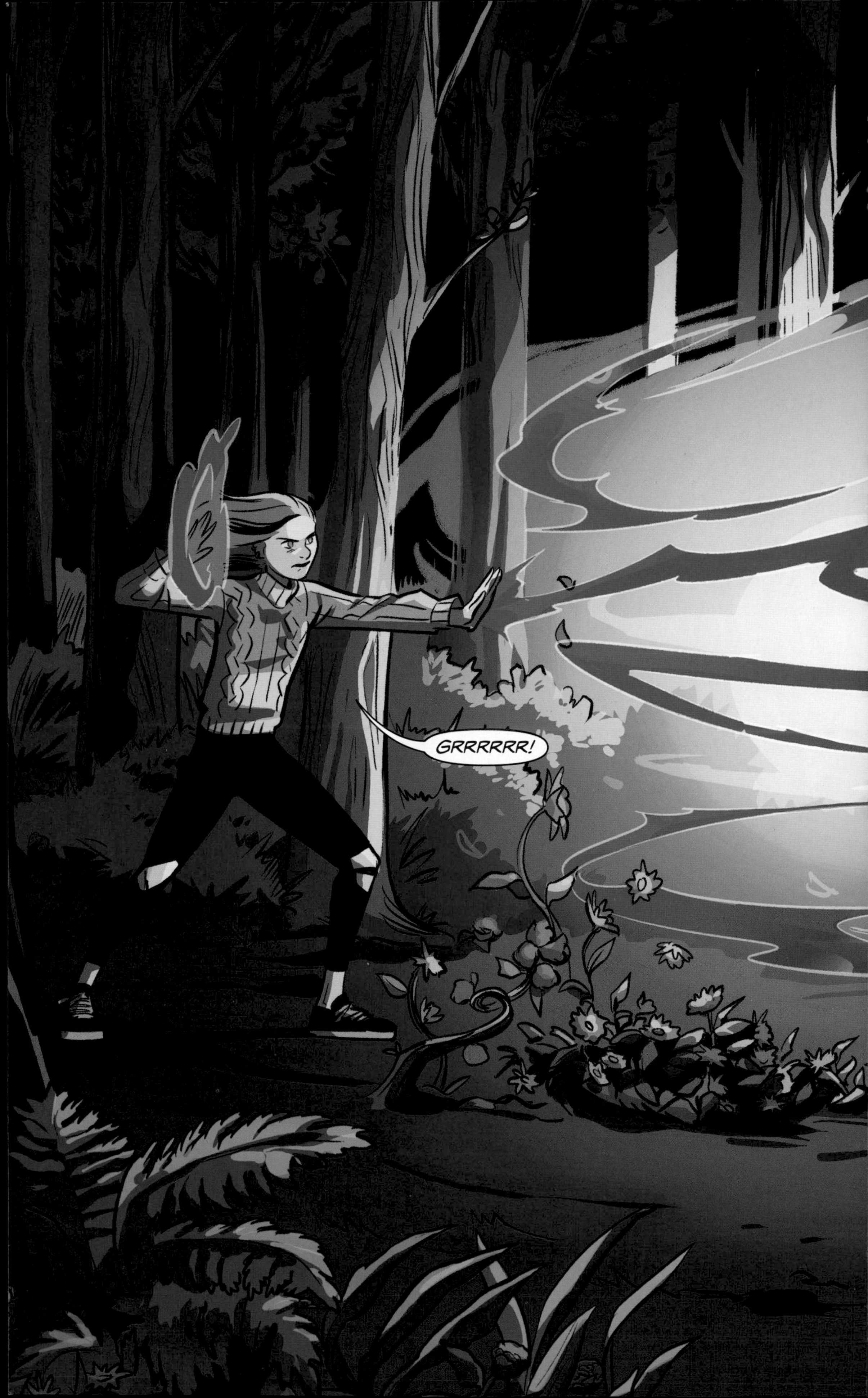
GRRRRRR!

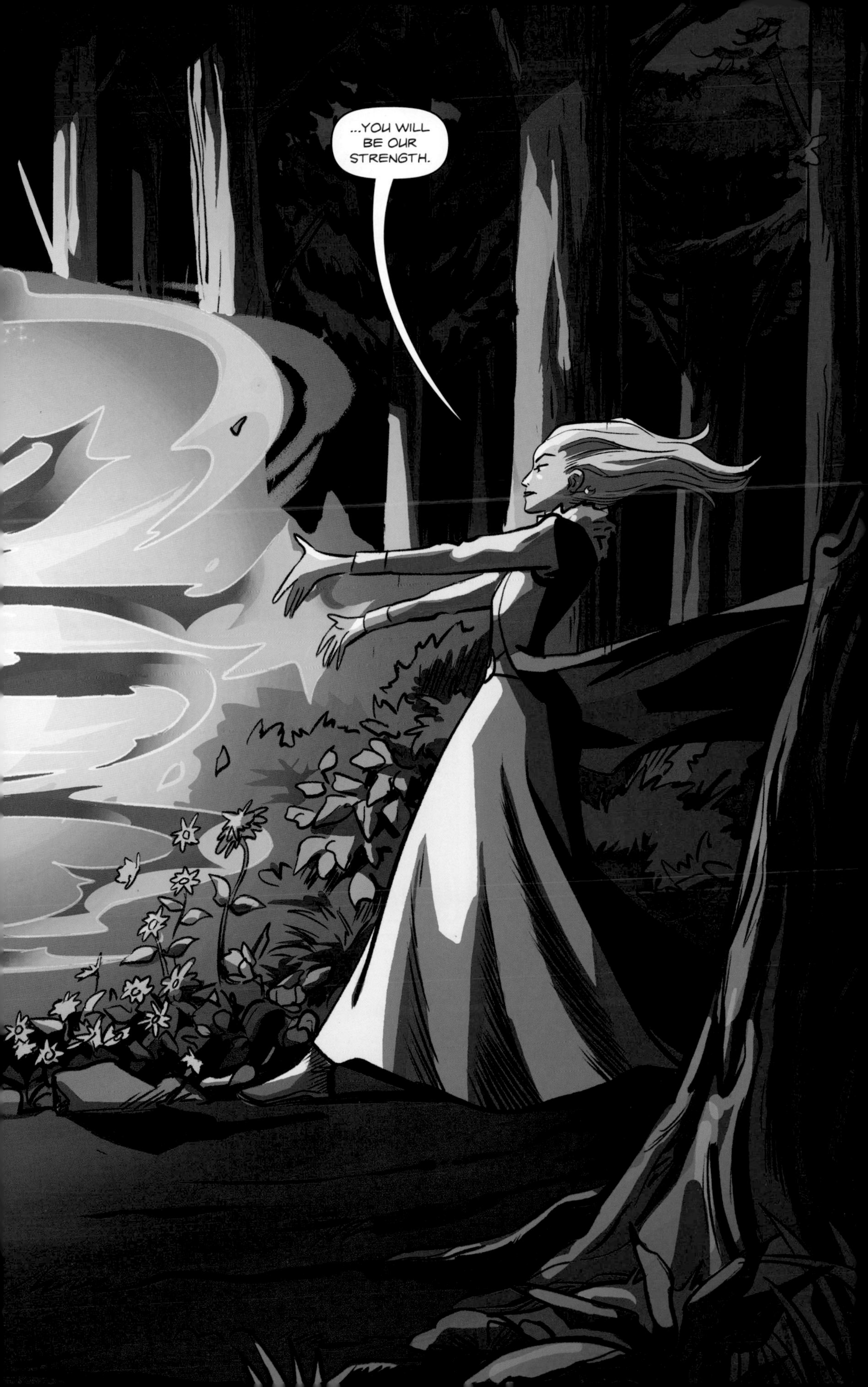
...YOU WILL BE OUR STRENGTH.

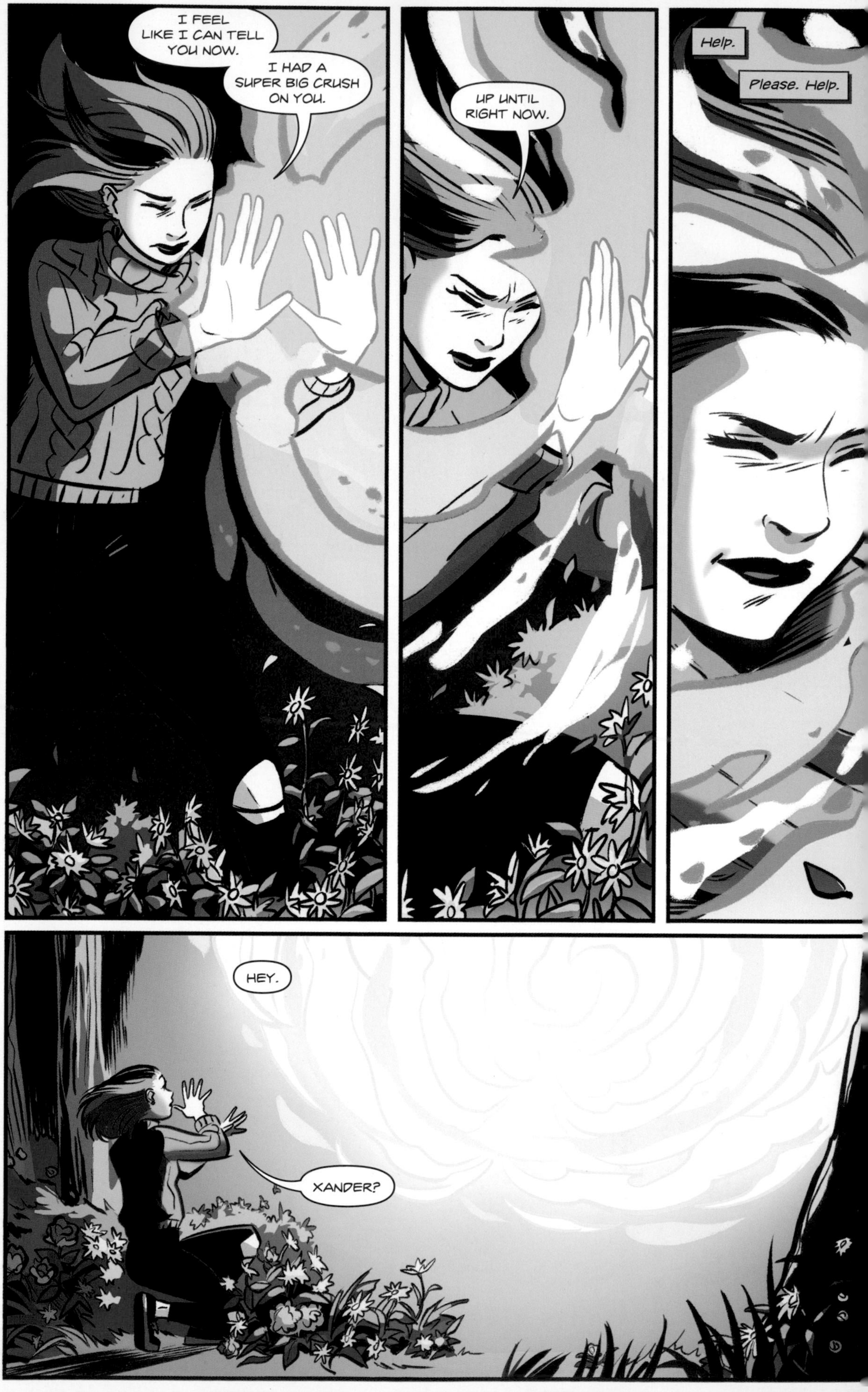
I FEEL LIKE I CAN TELL YOU NOW.
I HAD A SUPER BIG CRUSH ON YOU.
UP UNTIL RIGHT NOW.
Help.
Please. Help.
HEY.
XANDER?

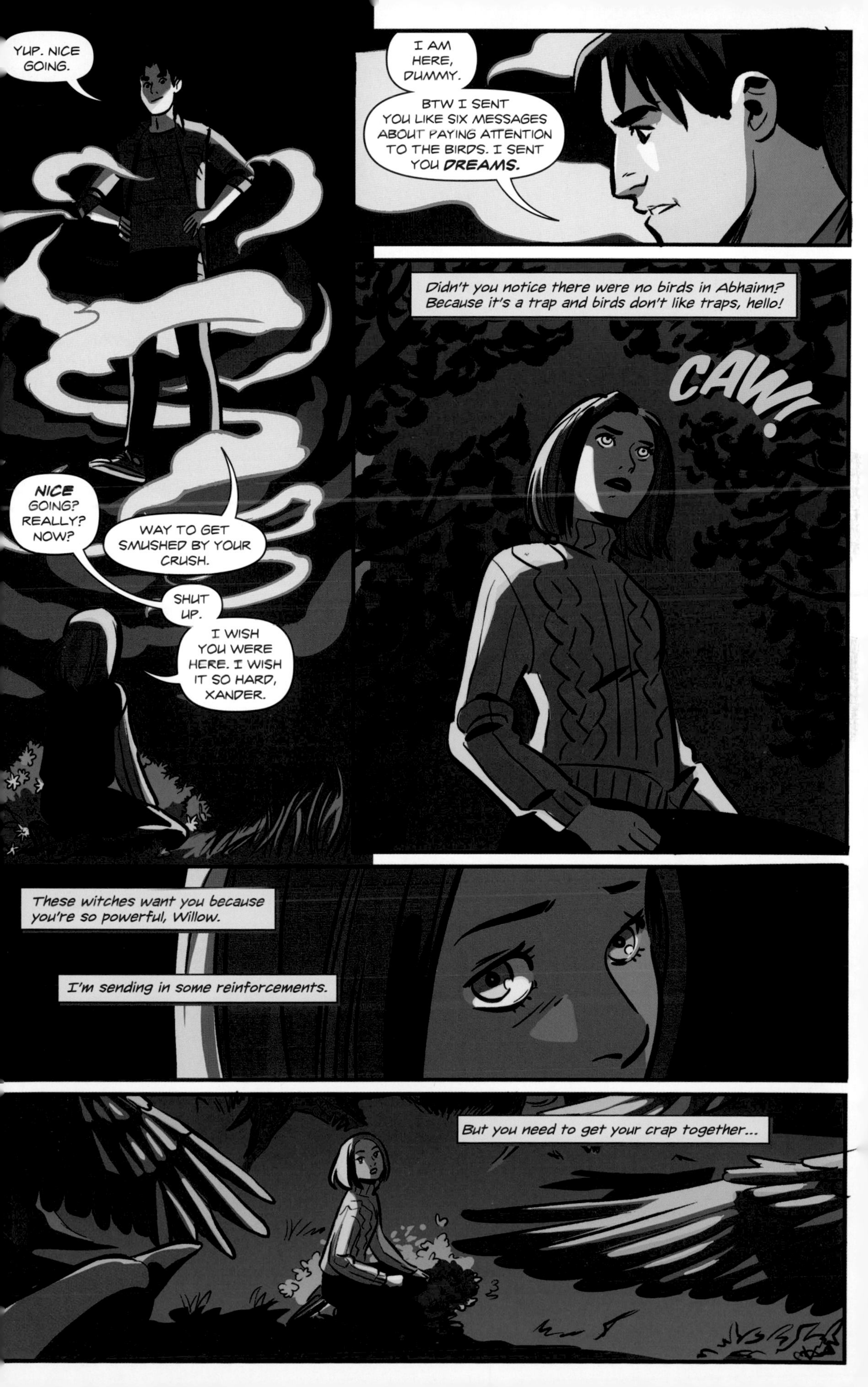
YUP. NICE GOING.
I AM HERE, DUMMY.
BTW I SENT YOU LIKE SIX MESSAGES ABOUT PAYING ATTENTION TO THE BIRDS. I SENT YOU DREAMS.
NICE GOING? REALLY? NOW?
WAY TO GET SMUSHED BY YOUR CRUSH.
SHUT UP.
I WISH YOU WERE HERE. I WISH IT SO HARD, XANDER.
Didn't you notice there were no birds in Abhainn? Because it's a trap and birds don't like traps, hello!
CAW!
These witches want you because you're so powerful, Willow.
I'm sending in some reinforcements.
But you need to get your crap together...

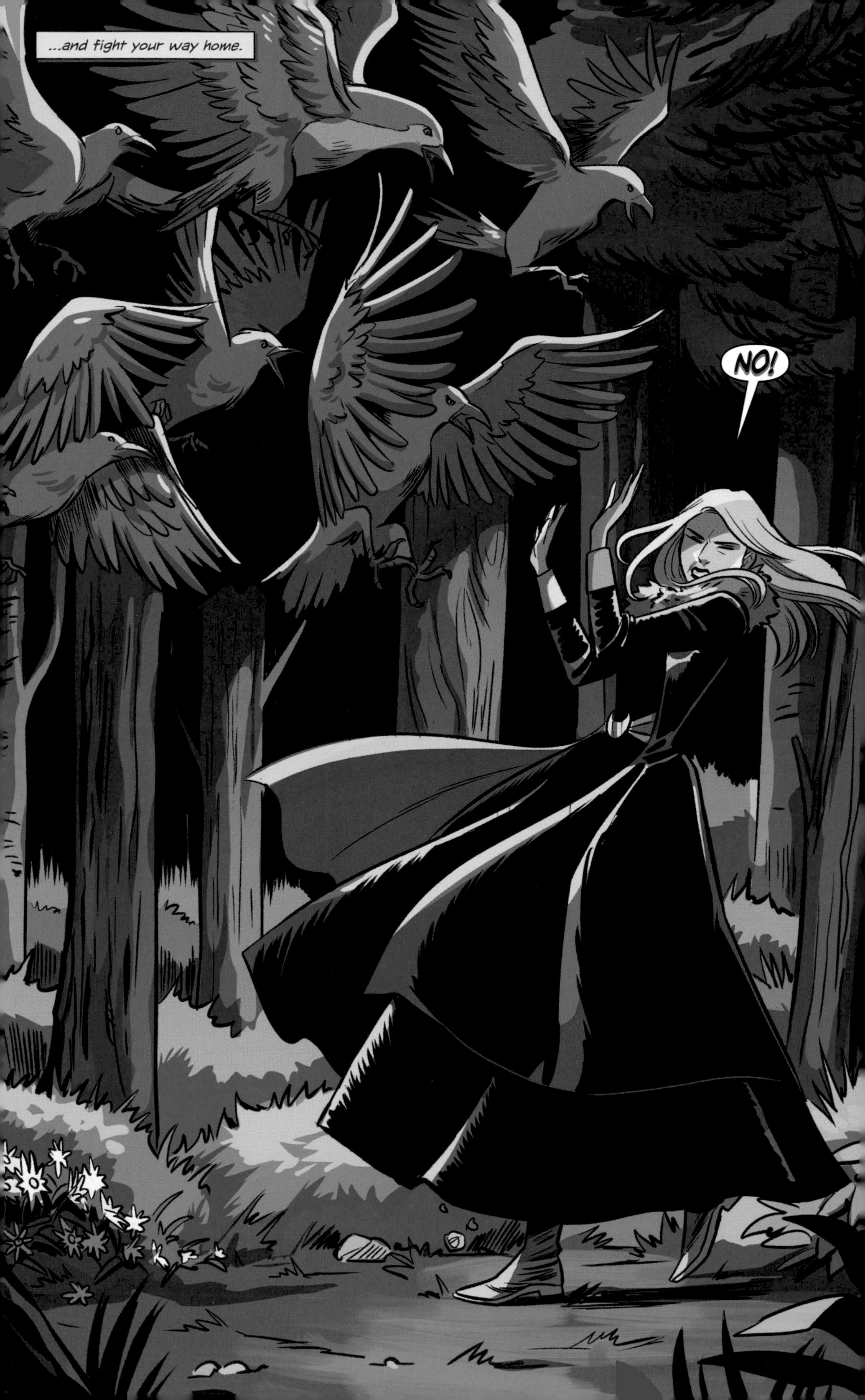
...and fight your way home.
NO!

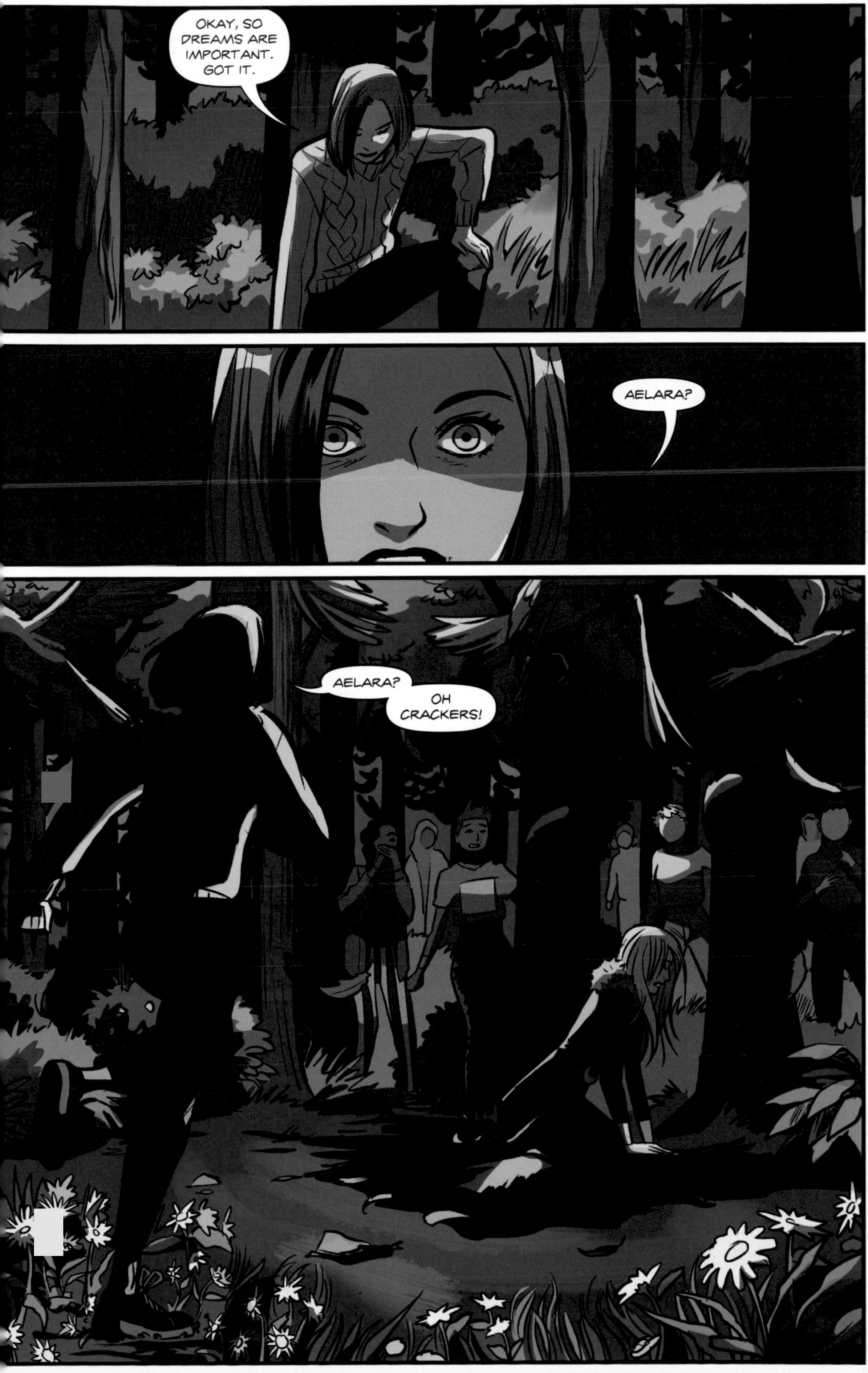
OKAY, SO DREAMS ARE IMPORTANT. GOT IT.
AELARA?
AELARA?
OH CRACKERS!

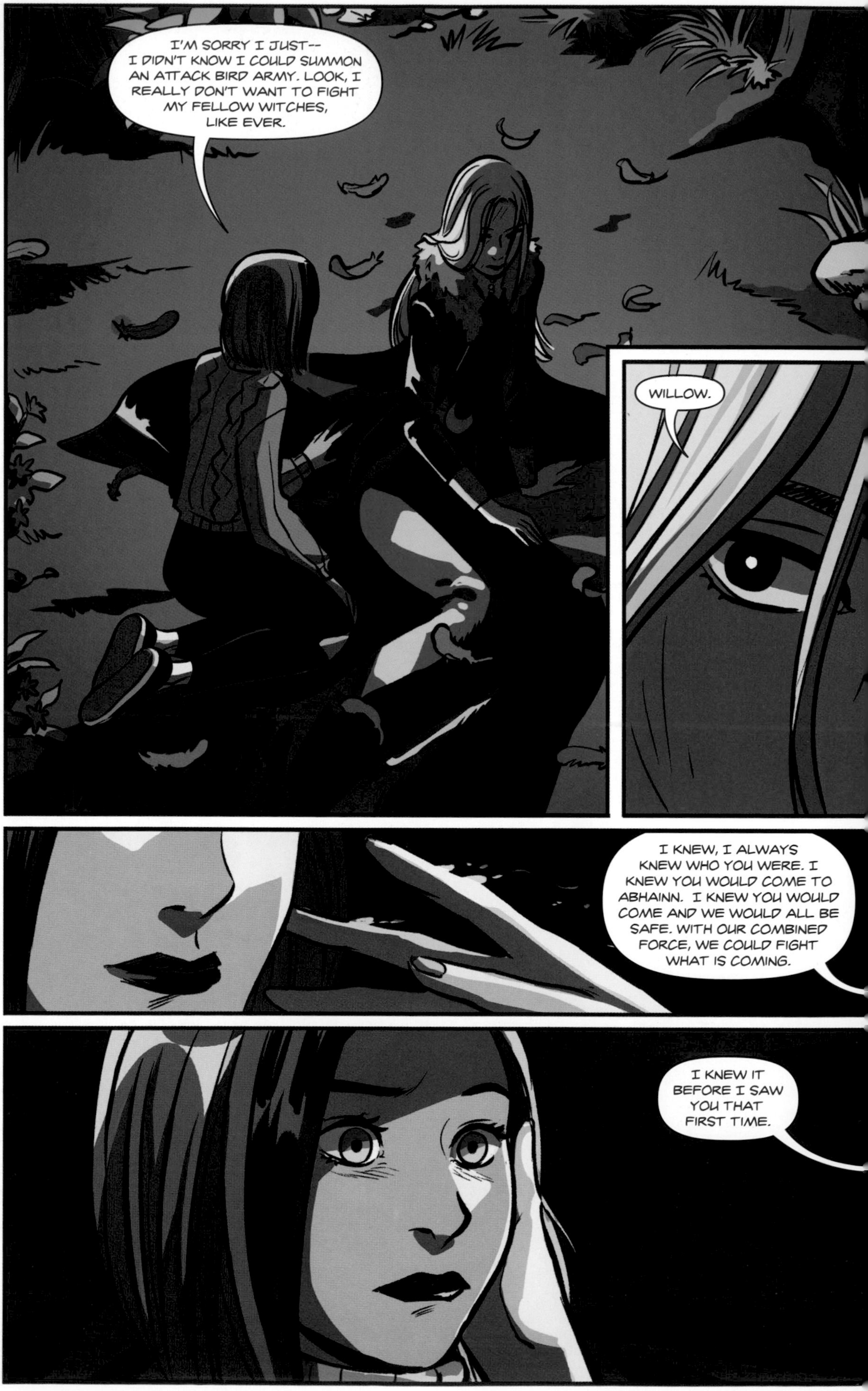
I'M SORRY I JUST-- I DIDN'T KNOW I COULD SUMMON AN ATTACK BIRD ARMY. LOOK, I REALLY DON'T WANT TO FIGHT MY FELLOW WITCHES, LIKE EVER.
WILLOW.
I KNEW, I ALWAYS KNEW WHO YOU WERE. I KNEW YOU WOULD COME TO ABHAINN. I KNEW YOU WOULD COME AND WE WOULD ALL BE SAFE. WITH OUR COMBINED FORCE, WE COULD FIGHT WHAT IS COMING.
I KNEW IT BEFORE I SAW YOU THAT FIRST TIME.

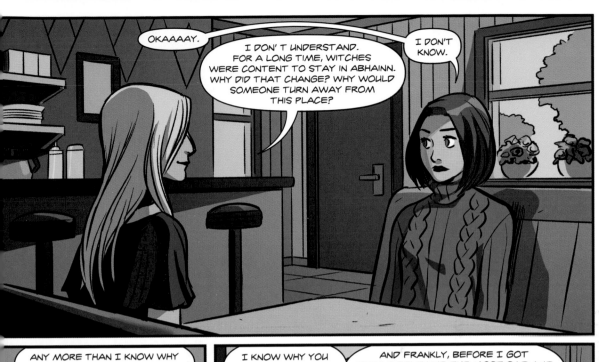

OKAAAAY.

I DON'T UNDERSTAND. FOR A LONG TIME, WITCHES WERE CONTENT TO STAY IN ABHAINN. WHY DID THAT CHANGE? WHY WOULD SOMEONE TURN AWAY FROM THIS PLACE?

I DON'T KNOW.

ANY MORE THAN I KNOW WHY THERE'S A MALT HERE ALL THE SUDDEN. YOU KNOW?

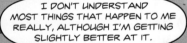

I DON'T UNDERSTAND MOST THINGS THAT HAPPEN TO ME REALLY, ALTHOUGH I'M GETTING SLIGHTLY BETTER AT IT.

I KNOW WHY YOU WANT TO FEEL SAFE BECAUSE I ALMOST NEVER FEEL SAFE.

AND FRANKLY, BEFORE I GOT HERE I FELT LIKE THE MOST SAD AND SCARED I'D EVER FELT. AND YOU MADE ME FEEL SAFE AND I'M SO SUPER GRATEFUL FOR THAT.

AND I'M LIKE 99.9% SURE I'M A BETTER WITCH FOR ALL THE THINGS YOU TAUGHT ME.

AND IT'S PROBABLY RUDE BECAUSE MAYBE YOU'RE THREE HUNDRED YEARS OLD AND I'M LIKE SCHOOLING YOU OR WHATEVER BUT...

THE WITCHES WHO WANT TO LEAVE ARE ONLY "RUNNING AWAY" BECAUSE YOU MADE IT A THING WHERE THEY HAD TO CHOOSE BETWEEN BEING HERE FOREVER OR "ESCAPING."

AND WHAT DO YOU EXPECT? BEING A WITCH IS ABOUT MAKING THE WEIRDEST CHOICE FOR YOUR LIFE POSSIBLE. AND IT'S A *CHOICE.*

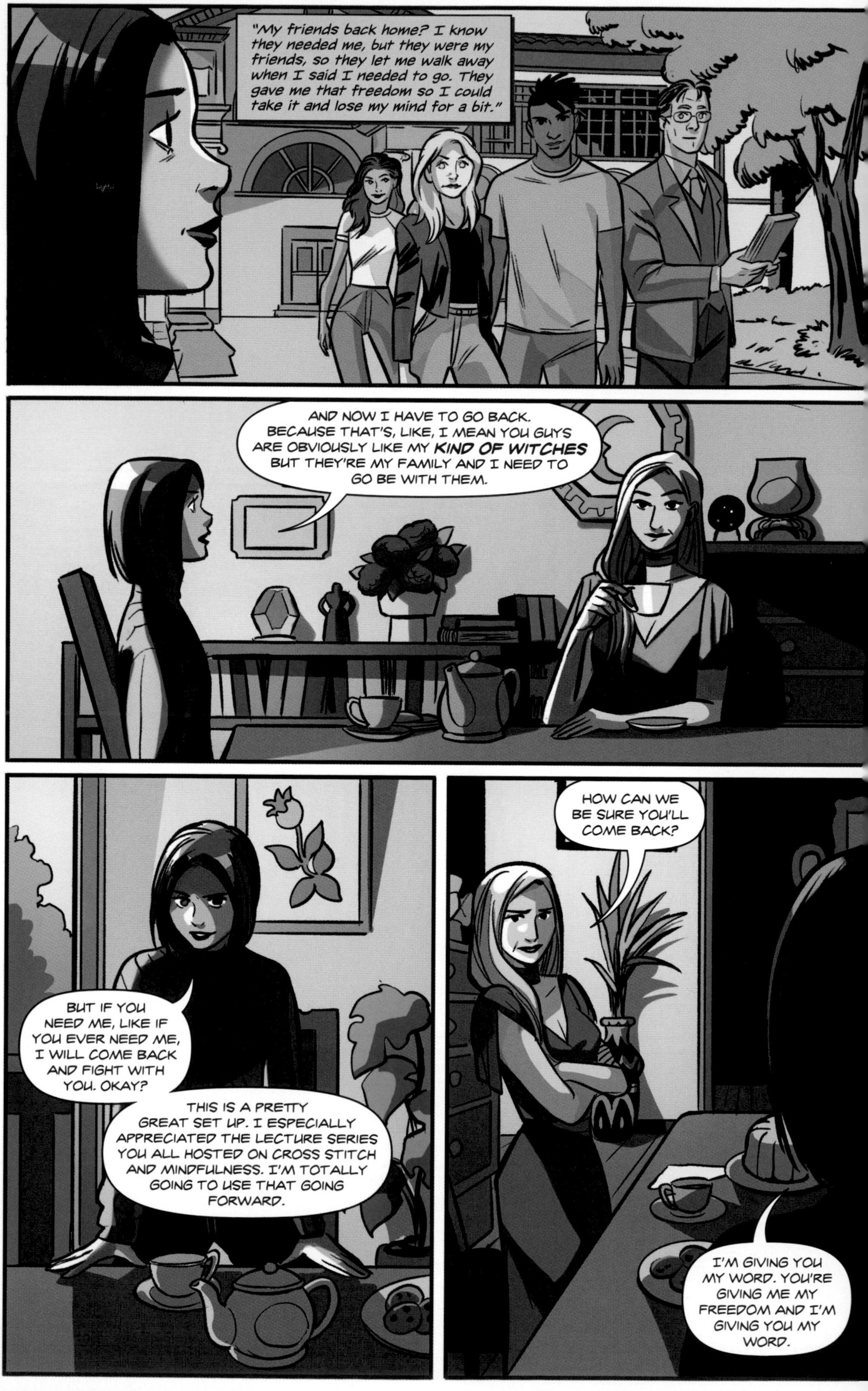
"My friends back home? I know they needed me, but they were my friends, so they let me walk away when I said I needed to go. They gave me that freedom so I could take it and lose my mind for a bit."
AND NOW I HAVE TO GO BACK. BECAUSE THAT'S, LIKE, I MEAN YOU GUYS ARE OBVIOUSLY LIKE MY KIND OF WITCHES BUT THEY'RE MY FAMILY AND I NEED TO GO BE WITH THEM.
BUT IF YOU NEED ME, LIKE IF YOU EVER NEED ME, I WILL COME BACK AND FIGHT WITH YOU. OKAY?
THIS IS A PRETTY GREAT SET UP. I ESPECIALLY APPRECIATED THE LECTURE SERIES YOU ALL HOSTED ON CROSS STITCH AND MINDFULNESS. I'M TOTALLY GOING TO USE THAT GOING FORWARD.
HOW CAN WE BE SURE YOU'LL COME BACK?
I'M GIVING YOU MY WORD. YOU'RE GIVING ME MY FREEDOM AND I'M GIVING YOU MY WORD.

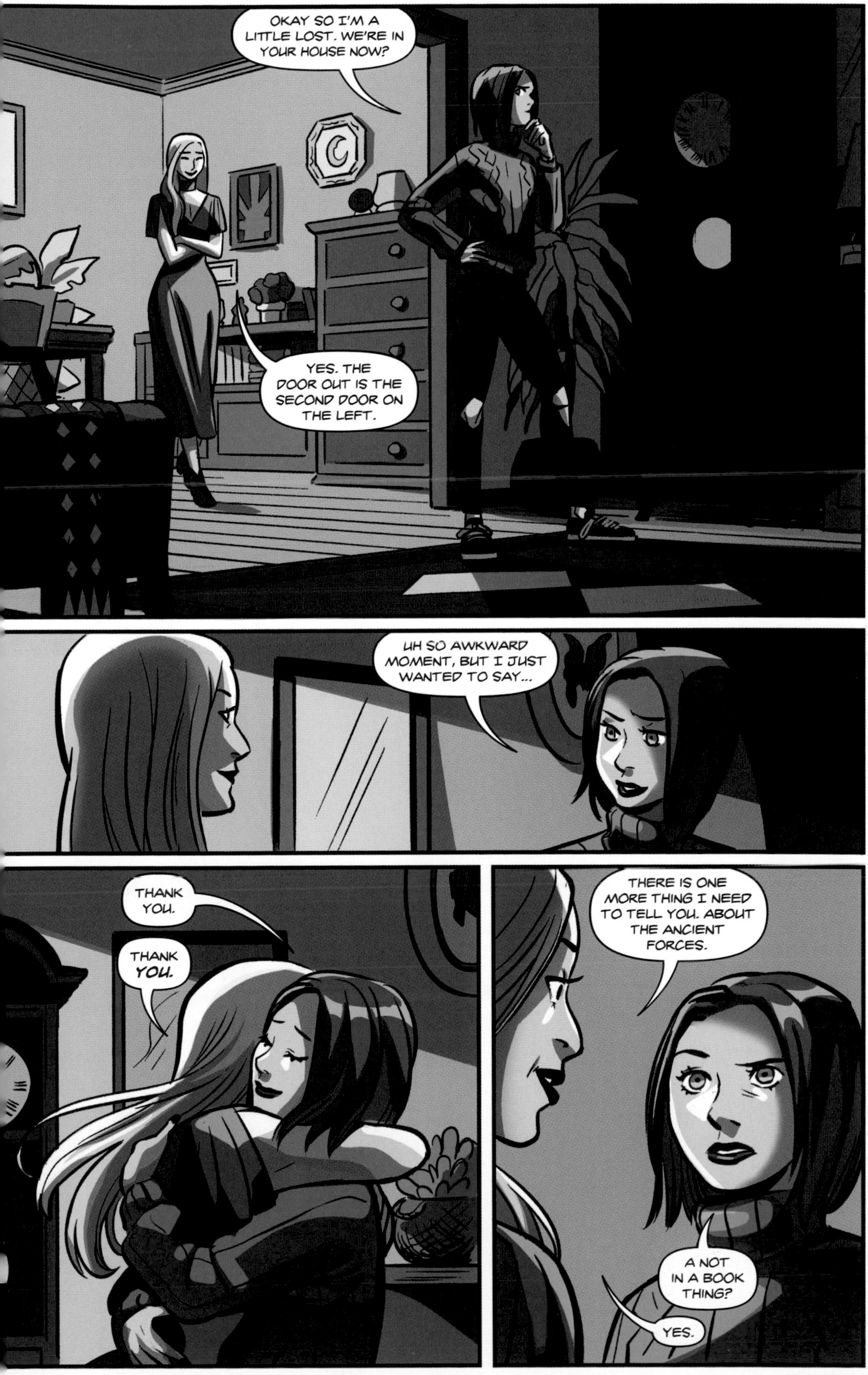
OKAY SO I'M A LITTLE LOST. WE'RE IN YOUR HOUSE NOW?
YES. THE DOOR OUT IS THE SECOND DOOR ON THE LEFT.
UH SO AWKWARD MOMENT, BUT I JUST WANTED TO SAY...
THANK YOU.
THANK YOU.
THERE IS ONE MORE THING I NEED TO TELL YOU. ABOUT THE ANCIENT FORCES.
A NOT IN A BOOK THING?
YES.

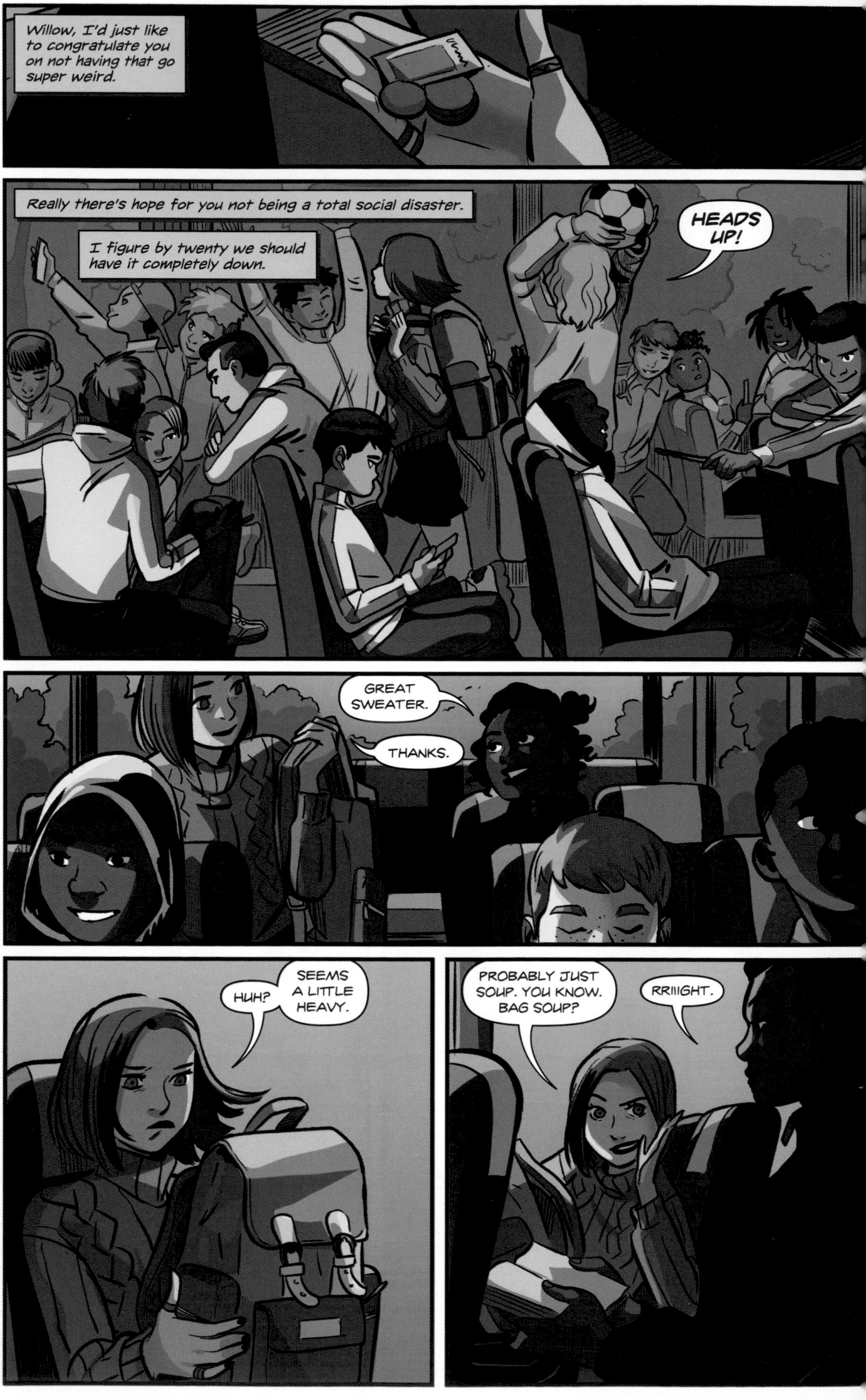
Willow, I'd just like to congratulate you on not having that go super weird.
Really there's hope for you not being a total social disaster.
I figure by twenty we should have it completely down.
HEADS UP!
GREAT SWEATER.
THANKS.
HUH?
SEEMS A LITTLE HEAVY.
PROBABLY JUST SOUP. YOU KNOW. BAG SOUP?
RRIIIGHT.

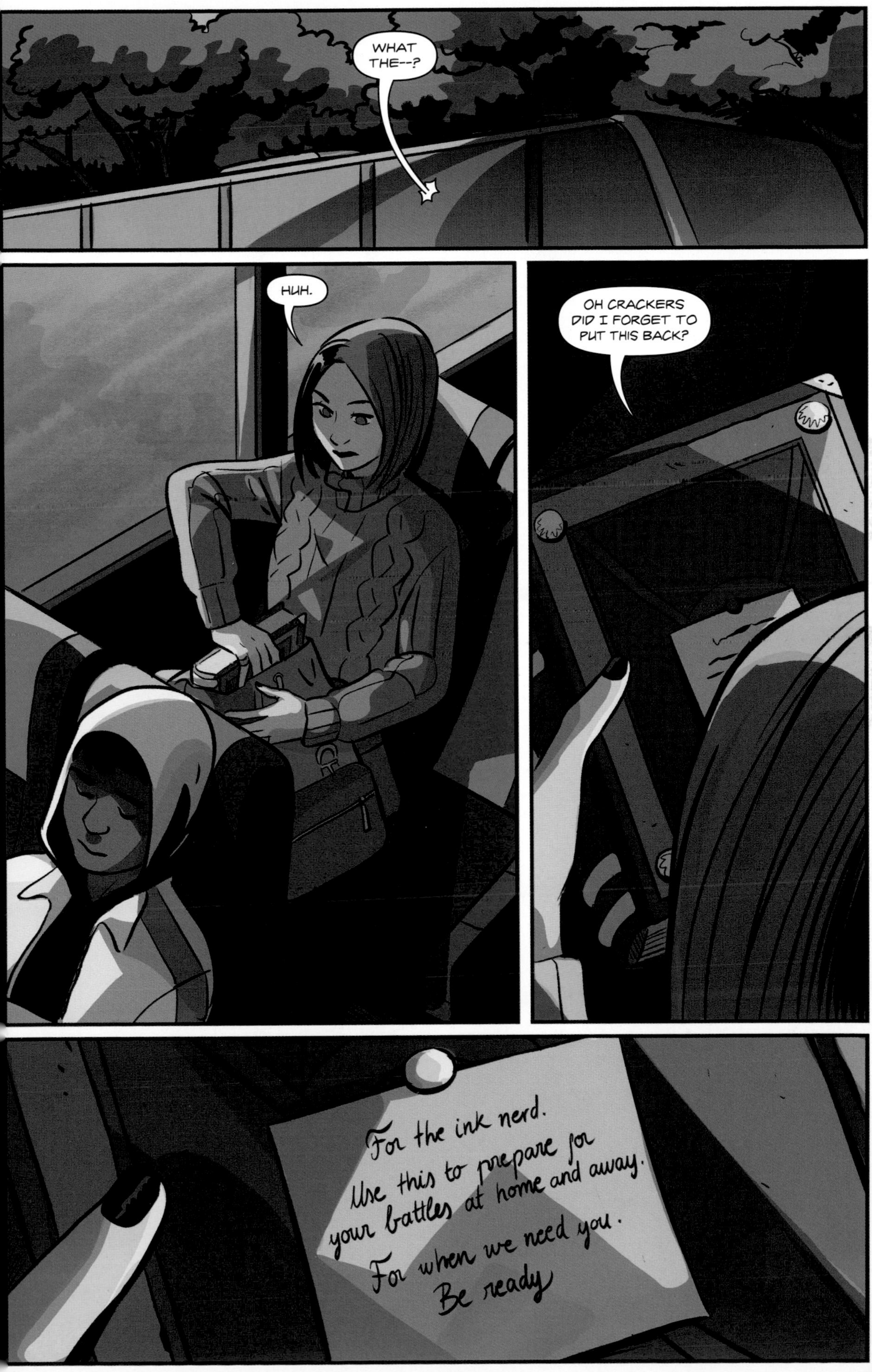
WHAT THE--?
HUH.
OH CRACKERS DID I FORGET TO PUT THIS BACK?
For the ink nerd.
Use this to prepare for your battles at home and away.
For when we need you.
Be ready

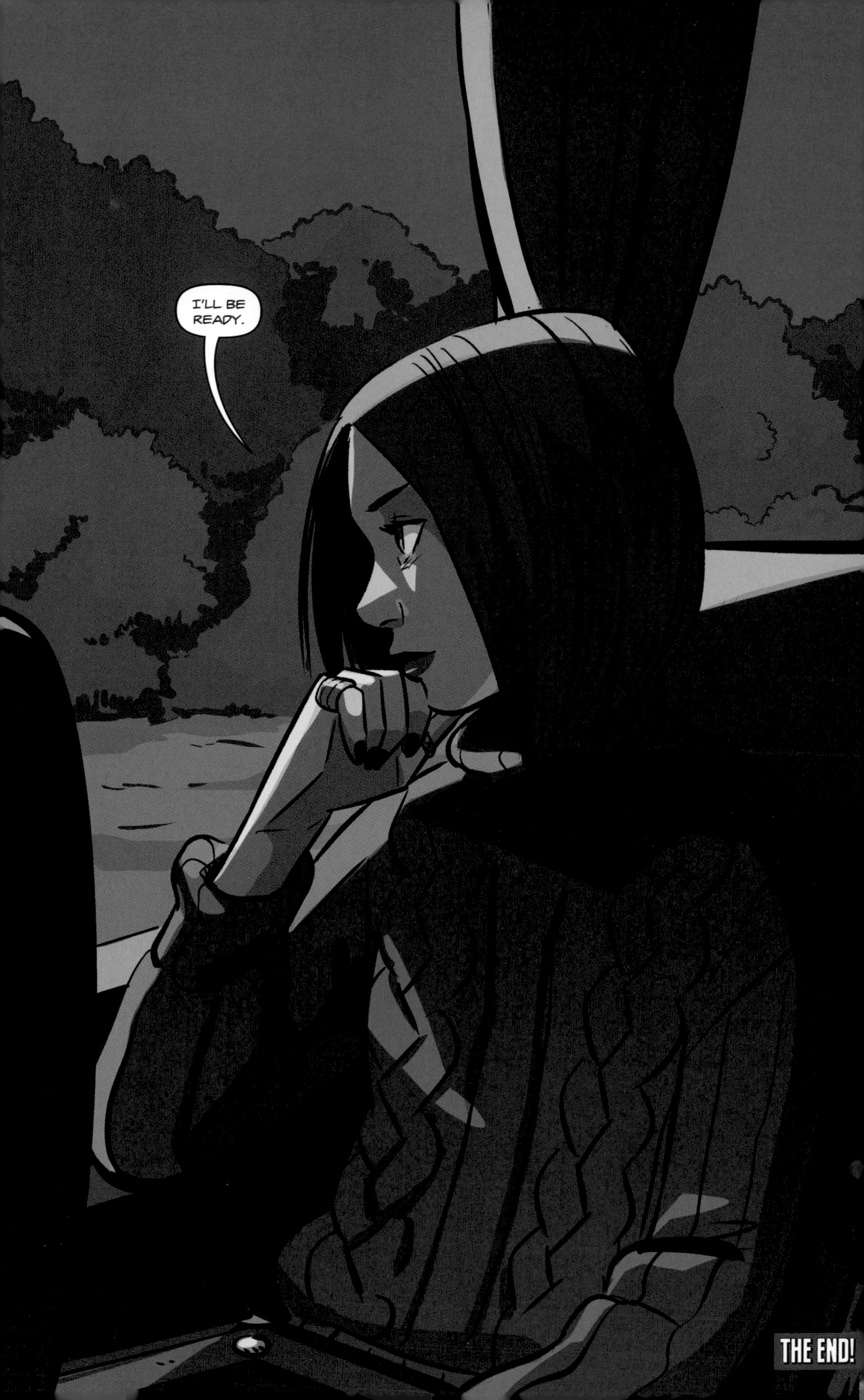
I'LL BE READY.
THE END!

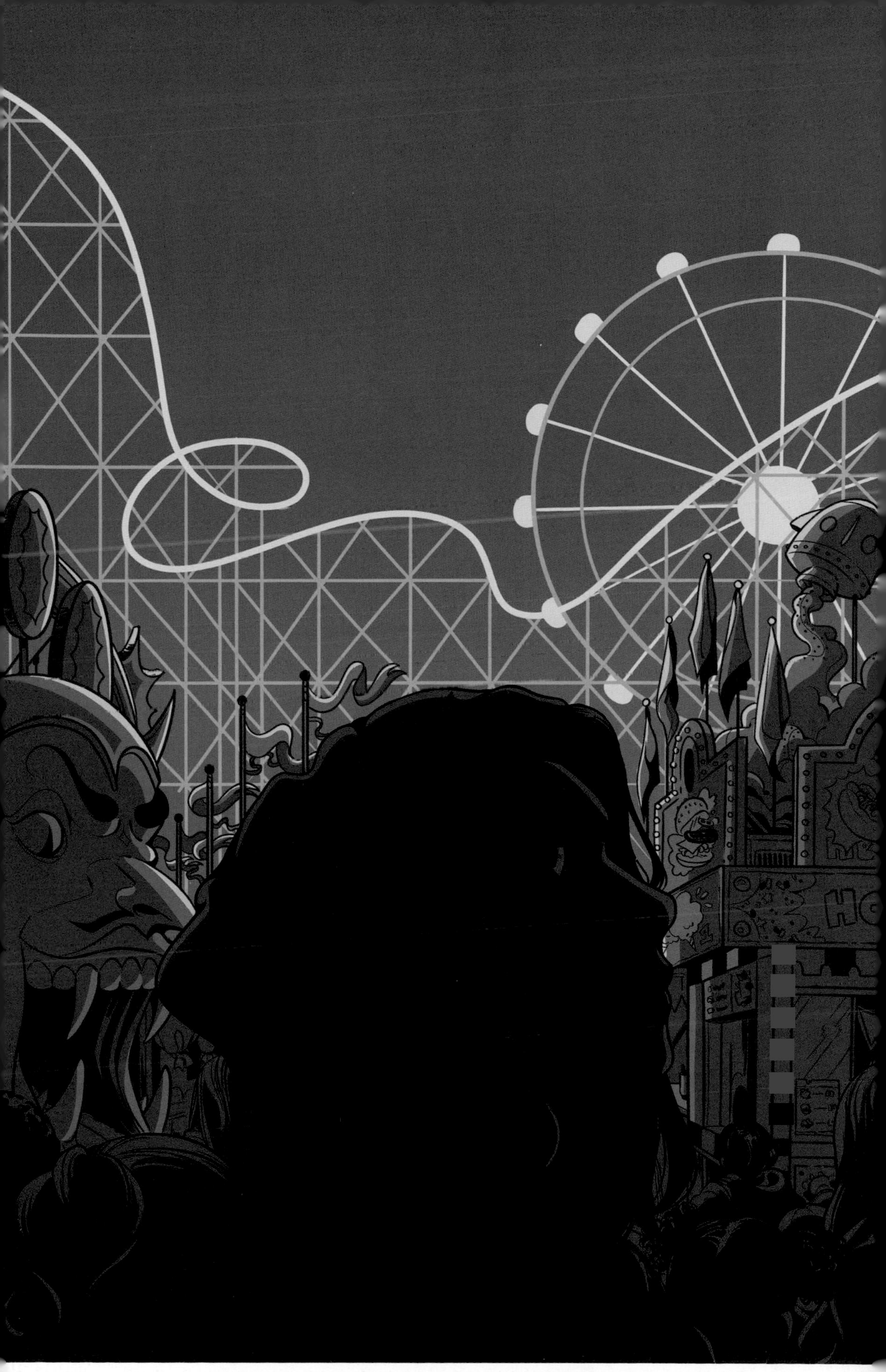

Willow #5 Variant Cover by **Rosemary Valero O'Connell**

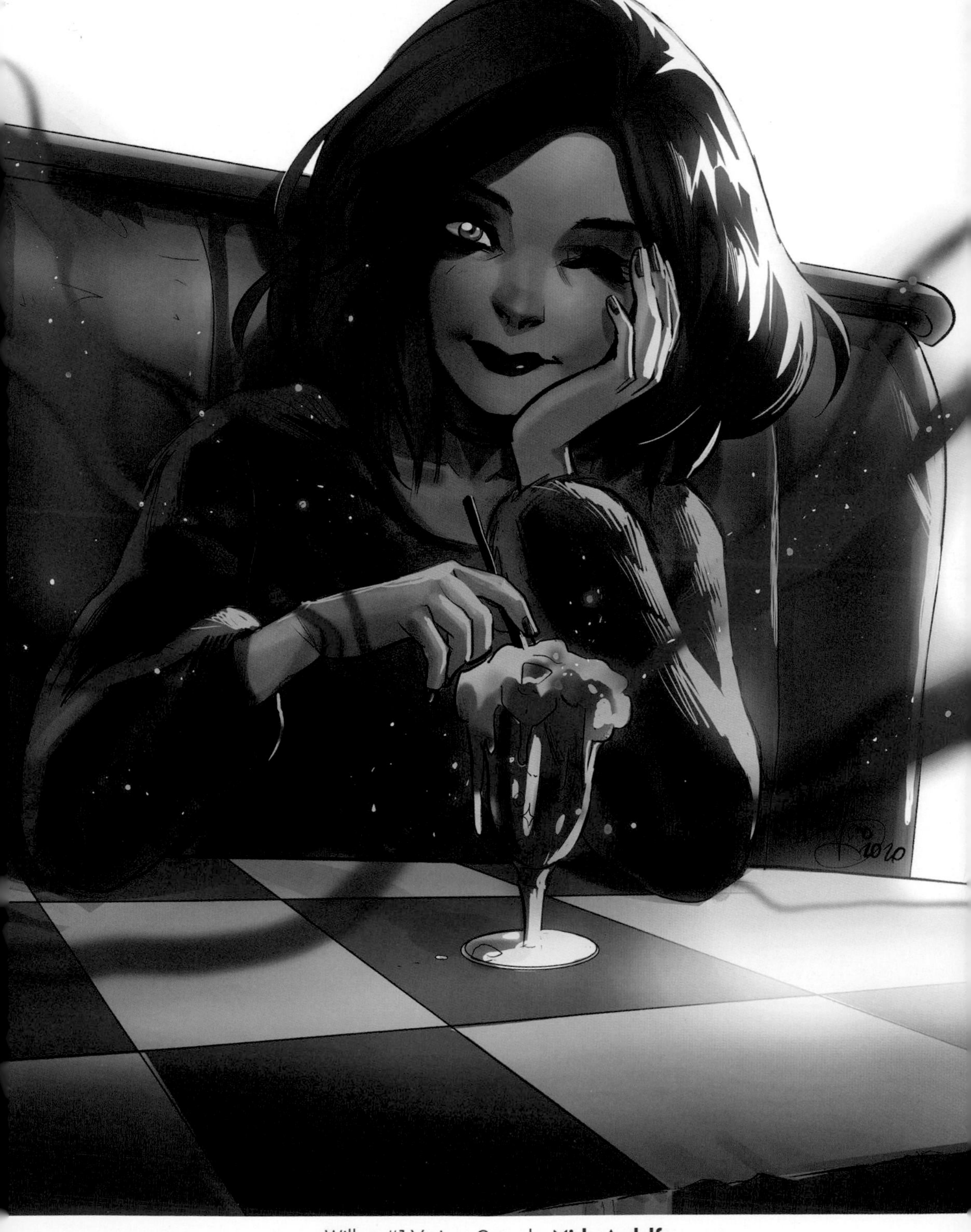

Willow #1 Variant Cover by **Mirka Andolfo**

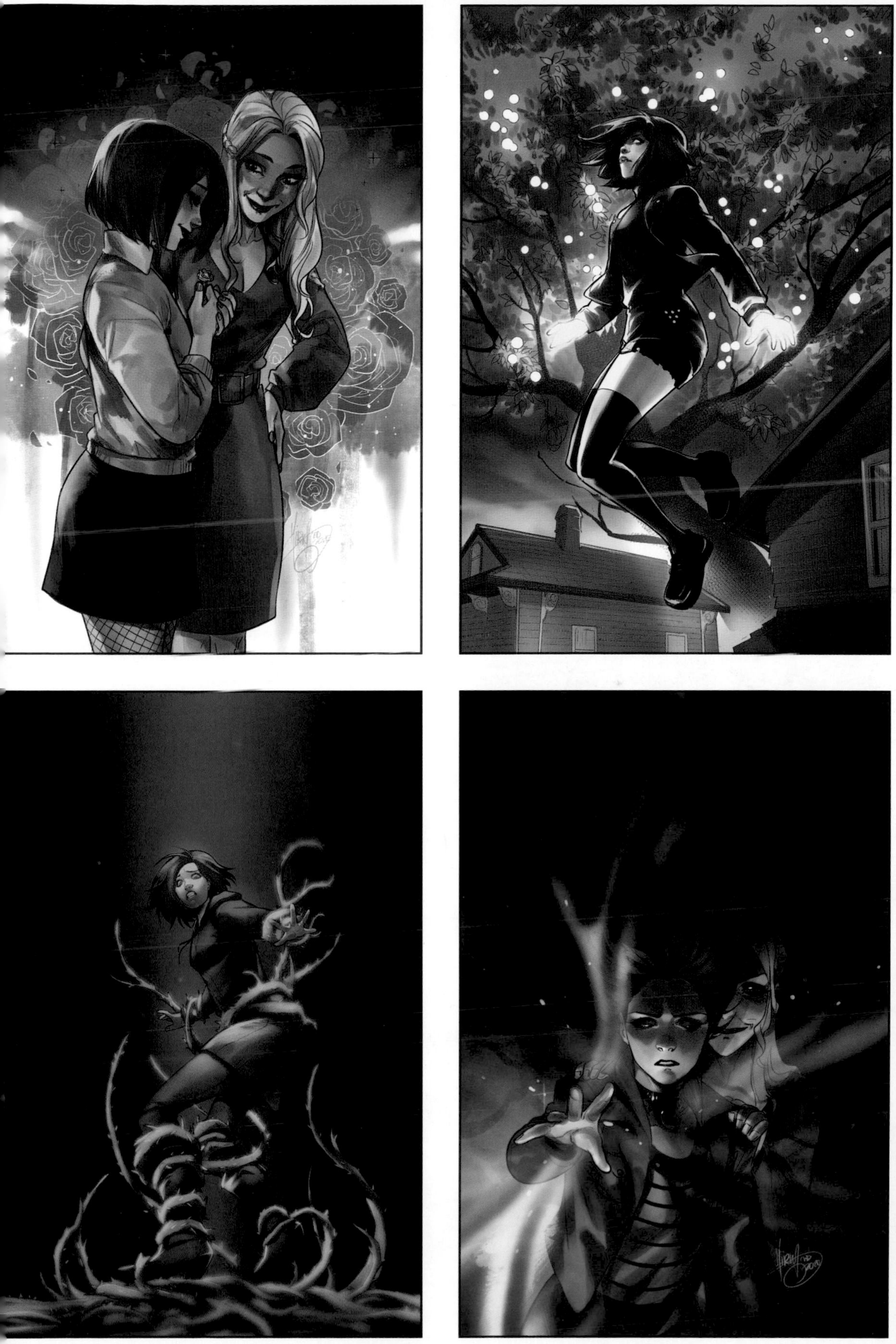

Willow #2–5 Variant Cover by **Mirka Andolfo**

DISCOVER
VISIONARY CREATORS

KIERON GILLEN DAN MORA
TAMRA BONVILLAIN
ONCE & FUTURE
VOLUME ONE
THE KING IS UNDEAD

JAMES TYNION IV
WERTHER DELLEDERA
MIQUEL MUERTO
SOMETHING is KILLING the CHILDREN
VOLUME ONE
SCOTT SNYDER

Brian Azzarello · Maria Llovet
FAITHLESS

GRANT MORRISON
DAN MORA
Klaus
How Santa Claus Began

SIMON SPURRIER × MATIAS BERGARA
CODA
VOLUME ONE
"This one is really special!"
—JEFF LEMIRE
(New York Times bestselling writer of Black Hammer)

matt kindt
tyler jenkins
GRASS KINGS
volume one

AVAILABLE AT YOUR LOCAL COMICS SHOP AND BOOKSTORE
To find a comics shop in your area, visit www.comicshoplocator.com
WWW.**BOOM-STUDIOS**.COM

Once & Future
Kieron Gillen, Dan Mora
Volume 1
ISBN: 978-1-68415-491-3 | $16.99 US

Something is Killing the Children
James Tynion IV, Werther Dell'Edera
Volume 1
ISBN: 978-1-68415-558-3 | $14.99 US

Faithless
Brian Azzarello, Maria Llovet
ISBN: 978-1-68415-432-6 | $17.99 US

Klaus
Grant Morrison, Dan Mora
Klaus: How Santa Claus Began SC
ISBN: 978-1-68415-393-0 | $15.99 US
Klaus: The New Adventures of Santa Claus HC
ISBN: 978-1-68415-666-5 | $17.99 US

Coda
Simon Spurrier, Matias Bergara
Volume 1
ISBN: 978-1-68415-321-3 | $14.99 US
Volume 2
ISBN: 978-1-68415-369-5 | $14.99 US
Volume 3
ISBN: 978-1-68415-429-6 | $14.99 US

Grass Kings
Matt Kindt, Tyler Jenkins
Volume 1
ISBN: 978-1-64144-362-3 | $17.99 US
Volume 2
ISBN: 978-1-64144-557-3 | $17.99 US
Volume 3
ISBN: 978-1-64144-650-1 | $17.99 US

Bone Parish
Cullen Bunn, Jonas Scharf
Volume 1
ISBN: 978-1-64144-337-1 | $14.99 US
Volume 2
ISBN: 978-1-64144-542-9 | $14.99 US
Volume 3
ISBN: 978-1-64144-543-6 | $14.99 US

Ronin Island
Greg Pak, Giannis Milonogiannis
Volume 1
ISBN: 978-1-64144-576-4 | $14.99 US
Volume 2
ISBN: 978-1-64144-723-2 | $14.99 US
Volume 3
ISBN: 978-1-64668-035-1 | $14.99 US

Victor LaValle's Destroyer
Victor LaValle, Dietrich Smith
ISBN: 978-1-61398-732-2 | $19.99 US

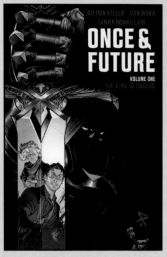

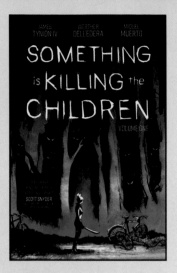

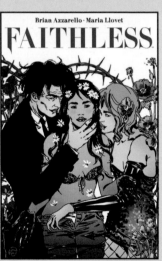

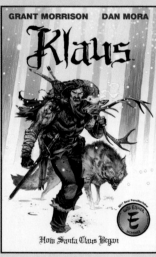

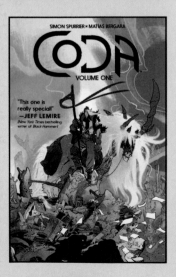

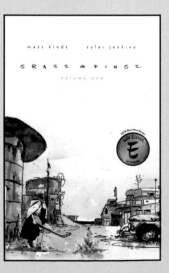

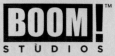